Death Activism

POSTHUMANISM IN PRACTICE

Series editors: **Matt Hayler** (University of Birmingham, UK), **Danielle Sands** (Royal Holloway, University of London, UK) and **Christine Daigle** (Brock University, Canada)

Ways of thinking allied with 'posthumanism' have received increasing interest across a number of disciplines, predominantly in philosophy and the humanities, but also in biology, law and ethics, and art theory and creative practice. Indeed, we contend that the field's potential implications extend to the majority of academic disciplines. Focusing on emerging trends, cutting-edge research and current debates, *Posthumanism in Practice* presents work in and across multiple disciplines that investigates how posthumanism can affect change.

The questions that posthumanism raises, of what it means to be human, the nature of our relationship with the world, our relative importance, our obligations, entanglements, potentials and limitations, speak to every aspect of life, This series will address questions such as: What are the implications and entailed effects of the revelations of contemporary science and philosophy? Can our laws, societies, and egos hold up to our becoming less special? What can we do, and how might thinking differently enable us to act differently?

Works in this series will pose these kinds of questions and offer practical answers, suggestions and provocations. The aim is to inspire work that isn't occurring often or loudly enough, and to promote a wide variety of voices which are left outside of the arenas where they might be most usefully heard. Disciplinary conversations also often remain siloed, but posthumanism is inherently an interdisciplinary concern; the field questions (but doesn't necessarily reject) the usefulness and stability of existing disciplinary boundaries. As such, this series will prioritize works which bring insights across those boundaries and which demonstrate the real-world potential and/or risks of posthumanist ideas.

Editorial Board:

Megen de Bruin-Molé (University of Southampton, UK)
Emily Jones (University of Essex, UK)
Yoriko Otomo (Director of Global Research Network)
Pedro Oliveira (Helsinki Collegium for Advanced Studies, Finland)
Rick Dolphijn (Utrecht University, Netherlands)
Isabel Galleymore (University of Birmingham, UK)
Craig N. Cipolla (University of Toronto, Canada)
Stefan Herbrechter (Heidelberg University, Germany)
Simone Bignall (University of Technology, Sydney, Australia)
Olga Cielemecka (University of Turku, Finland)
Dominique Chen (Waseda University, Japan)
Mickey Vallee (Athabasca University Canada)

Death Activism

Queer Death Studies and the Posthuman

Patricia MacCormack

BLOOMSBURY ACADEMIC
LONDON • NEW YORK • OXFORD • NEW DELHI • SYDNEY

BLOOMSBURY ACADEMIC
Bloomsbury Publishing Plc
50 Bedford Square, London, WC1B 3DP, UK
1385 Broadway, New York, NY 10018, USA
29 Earlsfort Terrace, Dublin 2, Ireland

BLOOMSBURY, BLOOMSBURY ACADEMIC and the Diana logo are trademarks of Bloomsbury Publishing Plc

First published in Great Britain 2025

Copyright © Patricia MacCormack, 2025

Patricia MacCormack has asserted her right under the Copyright, Designs and Patents Act, 1988, to be identified as Author of this work.

For legal purposes the Acknowledgements on p. viii constitute an extension of this copyright page.

Series design: Ben Anslow
Cover image: Ophelia, Sarah Bernhardt, 1880
(Contributor: History and Art Collection / Alamy Stock Photo)

All rights reserved. No part of this publication may be reproduced or transmitted in any form or by any means, electronic or mechanical, including photocopying, recording, or any information storage or retrieval system, without prior permission in writing from the publishers.

Bloomsbury Publishing Plc does not have any control over, or responsibility for, any third-party websites referred to or in this book. All internet addresses given in this book were correct at the time of going to press. The author and publisher regret any inconvenience caused if addresses have changed or sites have ceased to exist, but can accept no responsibility for any such changes.

A catalogue record for this book is available from the British Library.

A catalog record for this book is available from the Library of Congress.

ISBN: HB: 978-1-3503-7619-9
PB: 978-1-3503-7618-2
ePDF: 978-1-3503-7620-5
eBook: 978-1-3503-7621-2

Series: Posthumanism in Practice

Typeset by Deanta Global Publishing Services, Chennai, India
Printed and bound in Great Britain

To find out more about our authors and books visit www.bloomsbury.com and sign up for our newsletters.

*For Francesco and Circe
and all nonhuman victims of the Anthropocene*

Contents

Acknowledgements viii
Prelude: Cosmic Queer Death ix

Introduction 1

1 Danse macabre: Queer romances of fascination and fear 37

2 Global mourning: Pandemic, trauma and mass death 61

3 The denial of desire: Suicide and the right to death 81

4 Abolitionism: Mass death and the nonhuman animal 103

5 Capital zombies, death and disability 125

6 The unspeakable death (that is not death) 149

7 Goth culture, occulture, aesthetic death culture 171

Conclusion: The difficult joy of death activism 189

References 203
Index 212

Acknowledgements

This book is pseudo dedicated (after the actual dedication, exclusively for nonhumans) to my beloved Queer Death Studies Coven, Marietta Radomska, Nina Lykke and Margrit Shildrick, whose many hours of discussions, virtual and actual, both inspired and sustained the work. Thanks to the supporters of this project whose feedback allowed me to receive the grant for writing, Claire Colebrook and David Rodowick, both of whom have been inspiring me for decades personally and philosophically. Thanks to Christine Daigle who offered immense support both during the finalization of my previous book and whose editorial feedback on the manuscript has refined it in ways beyond my capacity. Thanks to Liza Thompson, my editor at Bloomsbury. Thanks to Circe and Francesco for sitting on the keyboard when they concluded I had written enough for the day. I am full of gratitude to my friends, especially the memory of Giovanni Lombardo Radice and Ana Djurdjevic, whose deaths were both a shock and reminded me humans can be tolerable too and dreadfully missed. Thank you as always to my Watcher Gabriel for believing and for tireless work for the animals.

The prelude to this book first appeared in Mythopoesis for Techne-Living Systems as 'Cosmic Queer Death Theory' (https://mtls.world/commission/patricia-mccormack/), and I am grateful for their permission to reproduce it here.

This book was written through a Research Fellowship Grant from the Leverhulme Trust.

Prelude
Cosmic Queer Death

What is so queer about death that it remains the one thing which unifies life but remains repudiated by the majority of humans and the very structure of anthropocentrism as under its perceived control? And how is art part of the catalyst which allows us to embrace death, thereby embracing the end of the figure of Anthropos, hence the Anthropocene, itself?

Queer theory has a long relationship with endings – both the endings of lives and the use of the end of species in homophobic discourse. The concept of the 'natural' and 'unnatural' is invoked in anti-queer rhetoric. Yet the 'unnatural!' as an exclamative intervention masquerades the very anthropocentric, especially Oedipal family, church, State and oppressively dominating, aspects of the power humans exert over nature: over the minoritarian, the other, the unlike, the gender, ability, racial, sexual, animal other, all of whom belong to nature. The truth is, we are nature. We are the natural. We are the queer fabulations and infinite differentiations that the metamorphic and evolving natural produces. The Anthropocene is against nature. Against life. Whether we invoke the capacity for reproduction or not in our queer becomings, queering the Anthropocene is a deeply creative, imaginative, artistic and ecological mode of expression that locates humans as pinpoints in a cosmic infinity, producing without reproducing, creating beyond capital. Queering our creativity embraces the death of anthropocentrism, through manifesting alternate modes of signification and understanding, through new escape routes via art (including the art found in science and technology, *ethics and theory). The Anthropocene sees itself as the centre of the cosmos, the colonizing phallic enforcer, repudiating death through technology, religion and reproduction, through lines of blood, familial and national, which persecute alterity and divide the world. The other already belongs with the nation of the dead for the Anthropocene – we are the unmournable, the killable, none so much as the nonhuman animal and the ecological environments destroyed for human encroachment and capitalist extractionism. The natural world is not divided, however, by the ownership of certain peoples based on blood and soil, devastation of colonialism or environmental rape-like exploitation. That is an anthropocentric trope. The world is divided into geo-strata of ages, to which we humans shall be relegated as another un-memorialized carbon collective within the Earth. Let's embrace that future available to us immanently, when we can give back to the Earth with our flesh and our care, our dissolution and our decay. Queer embrace of death laughs at the dominance of the Anthropocene, seeking to make the future of the Earth, of care and of compassion immediate, while attesting to the material devastation humans have perpetrated upon the Earth and its inhabitants as unnecessary and not inevitable. Queer death ends the age of the (now lower case 'a') anthropocene.*

The relationships of nature collapse the dialectics of Man. They are not dissymmetrical. They are not moral. Aberrations are normal. Perpetual repetition is perpetual metamorphosis. The relationships of nature occur in the spaces between each organism within each individual, as each individual entity nourishes its own ecosystem. Each entity forges strange participations with all other entities to constitute one another. Temporal. Geo-spatial. Ephemeral. A slice of life. A plane of consistency. We do not yet know how these planes operate cosmically, how gases and stardust and myriad molecules create their own relationality. What is there to know? For anthropocentrism, the impulse to knowledge is a will to power that begins with curiosity and ends with exploitation. It imposes a social contract onto anything there is 'to be known'. From excavation to manipulation. The natural wonder converts to resource. The impulse to artistic creativity in curious thought is different. It is at once an escape route from anthropocentrism and a seeking to gorge strange relations with the exhaustively unknowable. The natural and the cosmic are different in consistency, but resonant in their co-minglings, constellations of manifold unlike intensities. Or perhaps their resonance is simply a first step to thinking the ways we can go beyond anthropocentrism to embrace the wonder of alterity and the end of the master and slave, including the other as resource. In our curiosity how can we become resource? How can we desire curiosity with consent and reciprocity? In the terrestrial natural world this is more difficult. We can care for environments and for nonhuman animals. We can listen to non-anthropocentric utterances and share escape routes. Our tactics remain mammalian, predatory, problematic, perhaps irresolvable, but we continue because the most important ethical projects are of course the impossible ones. Yet if we wish to become host, to care with becoming-resource, and resourceful, we must learn to die. We must become queer to ourselves and unbind the self that we seek to refine or sustain in the increasingly capitalist pursuit of 'equality' or 'superiority'. While Eastern metaphysics has long espoused the joys of the death of self, Western metaphysics has overcome the crisis with God, Logic, Science, Capital. Always an overcoming. What if death of self was about desire instead of lament? Is this an artistic expression of radical compassion, caring for a world whose death we are causing?

There are so many ways to die. But for many of us humans, most in fact, we were never granted the full subjectivity and agency humanism peddled to us. So isn't it time we stopped trying to be equal by performing sameness, where women have to become men to succeed and people of colour have to erase their history, where the disabled have to adapt to prove worthiness and where species are treated based on their proportionality with humans, eat the pig, pet (or kick) the dog, wipe out the species or incarcerate it for our children's entertainment. This is a false ascendency. We should instead be sharing escape routes from anthropocentric superiority and its seriality (A is to B) and proportionality (A is to B as B is to C) to a full liberation from the structures that validate through recognition and 'knowledge'. We all already share escape routes, the woman walking home alone at night, the man of colour pulled over by the cops, the nonbinary person using a toilet, the disabled person figuring out how to ask for assistance without wanting to seem to need it and the billions of animals screaming as they cower from slaughter, or pace in their cages, or slink away in the dark because they know that to not be known is better than being known by humans. When we are silent and we exist in the dark, we do not have to consider ourselves absent. Yes it is important and pleasurable to be heard or seen in the right way. But there is artistry in all escape route tactics of alterity. The actions, always towards as well as away from, a multi-trajectory escape, are what define the self, instead of the signification and subjectification of our gender, race, sexuality, ability and, most importantly for Earth ethics, species. Our identities queer when we all exist as singularities in the silent darkness, because we know that we monsters can hear in this silence and see in the darkness. The enlightenment was an interrogation room for we witches. Our doings, whether they be science, literature, philosophy, must orient towards artistry and care for the Earth to flourish. Our doing. Not our being. Our constituting new escape routes and new spaces for the infinite others who cannot do or be because of the suffering imposed by human subjects, we who subject the Other.

So let's be monsters. If women are monsters, let's embrace it. If the woman, racial other, the disabled, the trans, all of us who have belonged to the arena of teras, wonder and terror, have always already been monsters, with high killability capacity, let's belong with our brethren the dead. There are many kinds. But they all share delightful distortions of ambiguity with genders, desires, the natural and the social, the human and the nonhuman animal. It is not our place to fetishize or co-opt the materiality of the otherness of an individual human or animal, so the new narrative of devolved becoming (becoming-woman, becoming-animal) is out. Instead let us think through and activate our artistry with the monsters of death: vampires with their femme phallic seduction (always preferable to the hero), to the witches from Circe and Hekate and Inanna to modern witches occupying the veil with unashamed womanhood and queer gendering, to Frankenstein's creature, that brown-skinned vegan empathic creation, whom Mary Shelley made far more ethical and articulate than his hubristic maker, to the zombies who critique and make account colonial violence while transforming from servile reminders of perpetual slavery to plague crazed reminders of the prioritizing of science towards the healthy white man, to the lycanthrope who shows the natural still lives in us, giving men a lunar cycle that means they eat their family. The world of art, literature, film creates animated dead who express escape routes towards life lived differently, who make humans the host, who sometimes enchantingly and sometimes violently treat us as we treat them. But instead we become the willing victims. And in this willingness our desires are queered, our death is a queer rebirth.

And what of the cosmic? There are certain monsters invoked by certain writers, whom I choose here to not name for their variously misogynistic, racist ableist blatherings, but, in true queer style, I both read and misread. These writers of what could be horror, fantasy, sci-fi, express their inner existential anxieties through externalized monsters and terrifying worlds. Except . . . many of these ancient ones and elder gods, these necromancers (only of the entrails of the human dead, mind) and, most of all, these non-anthropocentric scales, these enormities beyond human apprehension, these are us. The mostly white, male, heteronormative authors, just like the Ancient Greek heroes, are seeking escape routes from these cosmic beings and worlds. They exclaim the horror and try to flee without ever developing the compassion and empathy into which that impulse could convert. While we think how to become compassionate resources in our immediate surroundings, our multidirectional desiring trajectories can also become cosmically inclined to those incomprehensible worlds and monsters beyond our capacity to know or demarcate. These monsters, these cosmic shudderings, we feel. And in their absolute fabulation perhaps this is how we can become intuitively sensitive to those for whom we are the inapprehensible gods. For what else can billions of nonhumans be thinking, that they are led into unimaginable suffering and murdered? Without seriality or proportionality we can attend to an obligation (attendre) borne from a liberation (becoming queer-dead) taken from a horrification (of those writers with great worldings but tedious responses).

So what of the obligation of art? It is even deeper and more cosmically intimate. How can art view from a cosmic perspective while retaining the absolute critical intimacy of an animal in pain or of a gallery viewer in need of an affect that produces the ability to think without knowing and comprehend without apprehending? The mystery of the cosmos is also the abstraction of what art can do now. The history of women like Shelley and idiot stereotype white men has been queered by new theorists and theories of affect. What kinds of jolt can be produced to kill subjects? To kill the desire to be a subject? To be recognized? To climb the ladder of subjectification? That is an arena which belongs to desire and so the affect of art must quell that desire more than it reiterates subjectivity, even if it is in need of representation. Are the occupants of art, the figures, the characters, the forms, the outlines, the slashes able to show verbings, escape routes? Neo-capital has made art very small indeed, a tiny verisimilitude of value which has displaced affect or even the didactic and dialectic version of art we were relieved to see go. Can our ecosophical ethical art practices, in all epistemes, a queer, cosmic art, make the anthropocene die (or at least only one dying option among many thriving)?

Man seeks to defeat death. Or is defeated by death. For those never-Man, we run towards death as an act of love. To lose oneself. To be born. In acts of creativity through art we are lost to ourselves, we become immersed, not in the nihilism, martyrdom or sacrifice of subjectivity, but in the ecstasy of becoming-cosmic, of becoming-generative through each molecule and its unique trajectory of novel connectivities. Nothing is lost. Everything is its own potential through the unlike ways in which it connects with all else. What matters is our capacity to allow the other to be generative, to open up liberty for the other. Our escape routes are themselves liberated from being defined by the paradigm from which we seek to escape. Art metamorphizes escape routes into probing immersions in the mysteries of what can be when we are dissipated within and as the cosmos instead of bound by reactive diminishing anchors of subjectification and stratification. That is all we need ask of art – is it a dissipative practice of ecstasy, where 'the artist' themselves is dead because only imaginative action and affect matter as they transform the matter of those who witness and experience the art. The art is the escape route, we are mere psychonauts adventuring through what the art envelops us in, what enraptures us towards multiple ecosophical relations which encourage the human, nonhuman, vegetal, mineral to thrive. How can art create experiences of seeing in the dark, of listening to and hearing those utterances and cries inconvertible to human language? How then can these artforms ignite an ecstatic jouissance which allows our activism to be jubilant, even while we mourn for the unmournable and save the uncounted? Finally, how can we smooth the consistency of the many divergent and often dissonant collectives of activism in order to ensure we are always acting and performing artistry in ways which open new spaces for the other to express their own jouissance freely and without anthropocentric conditions? The answer to this is to die to ourselves, to call out the seductive lie that is the promise of subjectivity existing as equality in the anthropocentric world. To run towards the death of the subject as a coveting of new creative unions where intensities coagulate, where mucosal skeins and veils compress and expand and where the endless signifying divisions of the anthropocene are no more, collapsed instead into a cosmic universe of escape routes and infinite escaping towards pure potentials for otherworldly, and yet deeply natural, becomings.

Introduction

How post can posthuman go?

The seeming oxymoron of a concept such as death activism in a world teeming with unjust and dissymmetrical mass death, of humans, species and environments, manifests from queering the way we think about death precisely due to these circumstances. While not unique to these times, unjust and dissymmetrical death seems to be a multi-directional chaotic series of forces congruous with a new end-of-days anthropocene, coming from pandemic, environmental crisis, wars small and large, widening resource access gaps and increasingly industrialized mass death of bodies valued for their commodification, human and nonhuman. In many academic fields, the end of the world has already happened or been announced, particularly in relation to human exceptionalism and the death of Anthropos. However, semiocapitalism – the conversion of flesh and materiality to signifiers evaluated on capitalist exchangeability – and the virtualization of bodies and lives emergent through use value alone, mean material death is measured by numerical value rather than by individual life cessation or singular emergent energies. Material death as tragic or as a right of an individual is a shimmering illusion in the hands of neo-capitalism, a form of unthinkable death akin to times of great wars, but now including most earth life forms and deep-time earth events, themselves accelerated deathbound strata. Death activism proposes thinking death against its neo-capital heritage of signification through resource use value. There is no good or bad death; there are only ethical encounters that apprehend death as a troubled and troubling phenomenon vastly different between subjects, lives and connective environments. This book asks how the concept of death in a world where life is understood through hierarchies of subjectification and stratification can liberate material life from these anthropocentric signifying systems. It asks how self-death relations can be seen as joyful. It facilitates a different, queer death attitude to other Earth occupants, which prioritizes the gift of grace required to foster ethical interpersonal and interspecies encounters. For the field of Death Studies, this book offers an expansive and inclusive attendance to how different emergences of life are bestowed with equally different deaths. Taking the endowment of what counts as life and death further than humans alone, death activism counts all death, thereby counting all lives, be they in reference to the already vast spectrum of humans or to the even vaster and more precarious mass deaths of nonhuman animals, environments and ecological symbioses. Empathically but problematically, much of death studies focusses on the enormous dissymmetry in human deaths. Ecological studies often resonates this focus with the death of environments measured by their detriment to human populations and individuals. This book asks what happens when humans address the death of all lives and living systems and, more radically, how we can live for the Earth to thrive, rather than living as if the Earth exists for our thriving alone. Here is the place where death studies, in its nuanced evaluation of the ubiquitous fact of death measured with how very differently we measure the right to or value of life between subjects, meets posthumanism. As both a philosophy and a practice, the field of study which is posthumanism proper has sought to decentralize the figure of the human, especially as universal, eternal and superior. In its infinite guises, posthuman practices look to animals and nature, including plants, minerals and geology, to think new ways of living with the Earth. Technology plays various roles within this scope, from prioritized in certain incarnations, to allowing for a more flourishing relationship with the Earth against extractionist technology that seeks only to plunder to 'overcoming' humanist laments about mortality that can lead to a further level of human supremacy. Posthumanism also ranges from the pastoral, how to live with nature, to the futuristic, how acceleration towards extinction is inevitable. In this sense, there are a number of ways in which this book is both a book of posthuman practice and antagonistic to certain problems with posthumanism, namely the tendency to fetishize animals and nature for ultimate humanist purposes and the desire to save humans from potential catastrophes of our own making. In its optimistic incarnations, posthumanism dismantles the myth of human superiority and what it shares with death studies, the idea that there is one kind of human to represent all. Posthumanism as inspired by philosophy emphasizes connectivity and relationality with all life and technologies, with the infinite expressions and affects that allow any entity to emerge, and the many entities within one such as the human self, body and mind, as well as the one entity made of many, such as societies and activist movements. Death activism seeks to resist the anthropocentric impulse to know in order to allow to thrive, a humanist impulse also resisted by posthumanism. But it also counts all life as absolutely without hierarchy, a schema usually resisted by even the most hardened ecologist. This means the book takes the word *posthuman* as its most literal – how to no longer be human at all. In some chapters this is enacted with dances with aesthetics, which make strange our relationship with life through our artistic practices dealing with death. In others a more concrete relationship with death – our own and others – is called upon to suggest how we may end the arrogance of anthropocentrism by living actually posthuman practices, our lives measured by what they do for the Earth and the nonhuman other, and where counting as human becomes less relevant than forging relationships that produce thriving between species and environments. In between are discussions of how death can assist in alleviating the trauma of the demand we manifest as sovereign subjects, refining our selves into exquisite but empty simulations of life which capitalism demands. Each example is a posthuman practice because, against the simulation of sovereign subjectivity, real material practice is required as a form of art as activism (and vice versa) to pique becoming-posthuman so that the category of human simply does not matter anymore. The phantasy of equality based on counting as human, a ruse of semiocapitalism and neo liberalism, is left behind altogether, a tactic many posthumanists would find a step too far in our posthuman adventures but which, for the purposes of this book, shows the posthuman as attempting to find itself truly outside the term *human* and its associated concepts of humanism and human exceptionalism. The desire to count as human is the first death we must engage in order to become death activists. For many humans we never counted anyway and the energy expended to ascend to being counted as human is, in death activism, better utilized in service to queering ourselves and our fellow earthlings by resisting human-centred knowledge, human supremacy and human destruction of the Earth. Allowing the other who will never count to thrive is the foundation of practices outside the human entirely – the posthumanism which for many would be beyond the limit of how post- our posthumanism can go. The intensities and affects these produce are as poignant as they are joyful, affects beyond human language but surely preferable to the constant lament which threatens to atrophy our activism in the current ecological crisis. The posthuman experiments with our relationship with death are here presented as practical ways we can rethink the capacity for life to thrive – without counting, without being human, without conditions of knowledge or hierarchies of value. In an ecstasy of radical compassion, we die to ourselves to be born to posthumanity.

Anthropos and Thanatos

The inspiration for the concept of death activism was initially inspired by work with the Queer Death Studies (QDS) network. Queer death studies is an international network of researchers, artists, scientists and philosophers seeking to queer the way we think about death for an ecosophical future and to understand the status of death as it relates to and bolsters human exceptionalism in the continued exploitation of the Earth. It covers topics from algae to advocating for human extinction, with trajectories of care, of ethics and of dehierarchizing life on Earth, indeed rethinking the very concepts of life and death. During the first annual QDS conference in Karlstad in 2019 (pre-plague), as the various papers and panels unfolded, it occurred to me that many, if not all, of the 'lives' being discussed, as minoritarians, for infinite reasons, never really counted as living humans. And living humans are the benchmark for how we tally a life that matters and therefore a death that matters. The precision with which the majoritarian emerges as an instance of refined power, which includes the power of counting as a life, is relatively small. It is temporally contingent, and to an extent geographically so, although Western life and its consumer impact make that form of life more devastating, while each community has greater and lesser valued lives, often inextricably entwined with other lives utilized as consumable objects, human and nonhuman. Those humans who do not count, or count as diminished versions of Anthropos, as well as nonhuman life, environments, even cellular life where the very meaning of a living or not-entirely-living emergence is unclear, make up the enormous majority of the Earth's symbionts. What counts as life is, on the whole, more queer than not, if dominant anthropocentric definitions and instances of a certain kind of life are measured. Human exceptionalism, those exceptional humans, define the life denied to instances of life because those instances fail to fulfil the rigid criteria of life that matters. Failure, in contemporary capitalism, teeters on a precarious brink between consumable and consumer (especially for humans in the case of women and so-called 'developing' consumers), fetish and food (in the case of 'wild' life and farmed nonhuman animals) among other unstable or oscillating examples of a life, compared with life as a lived human subject. Anthropos, the living sovereign human subject, stands in opposition to the living 'thing' or a thing whose life is 'for' the living pleasure and experience of another. Pleasure is frequently claimed as need.

The emergence of life as a concept is contingent on the relation between organisms and their interpreters. There is an argument to be made that women, queers, BIPoC, disabled, monstrous, nonhuman, imperceptible instances were never alive to begin with. The field of 'social death' studies invokes the concept of 'liminal incorporation', which occurs when a human being is 'still part of society but socially dead' (Kràlovà 2017: 2). Beginning with histories of slavery, currently, social death can refer to death in the context of

> death studies and gerontology [which] concentrate on loss of role, of social identity, of social capital, and of social networks; refugee studies examine displacement, social exclusion, loss of citizenship, of economic capital and of access to resources; slavery studies look at interplay of power dynamics and examine the loss of cultural capital and of links across the generations, on which genocide studies also draw. (Kràlovà 2017: 2)

For social death to occur, it is unclear whether the status of social life need first be recognized to some extent at least, even if as intrusive social life (the enemy within model) or as extrusive (the fallen away or expulsion model). Jana Kràlovà examines slavery as the developmental example of these situated social life/death ambiguities. This example emphasizes the observational enunciation of the status of life and death from the dominant masquerading as neutral. For the slave, freedom, thus liberated life, is not available, even as a not-yet, and death has already occurred though in this conundrum life is yet to appear. Social death is by decree; the slave's status is neither self-proclaimed nor negotiated. The intrusive living slave is an enemy to what is counted as life, the life of the enslaver counts as a life, while that of the slave does not, in spite of being alive. The extrusive living slave is an enemy to what is seen as necessary in order to live; the enslaver maintains barriers of what proper life should be, yet the slave lives on. This is one example of the persistent and perpetual denial of life to lives converted to capital who have the perceived audacity to remain, especially if their remaining is not docile. The objectification of the enfleshment of the socially dead other is prioritized over autonomy. The seeming divide between the either/both inside/outside socially dead/alive entity is reflected in many critiques of logocentrism in continental philosophy regarding a shift from cognition to affect, logic to embodiment, demarcated conceptual *polis* to relational connection. Aspects of cognition include sensation converted to recognition, reason, repetition. Those of affect encompass virtualisation, difference unto itself, corporeality without signification. This general shift from Cartesianism to a form of Deleuzianism becomes more complex with the intervention of semiocapitalism. The concept of 'the' world is 'a' world. Claire Colebrook sums up the space between any apparent neatness of the Cartesian divide of mind/body that mirrors the world/a world:

> Maturana and Varela, insisting on the embodied nature of the mind, reject the notion of 'a' world that would then be pictured or known by a distinct self. There is no world in general, no subject in itself; the world is always given *for* this or that living system and *as* this domain or horizon of possible affects to which bodies would respond. The Cartesian subject is not only a philosophical error; it is embedded in a tradition of Western individualism in which minds are set over against a world that they qualify and master. (2014: 85–86)

Defenders may argue that the signified(s) of logic(s), the impetus for a political cognition beneath an affiliation tactical schema, while open for criticism within Cartesianism (though never entirely stable), retains a sharedness, a communicative series of social-cognitive firings, always misfires but tentatively expressive and affective. Cartesian economies of social subjective cognition in capitalism reduce the flesh of others to use value. According to Jean Baudrillard, the signifier designates economic value, the foundation of which is (or claims to be, or conceals that it is) in ideology. The use value is the signified; it disproves the signifier being driven by 'need' or by a certain consented morality. The sign itself thus reveals its arbitrariness, 'still, the arbitrariness of the sign is, at bottom level, untenable. The sign value cannot admit its own deductive abstraction anymore than exchange value can. Whatever it denies and represses, it will attempt to exorcise and integrate into its own operation' (Baudrillard 1981: 162). What is denied and repressed? Integration and exorcism of that which is denied and repressed – what I will term *anthropocentric motive* – resonates with the auto- and allo-social death of the intrusive enemy within and the extrusive abject exile without. The social contract of Cartesian individualism is undeniably one of shared individualism in competition rather than repetition. Majoritarian techniques and motives of power – the definition of the denied and repressed – may seem consistent between individuals, be they persons, states, political movements and so forth. These techniques reserve the luxurious right to remain in the realm of the world *for* and *to* them, rather than their occupation within the world acknowledged as a parasitic seeking of affects from competitors who may appear different, even antagonistic, but who play upon the same field of logic, cognition and economic signifieds. The other, especially aligned with flesh as commodity, is not individual so much as a unit of increment. Jean François Lyotard names this site of judiciary consensus the locale of the *differend*, the victim or plaintiff who cannot speak or cannot be heard.

> Reality is not what is 'given' to this or that 'subject', it is the state of the referent (that about which one speaks) which results from the effectuation of establishment procedures denied by a unanimously agreed upon protocol ... I would like to call *the differend* the case where the plaintiff is divested of the means to argue, and for that reason becomes a victim. (Lyotard 1988: 4, 9, original emphasis)

The minoritarian social dead cannot speak. If they speak, they will not be registered as speaking because their language or logic does not resonate with that of the signifying regime. If they are able to be registered as speaking, they cannot be victims, because they are able to speak and be understood as (failing to be) victims, either because they are not dead or because they are not so damaged as to be rendered unintelligible. The fatal conundrum of the differend shows beings, entities, organisms living, expressing, affecting, but to a world for and of humans, dead either as agents or because they are commodities, or both. As commodified beings, the flesh of the minoritarian is abstracted; 'it' is a unit *for* the slaver/exchanger but belongs to a non-Cartesian world of non-signifiable as real experience. It is present, to itself, in a way that is utterly divided from its presence to the world. A particular poignancy occurs in attempts to resolve the effects of Cartesian division and its capitalist manifestations when considering how very abstracted the differend other is to and for the world while simultaneously being sometimes excruciatingly corporeally present to itself. The agony of social death by means of slavery, genocide, of being the differend through gender, race, disability, species, is the precise revelation that though this being's being a being is not recognized, they continue to experience the affects of power. While there are many jubilant effects of this as a form of liberty, which will be explored in this book, it is easy to be first catalysed to think about death and the affects leading to death because of this poignancy. Elaine Scarry writes: 'as in dying and death, so in serious pain the claims of the body nullify the world. . . . Intense pain is also language-destroying: as the content of one's world disintegrates, so the content of one's language disintegrates; as the self disintegrates, so that which would express and project the self is robbed of its source and its subject' (Scarry 1985: 33, 35). In some instances, the other may learn the dominant language and perform it as a kind of charade, but unless the liberty to express and exist is available, the being does not exist and, as differend, is capable of neither pain nor technically death (this would be counted as loss of capital or at best tragic statistic for the person to and for whom the world belongs). Who can speak the world, expressed and lived by each nonhuman other, for and of itself? The wonder found in the utterly other world of the other, even while it is a shared world with us, threatens to reveal the nonhuman other's existence as a being while elucidating the world is for no one species or form of existence, from human to Anthropos. Teeming, mass presences of others are all around us within this world, which is their world yet as differends they too exist for the human. The language of the other is adamantly audible. Scarry writes: 'Physical pain is not only itself resistant to language but also actively destroys language, deconstructing it into the pre-language of cries and groans. To hear those cries is to witness the shattering of language' (1985: 172) for those species humans arguably most affect with parasitic suffering, farmed and vivisected nonhuman animals; there are corporeal and audible pre-linguistic cries and groans. Anthropos does not register the pre-linguistic; humans turn away. This is why Carol Adams calls the nonhuman animal the absent referent (1995, 2014). When the nonhuman animal is present, they are still absent. When 'ethics' are discussed between humans on the morality of behaviours towards the differend, they are still absent. The voluminous affective corporeal existence of so many human and nonhuman animals who are absented from these signifying regimes often conflates social death and anthropocentric death with actual death. Pain and suffering can also be included in this form of death (just as dying is included in death studies). The question of how to explore the liberties and joys of being embodied while not registering remains in the ever ominous light of the fact of being reduced to a commodified embodiment is what leads so many to pain, suffering and death. Because they are flesh, they don't count. Because they are flesh, we cannot register them. Because they are flesh, they are only flesh, and one must be either mind or flesh, social or natural. These are also arbitrary bifurcations that need negotiation, just as increasingly the 'we' and 'they' need negotiating in a world where victimhood is structured as incremental, too often leading to the prioritization of one form of victimhood over others, as if each victim must experience the world of and for themselves first in isolation. Thinking a simultaneity of liberty which enmeshes an enfleshed experience with the world between 'we' and 'they' when most of the world's beings are always together and both is further complicated by semiocapitalism's co-option of corporeal affectivity. While many theorists celebrate affective embodiment as rendering an emergence of enfleshed politicization, Colebrook flags affective existence as a risk of ultra contemporary addiction based on capitalism's desiring machinization of affective repetition without politico-collective context leading to 'narcissistic enclosure' (2014, 85). Pleasurable short-circuiting creates repetitions of jolts of signifiers utterly devoid of anything beneath, from social media likes, to purchasing disposable items (and everything seems disposable) until the signified for all of contemporary capitalism's jolts is 'next'. Franco Berardi (2015) sees this jolt as integral to semiocapitalist belonging. This could be a strange new turn of Lacan's desire that exchanges objects eternally until death, dematerialized because the physicality of the object is barely residual in its experience, except that the physicality of the slave labour, of the murdered nonhuman flesh, of the genocide leading to the social media post of 'support' for the absent referents is very real. Perhaps this pleasurable jolt is a numbing opiate, countering the affectivity of permanently and perpetually wound up capital precarity of living pay to pay, day to day, again raising the spectre of competitive victimhood to try make sense of the violent eruption of competitive super-exploitation. Berardi's term to describe the new affect, which is narcissistic, because the affect is selfish and neurotic, is the 'spasm' (2015: 217).

Life as commodity extends to life as fetish, symbol, representative idea or ideal. Life that exists as a living entity among and within other living entities can often seem reduced to or limited by anthropocentric versions of that life. How to think about life and living beyond human signifieds of life, even before the lives without any signification, means these lives are divested of the status of life proper, in spite of living. The seemingly easy difference between social and biological life belies the claim that all life is socially ordained, because it belongs to the social contract. Michel Serres states:

> The Philosopher of Science asks: but who, then, is inflicting on the world, which is henceforth a common objective enemy, this harm that we hope is still reversible, this oil spilled at sea, this carbon monoxide spread in the air by the millions of tons, these acidic and toxic chemicals that come back down with the rain . . . whence comes this filth that is choking our little children with asthma and covering our skin with blotches? Who, beyond private and public persons? What, beyond enormous metropolises, considered either as aggregations of individuals or as networks of relations?

> Our tools, our arms, our efficacy, in the end our reason, about which we're so legitimately vain: our mastery and our possessions.
>
> Mastery and possession: these are the master words launched by Descartes at the dawn of the scientific and technological age, when our Western reason went off to conquer the universe. We dominate and appropriate it: such is the shared philosophy underlying industrial enterprise as well as so-called disinterested science, which are indistinguishable in this respect. Cartesian mastery brings science's objective violence into line, making it a well-controlled strategy. Our fundamental relationship with objects comes down to war and property. (2002: 31–32)

In the social contract, life is the possession and mastery of what is living in order for it to be counted as life (and 'it' and 'counted' are the capital aspects of objects, spoils of war, since capitalism is economic combat). The division between life as sentient agential subject and living organism or object seems, from an anthropocentric perspective and equally from an ethical perspective, more immediately in need of negotiation than the division between life and death. Nonetheless, death, especially in certain organisms, has a unique form of finitude. My positioning of minoritarians of all species as already dead is not to conflate these designations (for any clarity in categorization still comes from possession and war even in times of reclamation) with non-living objects. The formation, after Serres, of a natural contract involves reimagining the very liminal and clinamen behaviour of a divide. The point of division is mythical, representing a definition gap that is both voluminous and the point of ethical opportunity: voluminous because the tipping point of the clinamen over from life to death is itself a legal, biotechnological one always alien to each individual organism's experience of that death, and utterly unknowable, a knot of interiority and exteriority that draws resonant binaries of culture and nature, observer and self. The clinamen reverberation area as a point of ethical opportunity arises because the clinamen is the turbulence from the general to the exceptional as it is from the material to the theoretical, an opportunity to rethink how we imagine life's passage to death in socio-political ethics and in individual considerations based on compassion.

> The question now is simple: does a streaming remain laminar? And the answer is equally simple: in fact, in practice, physically speaking, a flow always is or becomes, turbulent. The *clinamen* is the infinitesimal turbulence first, but it is *also the passage from theory to practice*. And once again, without it, we understand nothing of what goes on. It is thus a matter of experience. (Serres 2000: 83)

Serres posits that our relationship with the phenomenon of the clinamen, which tends to reflect how we relate in general, and how we see relations, can be described in one of two ways. The anthropocentric way is *foedera fati*, the Order of Mars. This structures all relations as that of combat, usually reducible to two (knowledge and 'everything else', humans and 'everything else'). Fati refers to the finitude of battles where the outcome becomes truth and the victor designer of that truth. The alternative is the Order of Venus, *foedera naturae*. This structure is a continuum of unconditional love. By being unconditional, love resists demand for knowledge, for finitude, for time, for a dialectic structure reducible to two, and for any form of combat, a being with rather than being against. This book will refer frequently to these two orders. However it is important not to mistake this as simply another dualism, or to place these two Orders into their own Order of Mars where we fight for one to be victor. These two Orders are ways of seeing or thinking of the same situations and relations. The Order of Mars demands conditions, oppositions and winners. It reduces the infinity of life to a reducible two and from an anthropocentric perspectivereduces all to knowability, control, ownership and power. The Order of Venus perceives through the inevitability of life itself, before and beyond knowledge, without demarcation or division that knowledge creates. It is simply how the Earth is, not how the Earth is apprehended with human perception imposed upon it. It is neither better nor worse, but shows that humanism is only one of infinite ways of relating with the world. It is not the opposite of the Order of Mars, it is the voluminous everything that exists outside of the limited scope that the Order of Mars produces of nature. Critically, it is nature without a contract,while the Order of Mars is a social contract. The love of the Order of Venus similarly is not love of an other or an object but the laminar flow which produces turbulences and shifts in multi-relational affectivity. The Order of Venus shows that the Order of Mars is an arbitrary signifying battle humans choose, and that there are other ways, thinkable and unthinkable, which far exceed human knowledge. The creative imperative of the Order of Venus is how we formulate the clinamen that best allows other life to thrive, in ways small and large. These Orders will be elaborated further, however at this point it is important to see them as ethical turns rather than another oppositional binary.

Serres's alignment of externally observed knowledge with the Order of Mars finds anthropocentric knowledge's particular interest in the rare as exception. By this technique, the ordinary is considered stable and homogenous. On the one hand, this means the rare is othered, so the other exists in order to be studied and known, becoming the fetish/symbol divested of unique existence unto itself. On the other hand, knowledge loses interest in the rare as knowledge subsumes it into epistemological orders, so the individual instance of an exception becomes a greater symbol for the entirety of many individuals. This is so in the case of gender and race but also the foundation of species and therefore speciesism, making it almost impossible to think of individual organisms, human and nonhuman, as having a dividuated, singular self. The organism as clinamen evinces that species, gender, race as consistent flow are incapable of attending to the complex turbulences which make up any entity and are able to describe the turbulence in the act of pronouncing knowledge as a meeting point of biological materiality, anthropocentric enunciation, the social and natural. The relationship between anthropocentric knowledge and 'its' object is only one of the multiple streams and trajectories through which any organism emerges, not even including those streams within an organism in excess of a demarcated self or enclosed system. Reminiscent of Gilles Deleuze and Fèlix Guattari's rhizomatic structure, life as clinamen and the pronouncement of what constitutes life and death as clinamen as well as the experience of life and death as clinamen (from precarity of life to the duration of dying) are a way of thinking the turbulent durational phenomena accounting for infinite variables and theorizing the spaces between – between bodies, between knowledges and between life and death. Christine Daigle and Terrance MacDonald state of Deleuze and Guattari's contribution to the field of posthumanism in the wake of the oppression humans wage on the Earth:

Indeed, the human's rationalistic attempts to gain control over oneself and live ethically have failed since ethical theories have all understood the human in terms of false categories and formulas which frame the human as transcendent. The mode of thinking is in utter disregard of the being of the human that fails to fit these rational and logical ideals. Despite its illusory power and its continued attempt to do so, human reason is unable to rationalise the irrational or, better said, the a-rational. Life itself, in its dynamic overflowing state of flux, resists and subverts as it unfolds as an auto-poietic force. (2022: 2)

Rationalized construction of subjectivities is intimately connected with not only gender, race, species and other minoritarianism but also 'killability', meaning the flow without turbulence claim can directly lead to death and a vindication of violence as 'necessary', 'natural' or any other motive gleaned not from need but from anthropocentric rhetoric in style as well as in proclamation. Jen Wrye discusses, in terms of the murder of billions of farmed animals by the pet food industry: 'Killability means that some lives do not count fully – those bodies are already transformed into the decimated, objectified object. This is so because narratives that justify violence toward, or the death of, others means that some lives become dead already' (2015: 100), Wrye acknowledges the already dead status of farmed animals in comparison with the status of the pet given an Oedipal, pseudo-relational status, be it baby or companion. The connection between the two is the creation of and for the world by humans on behalf of these two kinds of nonhuman animals. One is denied life, one independent liberty, both denied emancipation to exist unto themselves because the world created of and for them is a world created between humans. Neither domestic nor farmed species are allowed agency, and this before any attention to the individual who exists beyond the ontological limits set for them through species and salient function or use. Wrye's topic is especially interesting in that both nonhuman animals are positioned as existing for humans, in vastly different ways, yet the death practices following their killability are often almost opposite: the slaughtered farm animal, barely registering as a number except for the profit made, unseen, unmourned, within a factory setting where the murder is an inconvenient part of many in the mechanization of life as profit object, and the lamented pet, who is often gifted euthanasia, mourned and missed and whose memory remains indelible. The demand to choose a species in battling malzoan anthropocentrism reflects that of choosing a human minoritarian status to support. Both are false demands challenged by increasingly intersectional activisms and theories. Both show the translation of the turbulent flow of life of any entity converted to anthropocentric subject or object (often both), symbol, fetish or unit of profit also converts that entity's precarity in reference to their death.

Serres's Order of Mars is elucidated when wars are waged against lives and mass deaths occur within a nonhuman-to-human combat scenario, and where the other is not an enemy in conflict, but where these mass deaths are accepted precisely because the unique singularity of life is not registered. Studies of the lives and deaths of individuals, minoritarians and species can embrace thinking about the flow and clinamen of existence in varying fractal degrees, from the interiority of the individual to the practices that constitute lived existence and the becoming-dead (both conceptually and organically). Each turbulence may offer an opportunity for the practice of making-dead or becoming-dead (killability or 'natural' lifespan) to reroute the stream of that practice. Killability is as critical for activism as it is for death studies, because most protests focus on the injustice of entities, human and nonhuman, experiencing violence and death. The fatalistic construction of certain entities as deathbound or never alive means outrage over injustice is simply not audible in certain anthropocentric instances. This is another example of both the inextricability and the interdependence of life and death, as both constructed and usually opposed terms.

We, the dead

To suggest that minoritarians are already dead and never alive is a reclamation of how we imagine it feels to be dead as a qualitative fetish of human imagination – absent, forgotten, unseen, but also laid out, examined, a forensic artefact, a statistic, a homogenized type, be it gender, race, sexuality, species or group. From a vitalistic perspective, can we exchange patterns of war for consistencies of love, reclaiming death while acknowledging social death as a designation of kinds of life, and how they live, and for what they are used. Queer philosophy has a long and intimate relationship with death. Typically, queer death is affiliated with male homosexuality, for example the work of Leo Bersani (2009) and Lee Edelman (2004). Increasingly, thinking death studies through an active queering of attitudes and intensities of material, social and ecological death has come from feminism and ecosophical understandings, depriveleging the death of the figure of Anthropos. Just as the Vitruvian humanist white heteronormative able-bodied male Judeo-Christian god-simulacrum figure has been challenged as representative of the idea of what constitutes a human, so too the understanding of death is (often unspoken) the death only of that figure or evaluated comparative to the loss of the anthropic. Death is a concept emergent contingent upon the significance of the entity which brings it into being, including an anthropocentric relation with that being (the death of the object of value is raised, for example, when it is objectified by the dominant figure, but not for what it is in itself), creating more or less lamentable deaths. Ecological activism currently reorients towards an ecology of and for Anthropos, for humans certainly and especially Western humans. Sustainability seeks to guarantee the perpetuation of *those kinds of humans*. Mass death or enslavement of particular kinds of humans, and especially nonhuman animals, as well as environments themselves understood as organisms with an eco- and geological durational life, is not measured as equivalent to the lamentable death of the human. The address of death is beyond the death 'of' observation, the familiar Stalin comment that the death of an individual is tragic, while the death of millions is statistic. In counting only certain kinds of death as death and perpetuating a compulsory form of life as living at any cost for a certain kind of figure, what counts as both life and death is more qualitatively nuanced than just numbers, species, even gender, race, sexuality and ability. Queer understandings of death can intervene in both expected and novel ways. So-called extreme ecological radicals who advocate a cessation (or reduction) of human reproduction resonate in activism and perhaps moral attitude from the mainstream with queer culture. The former is immoral for suggesting the outrageous claim that the white Western human isn't compulsorily worthy of continuation at any cost, and the current cost for the Earth is exorbitant. The latter has been variously seen religiously, legally, medically and still morally as caught in the paradox of being illicit because reproduction is not possible 'naturally' (an example of raising of the mythical concept of nature against culture as a convenient anthropocentric rhetorical device). I would argue that in recent times feminism has also foregrounded reproduction as not a glorified uniquely female vindication for the existence of not-men, but as a form of drudge slavery to which women are defaulted, this before the contestation of the normative categories of gender. Reproduction as a battleground of queer feminist eco activism contra anthropocentric normativity is only one site where the privilege and deification of the anthropocentric worldview are challenged, but it is a useful site on which to start because the death of the idea of the inherent value of the Vitruvian Anthropos is what is being contested far more than actual material deaths of any and all organisms. Compulsory reproduction and antinatalism on the eco-queer feminist battleground can be understood as their own form of queer love story. The violent romance between humans and the Earth is complex in that it is a monodirectional struggle of resistance to response and reciprocity unless on human terms. Colebrook states: 'The very eye that has opened up a world to the human species, has also allowed the human species to fold the world around its own, increasingly myopic, point of view' (2014: 22). Complexity and chaotic clinamen balancing, which allows emergent lives to flourish and diminishing exhaustions to make way for new emergences, seem beyond the anthropocentric eye, even while its various manifestations in science, art and philosophy claim to know the Earth better than the Earth knows itself. There seems a deeply heteronormative phallogocentric aspect in this anthropocentric eye, which Adams (1995) critiques as arrogant, mirroring a Lacanian perception of the love object ultimately only for the benefit of the perceiver who is deeply incapable of apprehending or sensing any authentic and displacing alterity beyond its own uses or fascination, which itself remains in the realm of the ideational, not allowing the other its own materiality, singularity and expressivity.

Queering death studies becomes the study of the constellations of the dead, those who were never considered fully alive, those deaths which don't matter, because one must ask surely you have to be alive to be dead? Queer death studies in this book is about both queering death – mourning the uncountable through activism, embracing death for the death denied, creative understandings of never coming into being – and recognizing that categories of life and death do not mean the same for those who do not fulfil anthropocentric exceptionalist ideas of what constitutes a life to die. Each of these elements has its own contemporary human(ist) manifestations and potential queer reimaginings. Mourning the uncountable invokes a particularly poignant history of women and homosexuals as victims of technology (sterilization of desire, electric 'therapy'), of 'nature' (AIDS, but also the vulnerability of immunocompromise and of the increase in violence towards women and non-heteronormative persons during Covid lockdowns) and of a general social antagonism, preceded by a 'just' in front of subjectification – 'just' a woman, 'just' a queer. Race and disability are a key part of this general demarcation of queering, as queered versions of white imperialism and ableist understandings of the human template, so while not belonging to the realm of gender/sexuality per se, they belong to a technique of posthuman*ing* that counts humans who don't count historically while queer-y-ing the validity and ethical motive of using the category at all. This is seen in, for example, Zakkiyah Jackson's claim that the goal for Blacks should not be to become human since human is always coded as white to start with (2020). Embracing death elucidates the frontier of freedom for both the privileged and often the unrecognized in illegality regarding euthanasia, or euthanasia being conditionally regulated only for certain conditions, some lives being considered unliveable while others being observed as seeking a luxuriant or unnecessary death, both of which place the autonomy of death into the hands of external forces. The desire to die beyond the strict limits of these bio technological regimes is considered so utterly queer to a myth of ingrained life force that it emerges in discourse as a pathologization of the self due exclusively to the lack of striving to be a self in preference for a becoming-dead. Death as solace, non-being as peace are relegated to the realms of mental illness in need of a cure, just as homosexuality was once a curable pathology. Humans always exist within a continuum of the normal-pathological (after Georges Canguilhelm) regarding our experience of living the durational intensity of desiring life and desiring death, or absence, or respite, even though this existence is always and only one of living. One could state the normal being of living is a turbulent simultaneous life–death desire.

Death is a constant experience of unbeing, found in sleep, in catatonia, from drugs or exhaustion. These kinds of deaths-in-life are sometimes luxuriant and often necessary; without them we actually die. They do not belong to the order of death as a concept, be it the death drive, or existential angst, or la petite mort or the impossibility of death for a living subject. The deaths necessary to life are unromantic; they are simply a reduction in turbulence, a smoothing entropy within an accelerating and decelerating living. Those who suffer to an absolute limit, where life is intolerable, can demarcate the division between these deaths and the finitude of actual death as desirable and redemptive for alleviating life become unbearable. Creative understandings of never coming into being span a variety of ideas queer to anthropocentric compulsory desire-for-life. The most obvious, and ecologically critical, is the burden on the Earth and its nonhuman occupants – and many of its human occupants – of human population. In *The Ahuman Manifesto* (2020) I advocate human extinction from a perspective of care where Anthropos is asked to examine the perceived inherent value of reproduction of his form. Beyond the outrage this advocacy produces in many humans for myriad (usually arbitrary) reasons, and emphasizing that this is an advocacy neither eugenic nor about population 'control', challenging human reproduction as default has effects on issues of gender and sexuality. The expression 'compulsory heterosexuality' is a common term in queer challenges, and to that can be added 'compulsory breeding'. Inability to reproduce, pre-cloning but historically conveniently forgetting or leaving aside sterile heterosexual subjects, has long been the argument of the 'unnatural'ness of queer desire. The enormity of research on both queer histories of different human peoples and queer nonhuman animals and the challenges to reproduction as a concept through molecular biology have long made this claim defunct. The reversion to what is 'natural' and what is 'unnatural' is also a convenient conversion, of ideological prejudices into a pre-human order of what is right and true. Like the term 'queer', queer culture's structure of family chosen or created rather than biological or bred is part of a larger queer reclamation project that values creativity over the arbitrary alliances of bloodlines that themselves can insinuate resonances with patriotism and associated embattlement and conflict. Queer's choice of creative production of relations and either inability or lack of interest in maintaining reproductions shows the jubilant birth of new unlike affects and trajectories of living as a creative symbiosis that traditional human familial reproduction cannot. For women, the 'miracle' of birth is fed as a mandatory zenith of the grand heteronormative narrative of birth–marriage–reproduction–death. Though not always expected, this narrative remains strangely prevalent, having been repackaged with different, alternative and multiple simulacra of the 'miracle', while the foundational imperative remains relatively constant, to the point where biotechnology such as IVF supports this narrative rather than 'overcoming' its limit. Within this imperative is the insipid image of the unborn or yet-to-be-born child favoured by anti-abortion protestors, enhancing and making enormous the image of the foetus as an almost-quickened giant baby Anthropos at the expense of the forgotten vessel it occupies. The resonances between women's fertile bodies as nothing more than terrains for incubation and the Earth as a terrain for human occupation are historically common and clear.

When death is not death

My advocacy of human extinction, and I claim it as my own to answer for it even though it belongs to a number of different philosophies, including efilism and deep ecology activism, is strangely upsetting even though no actual death is being advocated beyond the death of a species. Violence and murder play no part. What is made dead is nothing more than a concept of not so much a not-yet as a never-been. It seems anthropocentrism is in adoration of the idea of the human species. Far from being a concept, which Deleuze and Guattari define as the navigation of a problem (1994), the human species is an ideal, even idol. The Human is a referent against which living humans are measured, rather than humans living their singular metamorphic being as a constant mediation of conceptual becomings through problem relations. We live against what it means to be human; the world may be for and of the human species, but so too actual human lives are for and of the human world. Human exceptionalism is the phantasm that destroys humans as well as the Earth and its occupants, that image against which we fail, but the constant measuring helps to keep us complacent, identity-oriented to the point of exhaustive narcissism and spasming, and strivingly docile, oxymoronically atrophied. It would be easy to see the escapees of this form of contemporary neo-capital, the posthumanist Übermensch, as the outliers who go beyond because subjectivity has no definition of and for them/us, in conflict with the horrific megalomaniac who uses the tools of capitalism to become a sort of Übermensch posthuman invasive species. Take Guattari's example of Trump:

> Now more than ever, nature cannot be separated from culture; in order to comprehend the interactions between eco-systems, the mechanosphere and the social and individual Universes of reference, we must learn to think 'transversally'. Just as monstrous and mutant algae invade the lagoon of Venice, so our television screens are populated, saturated, by 'degenerate' images and statements [énoncés]. In the field of social ecology, men like Donald Trump are permitted to proliferate freely, like another species of algae, taking over entire districts of New York and Atlantic City; he 'redevelops' by raising rents, thereby driving out tens of thousands of poor families, most of whom are condemned to homelessness, becoming the equivalent of the dead fish of environmental ecology. (2000: 29)

The nature/culture divide is again reorganised to be one involving the exploitation of the 'nature' of capitalism, seen not limited to Guattari's words of 2000, but Trump's 'legacy', among others which currently fester, and the viral 'nature' of micro-fascism in servitude of human hubris measured through the economic incrementality of both power and capital. Queer mortals and 'mere' mortals are allied in the fight against these kinds of posthuman warmongers. Economically enforced death is a collateral expense in the rise of power, creating divided oppositional pro- and anti-positions. Yet in the recent case of Covid, a collateral creation by humans borne of nonhuman animal exploitation, the virus is designated a moral value as 'evil' because it kills humans simply by encompassing the normative seeking to thrive, or it is denied as an absolute lie of world governments by conspiracy theorists who often happen to ally themselves with the separatist, power-adoring more-than-mortals (and it seems no coincidence that the closer these men get to the end of their life, the more voracious their desire for an accumulation of power becomes). To claim such heinous figures are posthuman sullies queer posthumanism as a practice of valuing lives as singularities and unique constellations in relation. It does affirm that there is no guarantee of posthumanism being more ethical. The phenomenon of the ageing white male in power becoming more parasitic, more imperialist, cannot simply be a coincidence considering his proximity to death. This is an ageist statement only defined by the proximity the subject has to power accumulation. It is untrue for most living and ageing humans.

The queer (un)dead

The already-dead-because-never-having-been experience of queer 'non-subjectivity' is posthumanism in practice, a living and joyful alive but possibly socially dead status. The amorphous state of experiencing but not counting as life collates the ways posthumanism bends time – we have always been posthuman, we are yet to be posthuman, humanism and time are non-narrative or linear. The non-definition of posthumanism favoured by material affect theory and activism, seen in feminism, postcolonialism, Afrofuturism, queer postsexuality and other deviations from definitions and identities themselves, is catalysed by the everyday embodied experience of what, for the privileged, can seem a futuristic fabulation or fantasy. Like posthumanism, what seems for some a fiction of being the living dead, or future human, is for others a banal and ordinary existence. This socially dead status is one intersection of what all these minoritarians, in their uniquely expressed incarnations, share. A multi-sharing being, it shares in an additional status of sharing, the unlike-but-like socially dead and nonhuman never counted, the killable. All form a connective collective where divides of nation, state, subject group and licit and illicit alliances do not make sense in the same way as those of majoritarian anthropocentrism. To be dead, queer in alliances and subject (de)formation means to be thriving in conditions often untenable, particularly porous to navigations, creative formations and escape routes. For those who do count, the thought of becoming actually posthuman, as in post-alive, seems to lead to a hoarding of micro-fascisms, a seeking of relations of self-with-self symptomatic of Bernard Stiegler's schema of the neganthropocene (2018), negentropy driven by power as desire and vice versa, short-circuiting alliances of desire with the unlike, whether human, animal, vegetal or mineral. Queer becomings acknowledge the involuted proximal affects in which we live with others, and the singularities which these others are, in excess of taxonomies of subjectification and species.

Take as an alternative to thanatos as the end of the increment of power as capital (subjective and economic), and even the thinking of generic species-becomings, this brilliant meta-anthropocentric imagining of the emergence of the coronavirus via singular encounters between unique singular emergences from potentially arbitrary species in desperate need of liberty from anthropocentrism by Nina Lykke and Camilla Marambio:

III. The bat, the pangolin and the virus: A modern fairytale

> A bat, a pangolin and a virus decided that they would give the Earth a break – to make it possible for her to breathe freely for some time without being burdened by CO2 emissions. So the bat, the pangolin and the virus developed a plan. They wanted to give humans, immersed in hubris and ideas about their superior and exceptional entitlement to treat all other Earth beings as resources, a lesson about kinship and shared vulnerability. The bat and the pangolin knew that it might cost them their lives to make the plan materialise because it involved yet another potentially deadly encounter with humans whose extractivist expansion, radical eradication of their habitats, and intensive poaching threatened both with extinction – not only as individuals, but also as species. However, both felt that it would be worth the try, because the situation for the Earth and all its inhabitants was so desperate anyway, and if they collaborated they might cheat the humans and be able to escape alive. (Lykke and Marambio 2020: 106)

Investing singular nonhuman beings with an agency of threat towards humans as a gift to the Earth mirrors the human fantasy that anything which is not in service to humans must be a malevolence if allowed agency. Alternatively, this is constructed as a chaotic accidental event. The bat, the pangolin and the virus can only emerge in this situation through their singular selves, not as beings but as conditions of human exploitation and responses to these. The unnatural participation (this expression is taken from Deleuze and Guattari, 1987: 240) produces affects, opening potentials for multi-organism Earth thrivings. Neither the bat, the pangolin nor the virus is speciesist or even organism-ist. They are entering queer becomings of species, and life and death collapse into an impulse of affective pedagogy. In the fairytale (because, like all fairytales, it makes the nonhuman think in anthropocentrically legible terms), the natural world makes the most unnatural manoeuvres, but 'these combinations are neither genetic nor structural; they are interkingdoms, unnatural participations. That is the only way Nature operates – against itself' (Deleuze and Guattari 1987: 242). Perhaps queers aren't afraid of death because we seek to become part of deep time, of perverse and entirely natural geostrata plateaus. Long designated by majoritarian subjectification as belonging on an 'unnatural' stratum, queer becomings form chaotic emergences of new formations of living, which may also include dying, especially in the case of parasitic organisms which require a host, like viruses, and humans. Far-right white leaders espouse their being as the pinnacle of god-like 'evolution' in the great acceleration of man's future (used very loosely); meanwhile, the earth is created on layers of microbes driving life creation through divergence and differentiation. The waste these men become in death creates greater flourishing than their lives could, on both a conceptual and a geo-biological level. Myra J. Hyrd and Kathryn Yusoff state:

> Scrape away a little of the humanist hubris in anthropocentric discourses and the era of industrialisation has a bacterial foundation that is less about great white men and more about a super organism that digests binaries as a matter of course, across aeons of time . . . The 'great acceleration' read from a bacterial vantage point is far more a case of the microcosmos relentlessly doing its thing – playing the long game of experimenting in diversification – with humanity naively hitching a ride in short time. (2021: 52–53)

Put simply, from certain vantage points of deep time and multiplicity entities, humans are more creative for life *in* death. Production of life comes not from reproduction but from decomposition. Conceptual navigations of life and death are, after all, a matter of perspective. Any horror of inconsequentiality this may incite in humans is neither more nor less than any other entity's reduction to use and consumptive value for them. As the fairytale concludes:

> The pandemic made conspiracy theories flourish in the human world. However, none of them came close to understand the real conspiracy –

or gift: the collaborative effort of a bat, a pangolin and a virus, who wanted to give the Earth an urgently needed break to breathe, and to teach humans a desperately needed lesson in kinship, shared vulnerabilities and new ethics of human and nonhuman tensegrities, caring and collaboration. (Lykke and Marambio 2020: 106)

The status of species in the fairytale speaks to human parasitism: the bat in this scenario is an accident, the pangolin is a killable commodity and the virus is outside knowledge. Each is measured against three anthropocentric indices: the intruder, the commodity and the unknown. The genesis of the novel coronavirus is itself turning apocryphal as this fairytale confirms. It illuminates the larger world of Earth as multiple tensegrities beyond and even without humans, at the same time showing the lives defined only through the intrusion of humans and the individuality of beings before species or knowledge. Like the inability to think of human extinction or Earth without humans with which many struggle, this fairytale converts natural unnaturality to a story intelligible to humans as its own form of unnatural queer pedagogy, showing up our hypocrisy and the inability of nonhuman beings to exist free of human ensnarement, its own less hypocritical way of defining the majority of entanglement. The hermeneutic self, demarcated from the world, is another form of hypocritical fairytale. Whether considered ensnarement or entanglement is up to any human ideology to decide, based on the level of self-sufficiency and extraction from the world the level of human hubris will allow the embodied mind to conceive. The tilt between mind and body is often the balance of measure in this case, the embodied entangled set at a distance from the cogito ego sum that seems envisaged as living beyond mere material incarnation. Margrit Shildrick describes human evolution and each singular human emergence as a bioassemblage of microchimerism. Shildrick utilizes the term *prostheses* to describe contemporary biotechnologies as well as the being of the human body as its own expression of billions of 'foreign' participants:

The component parts of the microbiome range across innumerable and highly diverse conjunctions of viruses, bacteria and eukaryotes, with a smaller number of archaea. Although microbes are commonly thought of as pathogens in everyday parlance, many are not and even those identified as

> pathogenic – such as some strains of fungi – may play an important role in maintaining healthy populations and even promoting inter- and intraspecies sociality through their effects on cognitive behaviour. (Shildrick 2022: 75)

Challenges to standard binaries of self/world, parasite/host and self/other are expressed in new biological understandings of worlds within the brain, gut, heart and other areas which still, in their loci of attention, take apart the body into larger worlds of occupation – the brain, gut and heart having physiological, biotechnological (especially transplant technology) and symbolic signifiers. An infinite mesh of worlds expressed of and for microbiomes independent of the host defies human perceptions of the invasive other remaining external. The geology of the Earth made of humans turned host through their decomposition (in idealized funereal practices) inflects inward where human is host as a world, as much as thinking the Earth is our own world. I use this example not to close potential humanist narratives with a scientific foil, but to open up multi-layered expressions of worlds teeming with life and death, for and with multiple entities, as operating on both actual and abstract levels. The worlds within we may imagine create a whole new form of fairytales challenging what constitutes life, death, sentience, singularity and multiplicity. Shildrick states:

> The notion of the human life span – the inescapable arc that begins in birth and ends in death – resonates strongly with the modernist move to put the sovereign individual at the centre of attention, but it begins to falter once we think in terms of impermanent assemblages. If posthuman embodiment includes technological materials and even insubstantial digital elements, as do many disability prostheses for example, then what exactly constitutes the moment of death? If organs can be transferred from deceased donors, or non-self cells transmitted over successive generations, is death an end? If the myriad organisms of the microbiome are both entangled with and distinct from their putative human host, where does life reside? (Shildrick 2022: 170)

While absolutely not diminishing or wishing to deny the material, real nature of the billions of nonhuman and human life endings caused by humans, the posthuman apprehension of what the centralized figure of Anthropos sees as the life counted because it is separate from 'the rest' is critically in need of re-evaluation because it challenges the anthropocentric fairy tales we dominating humans tell ourselves to vindicate dominion. For death studies, the clinamen of life and death, and self and other, has effects on the ethics of death-causing and designating 'killability' in others, while also assisting in developing more nuanced access to forms of death for humans who are considered beyond needing access to death through fulfilling the template of valuable life, be that through labour, familial connection or any other situation where death is denied.

In the fairytale of the bat, the pangolin and the virus, death is an act of creative (com)passion. Can thinking about human death differently deliver us from human exceptionalism in our unnatural participations and becomings? In rhizomatic becomings, always greater than the individual and utilizing micro-aspects of any individual's force beyond their own cognition, demarcating points of death can be more and less difficult to pinpoint. The affects which produce unnatural participations are already set in motion from multiple trajectories, and the creative expressions produced by participations as queer new forces together have reverberating polyvalent affects themselves. The beginning and the end of an individual in considering these becomings – whether socio-political, activist or biological – is contingent on a number of factors which, while sometimes difficult to attest to with precision, begin before that individual's beginning and end far beyond their end. This risks instigating a configuration of martyrdom except that accidental, tactical and desiring participations do not happen beneath a proper name. They belong to no structure of reified ideology or signification. Various chains of causality, obedience to the name or the word, become insensible or irrelevant. These becomings are both part of any organism's living and death. Cognition of purpose is a matter of degree, and reverberations always exceed purpose anyway.

Queer deterritorialization of Thanateros requires new declinations of normative territories as declinations of the matter and materiality of life and death and the yet-to-be-born as co-emergent. Heteronormativity, reproduction of the same, neo liberal operationality and use of lives rather than flourishing of lived emergences of singular organisms and their connections seem resistant to declination, even as novel viruses, mass extinctions, invasion, war and other irrefutable geo-age new aeons of life and death disprove the permanence of the anthropocentric human. This human is in perpetual acceleration *and* catch-up. In the case of wait-and-see bio-techno-capitalism, humans are too early, developing practices which, be it from motives of economy, luxury or simply hubris from the Frankenstein impulse of *because I can* experiments, arise whether in scientific or economic arenas, producing outcomes that can vary, most worryingly, from intense suffering, especially in psychological and vivisection torture of humans and nonhumans, or experimental intensive farming, for example (and diluting AI anxiety, which is basically humans afraid of human-like entities). Humans are too late in acknowledging and especially managing and transforming our affects in the Earth and ecologies, often the former causing the latter and vice versa. Through the too early and the too late weaves the accident, of discovery and of affect. Humans take authorship of the beneficial accident, and the perilous accident is designated as other, 'nature' striking back or similar re-designations of comforting binaries.

Loving the dead

Serres returns us to a Lucretian understanding of life, death and their temporalities as newly arranged turbulences of atoms always in states of flux: vortices, a perpetual *deviance* catalysed by a Venusian declination (Serres 2000). Venusian fecundity manifests creativity, lacks nothing and emerges as simultaneous schema of self within others and as part of larger collectives, as relevant for activism as for desire. Less relevant is the act of knowing, where according to Serres, the act of knowledge is ataraxy, the act of fulfilling of being a being. The world is perpetual turbulence, fluid unfulfillable and overflowing tumult in which our selves and connections are at best verbings, ultimately beyond anthropocentric grammar. Turbulence and its synonyms contain a residue of malevolence or trouble, arbitrary when all is turbulence of varying qualities and affects, some serene, all beyond the limits of language and attached moral evaluations. The clinamen is the moment of intersectings and emergent entanglings, which may offer an opportunity for tactical cognition but never finite measure. The world is perpetual deviation (*l'écart*) which can come to a frustrating awareness for knowledge that sees it as discrepancy/*écart*. Taking this concept as a mode of queering the world, as tactically encountering the world as deviation, morality intervenes as a claim of 'exact knowledge of natural things' (Serres 2000: 38). Knowledge for Serres accomplishes the Order of Mars, a battle that falsely creates a disjuncture between nature and 'science', or anthropocentric imposed reason, indivisible from moral motive and jurisprudence. Serres calls the law of anthropocentric knowledge a reiteration of death, violent, murderous, a plague (2000: 109). The Order of Venus, that of perpetual deviation and declination, swirls and circles around as an Order of both love and nature (*Foedora Naturae*), repudiating the fate and destiny (*Foedora Fate*) found in anthropocentric perception, which conceals in its claimed truths a faith in its own ordering. Put simply, the edict of the human on what is true is an ordering to the death of nature. Being an organism is being deviant. For queer theory, the order of death coincides with anthropocentric announcement, in the face of which – the actual territory of the white, male face – the rearrangement of atoms moves towards entropy, and change apprehended as the natural phenomenon of death comes much later. In prejudice, in killability, while shimmering with living and living connectivity, social death is both a liberty and a violation. To not be recognized as life brings all kinds of creative and oppressive affects. Deviants are dead before we are born; nature is dead before it is plundered. The Order of Venus finds fecundity in all meetings of matter in infinite and infinitesimal fractals between, within and beyond pre-emptive systems, regimes and knowledge. The natural order's fecundity is overwhelming in the complex ecologies of both life and death, increasing and decreasing, emergings and recedings, durations imperceptibly slow, fast, novel connections made perpetually. These inevitabilities of nature to which the human organism, but not the human subject, belongs are what lead to the infinite complexities of desire and to plague, to the viruses that inform and alter human evolution and those that shut down the world for a few years. Like viruses, there is no morality in nature. Morality is the infuriated hubris of the deviant perceived as disjunct. Queerness belongs to nature, to the Order of Venus, to love. The phenomenon of death included in this world is inevitable, sometimes lamentable, sometimes welcome, always beyond us as we live within its belonging. The death anthropocentrism brings means that for many humans and all of nature, our existence is conditional; it demands productivity and docility. Can queers, can others, can nonhumans, can nature be considered as having ever lived under this regime? The quality of life in anthropocentrism is often one of fulfilment and discrepancy, of a human simulacrum, a defleshed performance, anthropocentric drag, activism is a refusal to wear the anthropocentric garment. All organisms occupy a contested oscillation site of emergence and disappearance contingent with the morality of each human time and place, increasingly reducible to use value. Death has already happened for many of us, certainly for the Earth, for the billions of nonhuman animals who are murdered annually, often before they are born because they are born into killability or genetically born to become ill. The basic phenomena of life and death are conditionally and qualitatively very different under the Order of Mars than under the Order of Venus.

What purpose does already being dead/never having been alive serve for activism? Biotechnology has created new forms of deep-time death, in spite of the epoch of the anthropocene being newly birthed. Technologies of war that threaten mass indiscriminate death and bioengineering that creates lives for parasitic consumption without any attention to the internal suffering of the singular experience of the organism, nonetheless, show a romance with death beyond knowledge as a repudiation of difference in life, to creating life as a permanent threat. To live as suffering in the anthropocene is both collateral damage and a condition of life for many, having nothing to do with any pseudo-Buddhist or even efilist claims that all existence is suffering. In poverty, war, criminalization, neo capitalist slavery and especially for nonhuman animals in laboratories and farms, where slavery is of genetic make-up itself, unbearable compulsory suffering is a condition of being allowed a life. Under these conditions, understanding the enduring impossibility of death as unthinkable and defiantly undesirable is challenged. Does this create a resonance of responsibility between the never-alive queer and the better-to-be-dead other? Neoliberalism fosters activism in the face of the recognizable other that reflects an I who is not the dominant but who is a never-recognized awaiting recognition. Identity politics activism fails when being born means being born into Mars knowledge. Long have women, the colonized, the disabled and other-others been suspicious and outright refused the medico-legal claims to knowledge of our deviance. Queer, in its non-naming naming, embodies this refusal as meaning everything and nothing, a refusal of the noun itself, a queering and querying: a celebration of perpetual declination. The politics of remaining outside is one of both power as potential and resistance without definition via the resisted. We remain in the realm of the dead. Unutterable suffering is life without life and death without death, which may even covet death, though one can never claim the desires of the nonhuman. Queer biopolitics can be a politics that engages with the biopolitical Order of Venus, seeking to liberate the living-dead other, to overwhelm the Order of Mars. In their introduction to the first publication of queer death studies, Marietta Radomska, Tara Mehrabi and Nina Lykke affirm:

> In other words, in order to (re)think death and do it justice in its ontological, ethical and political terms, attuned to the present, we must refuse to perpetuate the epistemological and symbolic violence (with their practical, real-life consequences) of dismissing some deaths as not 'worth enough', not grievable enough, not even seen as 'deaths' in the full sense of the word. (2020: 82)

To this, I would add that we can perform this justice through a Venusian Order, a chaotic non-order driven by undifferentiated love, needing no valuation, economic, signified and subjectified or otherwise. Motive for impetus is hard to glean. Is it because we are queer, as are these other non-lives? We are not martyrs, though overwhelming compassion can cause a kind of death bound ecstasy alongside PTSD. Because we are definable as being desiring intensities in love with love of reshifting atomic configurations, and some need more urgent love, a love of care and of radical compassion. Love's qualities are not consistent. To the Hellenic seven forms of love we can add infinite others or remove titles of love altogether and accept that every molecular configuration of love is combined with a singular quality of life and death, and life-ing and death-ing. Is queer the love that ethically encounters each other as a singularity of life and death unto itself?

What death activism does: Chapters of the dead

Death Activism is formed, after this introduction, of eight chapters with a particular circular structure. This introduction sets the book within posthuman practice, queer death studies, queer theory and philosophy but also attempts to raise more questions than it answers. This tactic permeates the entire book. As belonging to the Order of Venus, the relationship of life and death with material organisms and collectives asks what happens when we interrogate death and life with love, what happens when we see all organisms as lives, what happens when we post not only posthumanism but also human exceptionalism without condition?

Chapter 1 is 'Danse Macabre: Queer Romances of Fascination and Fear'. While *Death Activism* is a firmly immanent book, useful only to the extent of rethinking death assists in questioning hierarchies of life, there is no denying the aesthetic and philosophical fascination the concept of death holds. Even the very idea of death as a concept, rather than simply an event that happens to almost all organisms, shows our impulse to convert death into that which it is not – a concept, a surmountable moment, something that happens to someone else, something our species will overcome, and in this chapter, something personified as a queer partner for all, no matter where in the hierarchy they exist. This chapter is not a historical text; it seeks to somewhat arbitrarily delight in the two phenomena of the danse macabre and death and the maiden in art. There are two reasons for this chapter's presence. By way of introduction to a rather grave book, I wish to open with an exploration of an art which shows the ambiguity of our emotions towards death in the face of its inevitability: death the seducer and death who drags us off, death the rotting skeleton with a smile and death the comforting angel. Most importantly for this book's queer turn, death who partners with us all, beyond gender, and dances us to the end of life in ways both horrific and comforting. The medieval context of dancing to and with death emphasizes the pure corporeality of a body's cessation, showing the Cartesian perceived supremacy of the human mind is ultimately irrelevant and fatuous. This could be seen as true today in the new Cartesians, the transhumanists, as for the wealth accumulators and 'bunker billionaires' who think overcoming death is guaranteed if one is anthropocentric enough in one's supremacy over both nature (as opposed to technology) and other lives. Dancing with death also supplants the difficult bargaining narratives we have with dying, especially in times of disabling or terminal illness. No semiotic narrative happens in the dance. This chapter asks how these images, taken out of their didactic historical context, can help us queer our way to dancing with death.

Chapter 2, 'Global Mourning: Pandemic, Trauma and Mass Death', uses Covid as a fulcrum upon which issues of trauma and living with a persistent fear of imminent death raise the understanding of vulnerability and obligations to abide with the living and with death. Expanding to larger concepts of the vulnerability of certain bodies against structures of citizenship and state, this chapter questions the location of life and the duration of living in the midst of death as both threat and cause of mourning, PTSD and other forms of trauma. How can these affects transform our individual selves into communal affects, in the hope that trauma can become a form of creative impulse?

Chapter 3 is 'The Denial of Desire: Suicide and the Right to Death'. Currently, very few theorists advocate for suicidality as being a valid desire. A step further than end-of-life assisted dying, increasingly some institutes are allowing those who wish to die due to what is loosely termed terminal 'mental illness', usually depression, access to end-of-life technologies. This chapter explores the ways in which those humans who do not show a life-thriving desire, through no external cause, have been pathologized, institutionalized, rationalized and otherwise disallowed their own desire to simply not be. Contentiously, the chapter is pro-suicide, at the very least because in Western neo-capitalism, while billions of others, humans and nonhumans, die from preventable causes, we are perceived to have freedom over most things except our own deaths. Safe access to our own death is prevented and illegal, yet the death of the poor and the disabled is seen as inevitable due to circumstances of inequality. The chapter asks what of those who want to die, and what is it about this desire that makes us turn to external causes or mental pathologization to explain and somehow cure this most aberrant of queer desires.

Chapter 4, 'Abolitionism: Mass Death and the Nonhuman Animal', explores the intersection between capitalism and the apocalypse nonhuman animals experience every day, even while humans dread a coming ecological apocalypse whose cause is exacerbated more than any other action by animal mass murder – animal agriculture. The chapter deals with the grief of animal activists in the face of our own species who seem to not care, and asks, Can a form of lament, a choral dance of liberation for the nonhuman other, be a way to prevent animal deaths while coping with the horrific affects bearing witness to animal mass death can cause for activists, risking atrophy or suicide? If the price of love is grief, how can animal activists transform their grief into action?

In Chapter 5, 'Capital Zombies, Death and Disability', certain disabilities, particularly those given a time limit at diagnosis, mean that many disabled individuals live after they were supposed to die or live in a way that can feel closer to being dead than alive. This form of living death makes many disabled people feel like zombies, and our relationship with death is very different from that of both able-bodied people and those with other forms of disability. Under these conditions, death can feel like a deliverance, while living a myth only fulfilled by humans entirely other to the zombie body. The interstitial space we occupy is a kind of twilight between life and death, which perhaps is the queer time of degenerative disability beyond able/disable, asking larger questions about the very categorization of disability.

Chapter 6, 'The Unspeakable Death (That Is Not Death)', furthers work on antinatalism, which advocates for the cessation of human reproduction. The chapter asks what dies if we as a species no longer exist, without genocide or eugenics. It posits the rhetoric of the need to breed as a form of genetic eugenics performed within the compulsory family structure. The chapter also identifies the racist, colonialist and rise of the right aspects of reproduction which currently attach themselves to human reproduction conditioned on markers of race and nation-state. Ultimately, the division of people reflects the divisions of the Earth, where we have taken ownership of land and transformed that into markers of war and opposition. All the while the rate of human occupation on Earth is the second most prevalent cause of ecological catastrophe. The chapter asks how we can transform our deeply anthropocentric perceived right to reproduce into practices of care for the lives already here, so desperately in need of thriving and so precariously at risk of death.

Chapter 7 is 'Goth Culture, Occulture, Aesthetic Death Culture'. By way of cyclically returning to the aesthetics of Chapter 1 to lighten and play with our relationship with death, this chapter explores two semi-contemporary subcultural movements which focus on death aesthetics and death practices to challenge our repudiation of death. Goth culture embraces the crepuscular and the charnel, appearing death-like in its visage and dancing as a chora of the dead. A primarily musical scene beginning in the late 1970s, goth continues to thrive as a subculture, mixing along the way film and literature to form a frivolous cult of the appearing-dead that challenges both traditional aesthetic beauty and aversion to the grave. Modern Occulture from around the same era, but currently experiencing new growth especially among queer people, embraces practices of deadening one's self and one's ego in order to cultivate a more creative series of relationships with the world, the seen and the unseen. In chaos magick especially, death practices such as the death posture and rituals which encourage losing oneself question the value of the refined identity advocated by neo-capitalism. The sections are briefly tantalizing rather than exhaustive and are designed to show that our danse macabre flirtations continue in our fun, queer relationship with death, even in the face of the overwhelming unjust dead-ing we currently witness.

The conclusion to *Death Activism* is 'The Difficult Joy of Death Activism'. This book is made up almost exclusively of ambiguities, of how to be an activist for both those who seek to die and those made dead against their will to thrive by our human practices. The final section emphasizes the necessity of death activism to apprehend the gravity of what we do, to individuals, to the Earth, while also asking how this eco-grief can be balanced with meaningful care and compassion. Like many of the affects in the book, joy here is also a form of grief, just as care is also a form of tentative grace and intervention, just as ethics is always a hopeful aspiration to benevolence and a risk of fatal outcomes. While death is a guarantee, how we relate to caring for the way others relate to death, with force or desire, is far more tenebrous. And yet we must persist in our joy in the face of sometimes overwhelming eco-despair, on scales planetary and for individual lives in insufferable conditions.

1

Danse macabre

Queer romances of fascination and fear

There is no possibility of representations of death. As the absolute limit of experience without the possibility of reflection upon it, death belongs to a realm of aesthetics that contradicts itself. Who can represent that which is both ubiquitous and incapable of any individual's reflection of their experience of it? Near-death, suffering until perceived dying, witnessing the death of an other are all about death, but surrogate to the purpose of representation from a traditional humanist perspective, which is that of converting the transcendental into the sensible, the idea into the materially affective. In many ways death is an ideal, aiming toward a transcendental signified defining death in the sentence 'what is death, what is the representation of death?' (there is no sufficient noun in this sentence . . . 'concept' and 'motif' are all poverty-stricken). Death is a 'thing' with which a relationship with art can develop due to it being utterly of the imagination even while belonging to every living organism, and utterly sublimated due to being unavailable except as an experienced finitude for every organism. In death, duration ceases and the self as concept remains as corpse, memory, relic, artefact, grieved object. For these reasons it can be suggested death is incapable of our representation of it while belonging to a realm of need or impetus to do so nonetheless. Although for various reasons that need resides in humanist impulses of allegory, catharsis, conceptual reframing and other navigating motives, there are opportunities to re-experience and re-present historical and contemporary images of death and the dead from a posthuman perspective – posthumaning the danse macabre. This chapter will do so, to elucidate the myth of the availability of knowing or capturing death through signification and to invigorate historical tropes of death by liberating them from various trajectories of Christian metaphor, fetishism of the other as thanaterotic catharsis and the residual division between life and death as love and horror. What I do not seek to do is to encounter these images as they were originally intended, or not strictly. Many images of the Danse Macabre, Death and the Maiden, the three living and the three dead, and other vanitas imageries, had richly specific contexts and purposes, asserting civic belonging, life eternal, compassionate dying among other purposes. This growing field of scholarship is fascinating, but rather than reflect upon the purposes of these images for their original audiences, I wish to explore the ways death can be thought through trajectories of love, thanaterotics divested of power as murderous, perhaps blasphemously, to delight in queering these images while touching lightly upon the medieval idea that there is something beyond about the figure of Death that is available for everyone. While many images of the danse macabre and other medieval death aesthetics were used to compound identity, status and regional belonging, the figures of Death themselves liberate our modern understanding of death-bringers (operators of tyranny, genocide and all forms of prejudice), and postmodern understanding of death-simulators (death-deniers, lives measured and mourned on their 'killability'). I will not be analysing individual images, nor as is the trend in contemporary death studies, regional or national areas. These studies have been done brilliantly elsewhere by medieval art historians and the area of study is growing. I begin the book with the danse macabre, in this opening chapter, for two reasons. The first is that for contemporary (likely secular or at least not of a medieval religious mindset) spectators of this form of art, we see it after the age of post-photographic, modern images of the dead. Our view is posthuman because our relationship with the dead has gone through the shockingly real-but-not-material images of the dead (an age of documentation, an age of snuff) to simulacrum perception (an age of belief, an age of disbelief, either way an age of apathetic response) to a point where individual images may be shocking, but they do not represent 'us' unless as testimony of events passed. The danse macabre is the us of the future which solicits a relationship of compassion and love and jouissance. As a queer form of desire – desiring a relationship with Death as a figure that is one of compassion and acceptance rather than horror – the danse belongs to a different representational schema than those of power and violence found in othering the dead. (Indeed, the purpose of Death in the medieval allegory was to disprove the value of wealth, power and beauty, of 'counting' as an unkillable human life.) Contemporarily, even if we witness those real images of the dead other, the separation of witness and object remains. We may seek to prevent future deaths but the dead remain symbolic. Just as posthumanism utilizes monsters to think different human immanence and futures, connectivities and intensities, devoid of traditional significations of subjectivity, I will use Death as a figure that reconsiders our becoming-dead as a unifying plane of desire and love. Themes of teratology also belong to collapsing this doubled division, so teratology and the monstrous other belonging to the realm of the dead will also be invoked to confirm the status of many minoritarians as both fabulated and already dead/never been alive. Art provokes the limited and liminal access human representation, including thought, has to death. Emmanuel Levinas states:

> Here we leave the limited problem of art. This presentiment of fate in death subsists, as paganism subsists. To be sure, one need only give oneself a constituted duration to remove from death the power to interrupt. Death is then sublated. To situate it in time is precisely to go beyond it, to already find oneself on the other side of the abyss, to have it behind oneself. Death qua nothingness is the death of the other, death for the survivor. The time of dying itself cannot give itself the other shore. What is unique and poignant in this instant is due to the fact that it cannot pass. In dying, the horizon of the future is given, but the future as a promise of a new present is refused; one is in the interval, forever an interval. The characters of certain tales by Edgar Allen Poe must have found themselves in this empty interval. A threat appears to them in the approach of such an empty interval; no move can

be made to retreat from its approach, but this approach can never end. This is the anxiety which in other tales is prolonged like a fear of being buried alive. It is as though death were never dead enough, as though parallel with the duration of the living ran the eternal duration of the interval – the meanwhile. Art brings about just this duration in the interval, in that sphere which a being is able to traverse, but in which its shadow is immobilized. (Levinas 1989: 141–2)

Death represented may take the form of a Charonic, Hypnotic or Chronotic entity, spanning metaphors of traversal, sleep and duration, or of a vitalistic corpse or skeleton dancing their way to eternity or enticing the corruptibility of vanitas. Death is a happening, as a noun how can it be shown? And yet representations of certain figurations of Death as an entity are deliriously seductive, comforting, horrifying all at once. For this chapter, Death as figural is capitalized, while death as a phenomenon is not. Death in art, whether as purely aesthetic or as a morality motif, is a pique for making ambiguous many bifurcated affects – not only desire/terror but also beauty/ugliness, licit/illicit, immanence/eternity, pleasure/fear and, in this chapter, desire and gender as thoroughly queering our relationship with bodies, death and desire itself. Levinas's statement shows that while images of the dead belong to another realm, especially forensic or representative documents of war, genocide, homicide and slaughterhouses of all environments, Death is a figure of delight. In art, from Poe to Damien Hirst (responsible for the death of conservatively 913,450 nonhuman animals, see Goldstein, 2017), the death of the other is a critical creation to alleviate the (usually immortal masculine) denial of the coming of finitude for self, and the unimaginability of after-one's-self. Like pornography, the corpse of the other is the money shot which denies the other's living in order to vindicate the self's belief in their own immortality. To this potentially, I would add hunters (trophy or not) and malzoans in general. Technically, it is not the death of the other which repudiates the majoritarian's death but the dead other, precisely because the other belongs to the realm of the killable. These devastating kinds of spectacles coming from equally devastating practices will return towards the end of this chapter. For now, it is the figure of Death that occupies a more ethical manifestation of the 'death that is never dead enough' in Levinas's words, because, unlike the femicidal, ecocidal denier of death who actually makes the other dead, Death makes the living spectator dead, and through art frequently seeks to tantalize us into their realm (more on the difficulty of Death's pronoun later). The anthropocentric bringer of death for art is the maker of a world he perceives for and of himself. The dance of death brings us into worlds of death, as an example of accepting and embracing death, rather than cause suffering through its denial. Though manifested in many varying anthropomorphic and pseudo-anthropomorphic representations, Death can be layers of Anthropos themselves denied, strata of cadaver, skeleton. Death can also come in Therian/Thanatos forms, such as the vampires, reapers, demons and succubi of art, literature and film. A relationship with Death as figurative in art is a queer death encounter. While it may seem to lack the philosophical negotiative sophistication of conceptual artistic presentations of death, and also deny the finitude of being/becoming-dead, it is a different way to think with and through death that does not involve the perpetual anxiety which leads to violence invested in majoritarian practices of refusing one's own death. There is a sense of playful joy in Death as the lover, the friend, the creature of thanateros beyond Anthropos but related to them in an uncanny, transformed form. Relationships with Death often do show a beyond, a future in death. Reading from a posthuman antitheist position, this is a celebratory apprehension of the memento mori. There is no truth to be found in representations of death. Death has no transcendentally signifiable truth and is simultaneously absolutely true in that it simply is what it is. As a reactive affect, this leads anthropocentric hubris to violence, under whatever name, be it art or war. The reactive affect of posthuman artistic representations of death sees practices of art involved with communities for mourning, for grievability most often found in images of the dead. Death itself in these images comes from anthropocentric actions. The dead are more than symbolic, conceptual and metaphoric; they are visceral, living singularities ceased by humans. Death in nature is beyond ethics because it cannot be subsumed into human signifying regimes, but the deaths we cause belong to our responsibility. Death in art as a figure is a conceptual fabulation of a phenomenon known to be unknowable, so able to be imagined as imagination. No catharsis is achieved; Aristotle and Apollo are replaced by Plato and Dionysus. Fear of death is shown as hubris, as self-deceit at the possibility of immortality. In *The Apology*, Plato shows the death of the other to displace mortality in the name of justice as a catastrophic hypocrisy (2010). Plato shows that denial of death transcends epistemes and orders, which in contemporary understanding would mean that the court, the art gallery, the home and the restaurant are no different in designating just and unjust murder when the victim stands in for the acceptance of the death of all humans as inevitable. Posthuman embrace of Death is a way to creatively imagine death of the self as a queer romance with a gentle, often disinterested other, without expiation or 'sacrificial' victims in one's own place. It may seem 'light' but just as the arbitrary nature of religions navigates death through fabulated narratives, death seems the time for such tales in confronting the unknowability of what is to come, whether far or close. This allows life to continue to flourish in the being of one's own death, life as the energetic pulsation of billions of flows of which each singularity is a fleeting moment or point of interactions.

The double moment of death as an event, the event of death and the reflection, testament, representation of 'what happened', cannot exist for our own death. Deleuze states: 'Death has an extreme and definite relation to me and my body and is grounded in me, but it also has no relationship to me at all – it is incorporeal and infinitive, impersonal, grounded only in itself' (Deleuze 1990: 151). Death as non-signifiable means it comes into play as a playfulness with representation beyond logic, narrative; it just *is*:

> Our words reach only as far as the instincts, but it is from the other agency, that is, from the Death Instinct, that they receive their sense, nonsense, and combinations thereof. Underlying every instinct is the epos of death. We could say initially cover over death and cause it to retreat; but this is temporary, and even their noise is fed by death. (Deleuze 1990: 326)

Deleuze's examination of death in DeFoe compared to Zola claims that thinking death literally leads the subject to either murder of the other or to a crack-up which may break or transform the self (or each as forms of the other). Existence is a perpetual crack-up which certain fictions, as works of art indistinguishable from/as theory, work with (rather than through). These take various forms of working with/through the other. But the other is the a priori possible, incapable of being converted to a pre-ordained symbol or fetish of one's own already-known. Deleuze emphasizes that for Lacan this indivisibility of self and/with the 'big O' Other is a form of perversion, beginning with disavowal of difference between the sexes and continuing through the otherwise-Other, beyond signification either for self or in the world as oppositional. Perversion is a condition of being that denies Death as a non-oppositional Other, because for Deleuze perversion is not defined by a set of practices which uses an other (e.g. voyeurism) but

> from the point of view of the structure, the contrary must be asserted: it is because the structure-Other is missing, and is replaced by a completely different structure, that the real 'others' are no longer able to play the role of terms actualising the lost primary structure. Real 'others' can only play now, in the second structure, the role of bodies-victims. . . . All perversion is an 'Other-cide', and an 'altru-cide' and therefore a murder of the possible. (1990: 320)

It is plausible to see perversion (though I am reluctant to use the word as it has a reclamation value for queer theory) as inherent in all forms of heteronormativity, practices that utilize the other reducing them to a prop or use value for the self, and general majoritarianism in service of a drive for power. Majoritarianism is the normalized state of perversion when the subject repudiates its own integrity being inherently cracked-up, and, most critically, when a subject refuses the possibility of their own death. Utilizing self-referentially fictitious, celebratory nonsensical figurations of Death to think the structure differently allows for an acknowledgement of death as the dissipation of the already schizoid self into a greater definition of life than one's own life, while instigating imaginative possibilities of others Death could be, even knowing they are not Death, because there is no Death other than death. A little madness, a little childish need for anthropomorphization without actual belief in its reality. Creating figurations of Death and revisiting representations of Death while not necessarily adhering to their initial purpose queer our relationship with death without denying it or making the other suffer to ablate it. This is the tactical queer relationship with Death as Other, where the majoritarian pervert's is a denial of death as part of self through techniques of causing the death of the other. Figuring Death mingles the wonder and terror of life and its cessation as co-emergent and undifferentiated.

Danse macabre: Cacophony, polyvocality, multiplicity and memento mori

According to Immanuel Kant, certain intuitive imaginings necessitate representation even while being of their very nature, beyond the capacity to be represented.

> Such presentations of the imagination we may call ideas. One reason for this is that they do at least strive toward something that lies beyond the bounds of experience, and hence try to approach an exhibition of rational concepts (intellectual ideas), and thus [these concepts] are given a semblance of objective reality. Another reason, indeed the main reason, for calling those presentations ideas is that they are inner intuitions to which no concept can be completely adequate. A poet ventures to give sensible expression to rational ideas of invisible beings, the realm of the blessed, the realm of hell, eternity, creation and so on. Or, again, he takes [things] that are indeed exemplified in experience, such as death, envy, and all the other vices, as well as love, fame, and so on; but then, by means of an imagination that emulates the example of reason in reaching [for] a maximum, he ventures to give these sensible expression in a way that goes beyond the limits of experience, namely, with a completeness for which no example can be found in nature. And it is actually in the art of poetry that the power [i.e., faculty] of aesthetic ideas can manifest itself to full extent. Considered by itself, however, this power is actually only a talent (of the imagination). (Kant 1987: 182–3)

While Kant's ideas of universal modality and will as reason are not consistent with the Spinozan concept of ethics this book utilizes, this small excerpt shares with death activism some elements which set death apart from any striving for intentional and rational formulations for transcendental logic. Kant is useful in that the absoluteness of death is universal, but it is beyond logic. Thinking death therefore requires a turn to poetry, to art, to aesthetic imagination because while death is absolute, representing it and especially reflecting upon it experientially, thus, authentically or logically, are impossible. It is beyond the limits of experience. Dying may be exemplified, but this would require a close call to death, a return, a calmer clinamen than the torrential turbulence of dying even in its quietest forms and acknowledging that many experiences of dying are partnered with a self-preserving amnesia. So let us follow Kant's proposal that to experience the realm of death, to venture to hell, or heaven, or Elysium or Tartarus, we venture into the world of aesthetic imagination, potentially reaching a realm of the sublime.

For Western Europe in the thirteenth to fifteenth centuries, the danse macabre, or danse of death, was a popular artistic allegory for the ubiquitous phenomenon of death. Most commonly, the danse macabre is an etching, painting or sculptural frieze of Death, as skeleton or cadaver, leading a dance with either another figure in a courtly configuration or in a procession with many humans, sometimes punctuated with a few extra skeletons or cadavers (see Clark 1950). Its popularity never really disappeared, but its allegorical use is amorphous in that whether or not death is attached to a revenant afterlife, the democracy of death-for-all remains galling to anthropocentric ideology. The purpose of the danse macabre was morally pedagogic, an encounter operating as a constant reminder of the memento mori, don't forget that you will die, also seen in many sacred spaces, churches and catacombs, as 'what you are now, we once were; what we are now, you shall be'. This operates as a reminder and a mirror, but the reflection is not guaranteed beyond the unified and putrefied end for/of all. I will tactically remove the theistic allegorical morality while retaining some of the more queer aspects of the danse macabre. I do so both in flagrant disregard for rigid historical purpose to an extent, because some elements of medieval imaging of Death as a figure challenge the contemporary attitude to death, but also show that Death does historically belong to a rudimentary and sophisticated form of creativity that defied science, even religiously driven knowledges, and aligned more with aesthetics. Death belongs to art. The allegory's purpose, to make people docile and humble and curtail excess and living, life itself as a form of vanity, seems counter to our modern understanding of living life to the fullest. What I am interested in is not so much the purpose of this allegory as what its depiction can say about our relationship with Death the figure, and death the phenomenon. There is also something irrefutably enigmatic about these representations that elicits the teratological wonder of both beauty and fascination at the repulsive. Going beyond – beyond knowledge, beyond representation and beyond experience – is where Death the figure takes us. All the while we, like Serres's definition of the one who is gracious, are dancing, as a stepping aside and are therefore nobody (1997: 35, 47). In medieval representations of the danse macabre, other challenges that take the subject beyond are also present. Death prefers dancing to linguistic expression, and while many original witnesses to these artworks would not have been literate, the concept of The Word would be, as spoken, prioritized. Death does not speak; Death dances. 'I dance naked, I am nothing' (Serres 1997: 35). The primary configuration of the danse macabre is somewhat illicit, dancing being attached to forms of excess, disease and the liquification of the body's legible parameters as oppositional and chaste. Guattari states of a semiotic semiologies:

> It seems necessary to distinguish between the pre-signifying semiologies – for example, of archaic societies, the insane and children – and fully signifying semiologies of modern societies that are all over coded in the writings of social and economic laws. In primitive societies, one expresses oneself as much by speech as by gestures, dances, rituals or signs marked on the body. (1996: 149)

The dance of death calls to mind both the horrors of St Vitus's dance and the revelling of Maenads, the convulsions of the black plague and orgiastic carousing of any kind not restricted by the rules of courtly dancing. Death does not speak, but sometimes plays music, albeit in an inverted way, such as pipes blown backwards. Often instruments are made of human remains – bone pipes, skull drums, in, for example, Death playing the shawm at the start of Bernt Notke's 1463 *Danse Macabre*, formerly in the Marienkirche, Lübeck; Four musical corpses, an additional woodcut in the expanded *Danse Macabre* edition published by Guy Marchant in 1486; and the 'Dantz hus' scene with musical and dancing corpses, opening woodcut in *Der doten dantz mit figuren clage und antwort schon von allen staten der werlt*, attributed to the printer Heinrich Knoblochtzer after 1485 (see Warda 2011).

In the multi-person dance of death, there often appears a hierarchical procession, pope or bishop first, then cardinal, merchant, leading down to the farm-working peasant. This is most notably seen person by person in Hans Holbein's woodcuts for *Les simulachres & historiees faces de la mort* published in 1538, but also a driving structure of Marchant's original revision of *Danse Macabre*. Various arguments as to the significance of this order make the dance only more enigmatic. While some see the hierarchy as a line to access to God or entry to heaven, others see it as those who shall be judged and presumably punished in order. Either relies on a left-to-right or front-to-back literary narrative reading of the dance. What matters most is that Death, at the front of the procession, is the gateway to the end of hierarchy, the threshold of signification and subjectification; all who pass this threshold become food for worms. Death's orbless sockets cannot see regalia or vestments. Death sees only as a making-dead, an entity as a verb*ing* or a clinamen. Death is the horizon partner where all becomings align in a singular consistency. How can the danse macabre show Death as a queering while being the deading of all subjects? In some ways, becoming-cadaver reduces all ties of status and even family to the nameless, faceless matter of the earth. Fathers may produce lineages, daughters may be commodified as suitable objects to create allegiances, but these cannot stop what we all become. We may all come from sources we like to oversignify, or conceal, origins being an obsession with anthropocentric subjects. But we all go to the same figure, be they understood as father/mother or God(s) – Death. Queer death is the progenitor of all.

> The dead father thus serves his living son as a mirror, just as the Three Dead are the fathers of the Three Living in some versions of the Legend. The son knows that it is his father's corpse because the tomb is recognisable through its heraldry and the imperial effigy, but these only disguise the ultimate brutal truth below, viz. the real corpse (not a cadaver effigy!) in its putrid state. Putrefaction has other implications apart from an unpleasant smell and sight: it erases the possibility of recognising the deceased once the face

has been reduced to nothing but a skull, perhaps with just some tufts of hair clinging to it. Skulls are normally anonymous. (Oosterwijk 2011: 32)

The significance of the proper name is shown up as little more than cadaverous in medieval death art. The tale of the three living and the three dead is another allegory of memento mori. Three people, usually young men but sometimes of each age of man and occasionally two men and a woman, in their pleasure travels (hunting, drinking) encounter three dead upon the road. The three dead are often in varying stages of putrefaction. Various poems of this story designate three different responses from either side of the encounter. The men will express fear or repudiation or believe these are demons, while the dead may state their status, or beauty in life, with the ultimate warning: 'beware'. This medieval idea is in direct contrast to Heidegger's 'being-toward-death', which, according to Kathleen Higgins, is 'keeping death always in view, he had in mind the way that aesthetic framing of our experience as an ongoing activity can assist our ability to find rich significance in living' (1998: 48). The admonishment of the dead is for the pleasure-seeking to become pious, for their death awaits. Life is truncated with a haunted sense of both impending death and the death that is the capacity to understand life defined by its finitude and its purpose as pious, or moral. So perhaps Heidegger's being-toward-death is a self-sufficient, Dasein version of the same warning after all, both remaining an abstract warning nonetheless. Similarly, while religious, this message is not so different from Kant's moral imperative or contemporary drives to live ethically in philosophy and justice theory. The admonishment expresses the double idea that the men should beware both because a life lived without piety defies the purpose of living and risks an eternal damnation (and who wants to spend eternity wandering byways scolding revelling men? Some would prefer the more traditional hell). These Dead Three are a more terrestrial version of Death in the danse macabre, in that they are not Death or representative of the figure of Death but are the living dead. They are animated yet dead, their expressions of their lives are all in the past tense, and if clothed they are ragged in textile, hair and flesh. They belong to the post-life world, yet here they are on the road. There is something wrong with the encounter beyond the admonishments because these three are the beyond – they *are* but they *shouldn't be.* There is a sense of pagan eternal wandering on the banks of the Styx in these three. All signification is lost, and binaries are collapsed – their gender, social status and even state of putrefaction are gone or made ambiguous and they nonetheless remain. And for the living men and occasional woman *they are themselves* (e.g. the fourteenth-century 'De Lisle Psalter' [*Arundel MS 83* see Biggs 2014] shows three women separately from three men, but the skeletons are all identical even though one skeleton in each panel is naked. Death makes our genders and verisimilitude very queer indeed.) Just as the end of the world always has residual survivors who must then survive the after-the-end-of-the-world, these are the survivors of death who are dead, an apocalyptic existence. Like Death in the danse macabre, these three are sometimes dynamic, their attacks if they are aggressive are often luxuriantly aerobic, seen in 'The Office of the Dead' in *Add MS 35313* (See Biggs 2014). Encountering these images as a form of posthuman practice, especially from a queer teratological perspective, the dead, whether dancing, scolding or attacking, whether robed, corrupted or skeletal, are consistently aesthetically more pleasing and interesting than the tediously flashy living. They belong to the hugely popular genre of 'zombies' (scare quoted because these Deaths are not testaments to the horrors of slavery and racial exploitation and murder), of revenants, of the living dead, of monsters and of Death as a seductive figure.

Whether singular, triumvirate or multiple, Death(s) in the danse macabre plays with and on concepts of gender and desire within and in excess of any moral allegory. Death is decidedly queer in many representations of the danse macabre and death and the maiden.

> Yet the dead are not necessarily mirror images of the living, for some artists (and patrons) were morbidly fascinated by the potential for sexual tension between a male corpse and the luscious body of a young female, or the horror that the decaying female corpse must inspire in a living man. The gender of personified Death was not always fixed, either. The early association of sin with death meant that Death often assumed a female appearance. A late example is the presentation of Death as a longhaired female demon in the fourteenth-century fresco in the Camposanto in Pisa, nowadays attributed to the painter Buonamico (Buffalmacco). (Oosterwijk 2011: 12)

Imagining the likely male artist and patron does not limit the gendering of Death, though the function may. Very little is offered by way of what a woman may experience upon witnessing the danse, and, usually, death and the maiden are, for women, limited to a rudimentary warning against vanity, though at a time when vanity belonged to a limited few and the danse was for all who partook in religious ceremonies, literate or not. A simple anti-vanitas message does not encompass the ambiguities of these images. Presuming that there was no lost female gaze, the viewer may be perceived as male, yet all who attended church bore witness to these images. The decaying corpse of a male with a luscious woman can be attested to in certain representations, especially those cadaverous Death figures with rudimentary corrupted genitalia, but many others show a generic Death figure that has a corrupting element upon the living maiden but is not necessarily male per se, such as Niklaus Manuel Deutsch's two sixteenth-century *Death and the Maiden*, one of which is lewdly grabbing the maiden's groin, while in the other Death has their head up her skirt. Death offers seduction as inevitable rather than amorous, both a mirror and a courtier (deeply queer in the ambiguous oscillation); the death they bring is a kind of viral decimation of life represented as beauty and beauty as life. The purpose of making these kinds of Death figures fascinating is to illuminate a different form of aesthetic value, and different ebbs and flows of seduction, intensities of desire and the clinamen of life and death themselves – as the maiden corrupts, Death vibrantly gleams, grins, rots in animated didactic or lugubrious glee. Those Death and the maidens which are clearly erotic still do not guarantee this death is male, seen in Hans Sebald Beham's winged angel-skeleton, or in the work of Hans Baldung Grien, who seems to have a Death and the Maiden for every occasion and relational intensity. Hans Baldung's 'The Three Ages of Man and Death' is actually at least two women, a baby and an androgynous revenant. Death brings strangeness to identifiable subjectivity, and their presence makes all devoid of modesty considering the amount of nudity in many of the sixteenth-century paintings. When we enter the nineteenth century, Death becomes irresistibly and gorgeously attractive, the pinnacle of which may be Marianne Stokes's 1900 *Death and the Maiden*, where Death is still adamantly androgynous. The reverse equivalents of Death and the Man/Courtier seem to be more suggestive of Death as a woman due to the residual flesh and hair indicating breasts and the middle stage of femininity, the fecund mother. To be fecund with death is a further ambiguity that extends to Death becoming both a warning repellent, as in the three living and the three dead, and irresistible, as in some versions of Death and the maiden or young man, especially in courtly, one-on-one danse macabre.

> In the German Danse Macabre tradition women usually appear only as female counterparts to certain male personages such as the King (Queen), Count (Countess), and Duke (Duchess). Furthermore, women can be included as an Abbess or Nun, matching the male ranks of Abbot and Monk. Alternatively, they may make an occasional appearance as a Mother with her little children. The only other cases in which women are not presented as mere counterparts for male figures occur when they appear as girls and young women in the motif of Death and the Maiden, or when they are used as personifications of vices that were seen as typically female, such as vanity or a predilection for wordly pleasures like dancing. . . . Therefore, there are two possible interpretations of the positioning of le mort on the female side of the couples in Marchant's Danse Macabre woodcuts. He may indeed be 'leading' in the position of a superior, but he may also be 'choosing' or inviting a partner as we have seen was the custom of female carollers. (Eustace and King 2011: 58)

For every example of Death and various dialectics of allegorical warning/seduction being heterosexually configured, there are exceptions, just as there are exceptions and oscillations between choosing death and being chosen for the danse. Eustace and King offer many visual examples, and the nuances in gesture, posture and allegorical items included are magnificent. The increasing availability of danse macabre and death and the maiden studies through a critical theory lens show a genre with very few absolutes in structure, narrative, figural representation and opposition (or at least we are limited in our contemporary access to the medieval mindset of such). Death is a woman, a man, indeterminate, opposed to a woman, opposed to a man, as a mirror, as seducer, as warner, to be feared, to be desired. In the danse, Death is weaponed (scythe, spears, violence tailored against specific subjectification/vanity of position) or Death offers deliverance (seduction, sleep, the gentleness of the danse). As the potential for death the phenomenon, Death is available by many means. From a postmodern perspective, Death is queer. From a posthuman perspective, Death is a practising posthuman figure, the horizon of signification and subjectification, the shape-shifting, adaptable figure who, unlike the metamorphic dancing Devil, has no moral value in themselves, so ultimately between and beyond good and evil. In living, we cannot see the horizon of death. It is figuratively not accessible; it is neither visible nor invisible as a cessation of turbulence. Temporal and final all at once, death needs something to prop against because it is inconvertible to signification. Kristeva states:

> The corpse (or cadaver: cadere, to fall), that which has irremediably come a cropper, is cesspool, and death; it upsets even more violently the one who confronts it as fragile and fallacious chance. A wound with blood and pus, or the sickly, acrid smell of sweat, of decay, does not signify death. In the presence of signified death – a flat encephalograph, for instance – I would understand, react, or accept. No, as in true theatre, without makeup or masks, refuse and corpses show me what I permanently thrust aside in order to live. These body fluids, this defilement, this shit are what life withstands, hardly and with difficulty, on the part of death. There, I am at the border of my condition as a living being. My body extricates itself, as being alive, from that border. Such wastes drop so that I might live, until, from loss to loss, nothing remains in me and my entire body falls beyond the limit – *cadere*, cadaver. If dung signifies the other side of the border, the place where I am not and which permits me to be, the corpse, the most sickening of wastes, is a border that has encroached upon everything. (1982: 3)

The suppurating sicknesses of the living are testaments to life's continuation and threshold punctuations between potential life and death, though more for bubonic plague times than our own (the living sick will be addressed in Chapter 5 on disability and death). Yet the fascination the wound elicits has little to do with actual death, especially in contemporary arena where a wound signifies volitional agency as often as an accident. The abject persists in seducing fascination on the part of the within without and the without within, as well as the self as other, and other as self. The corpse belongs utterly elsewhere. I would argue that the flat encephalograph may register as more logical to the living, but the concealment of corpses in general, and their use as testament, testimony, bearing witness more than as representative of our own death, leaves them away from the self. Additionally, most of us will see fake death so often that if we do bear witness, the moment of the 'arrival' of the corpse will be as a result of a medico-legal annunciation more than an authentic a priori ability to register death arriving. In this sense, the corpse may represent death, but only as an exacerbated version of the danse macabre as a mirror. The problem here, which will be discussed throughout this book, is that ethics cannot take the impetus to act if that impetus comes from the potential of the self to experience the suffering or finitude of the other. Speculative narcissism is not a means for ethical interaction. The flat encephalograph is designation of death converted to pure third order signifier. The suppurating wound reminds us we are fascinatingly disgusting, thus still alive. The corpse encroaches on all but can be converted to nothing thus everything. The overwhelming nature of the corpse in its simplicity is absolutely expelled in contemporary culture – from those corpses who do not look like me, so don't count as corpses, to the corpse who could be me but is now converted to a testimony for the living's sense of judicial equilibrium, to even the saturation of aesthetic representations of death in all artforms made shiny simulacrum, protected from lamentation or affective capacity. Death in the danse macabre can occupy the place of both death and the dead, the jubilances and sorrows and griefs and demands for actions, seductions and aversion beyond our own dying. From modern eyes, the playful terrifying figure of Death or Deaths in the danse macabre are all the borders of gender and desire, as well as ethical demand and repudiation that more so-called modern representations of death – flat encephalograph, judicial enunciation – close over into hermeneutic phenomenon easily digestible in their form and function. There is an 'everything'ness about Death in the danse macabre – aesthetically, conceptually, ethically – which is liberated from pure allegory and didactic warning, seductive or otherwise. Death is closer to the 'every-human' than the Vitruvian Man. In Death's queerness of form, function and 'occupation' or purpose as figure and concept, representative of 'the dead' gone before and still dancing and living anyway, revisiting the danse has a posthuman enigmatic attraction, itself a queer posthuman dancing with death.

Pietas and thanaterotics

Kristeva states: 'The corpse, seen without God and outside of science, is the utmost of abjection. It is death infecting life. Abject. It is something rejected from which one does not part, from which one does not protect oneself as from an object. Imaginary uncanniness and real threat, it beckons to us and ends up engulfing us' (1982: 4). What of the corpse of art? The corpse made art? Paul Virilio (2003) claims that the twentieth century saw art align with a form of fascism that made the body of the other redundant flesh for use and manipulation, where eugenics and aesthetics, bio-science and 'extreme' or what he calls snuff art – everything from German Expressionism through to Gunther Von Hagen's *BodyWorlds*. Virilio sensitively but somewhat religiously laments the lack of pietas in art, emerging simultaneously with the 'look of death' (44), death existing to be looked at, whether through advances in aesthetic technologies, such as the camera, to the camera testifying to the imminently murdered in various death camps from the Holocaust to Cambodia. Virilio's collapse of fascism and 'extreme' art mirrors the collapse of aesthetics with bio-sciences themselves, techniques of power involving the manipulation of bodies divested of autonomous life to both aesthetically and commercially accelerate the often murderous ideology of individuals or regimes. Even self-expressed representations of tortured bodies in dance which could be considered feminist and recuperative are offered as examples of contemporary delight in spectacles of the promise of death (offering Ann Hamilton and Meg Stuart). Much of Virilio's ideas verge on Christian crank (and he does not mention the spectacle of Christ in this litany of suffering bodies) in that he aligns the human form as sacred with piety, and any distortion of that form is profane, with an attached insinuation of being also unethical. The question Virilio does ask, which remains undeniably urgent, is how has the materiality of twentieth-century art's use of actual bodies (he does not mention nonhumans except as 'if animals, then when human') become indistinguishable from a drive to distort bodies to aestheticize their manipulation in the name of profit, power and sensationalism in the suffering and ultimately superiority over others. An unspoken suggestion in the many representations of death Virilio discusses is that while the twentieth century did invent an absolute real dance of death – real bodies inextricable from the technologies of their demise – the witness who remains is never included as potentially one of these bodies. There remains an adamant dialectic of us and them, of those worthy of killability and we who remain to be titillated or have our fascism vindicated or our scientific patents profitable. For this reason, biotechnology's new relationship with 'real' death, be it of nonhuman animals or humans, in service to fascist majoritarianism, be it prejudice or neo-capital profit, offers a vindication of re invigorating examinations, even superficial enjoyments, of medieval danse macabre and deaths and the maidens. These earlier danses lack the invisible referent of those who remain after death: for the medieval danse macabre it is God alone; for the modern it is Man-as-God. The distance between the dead in the kinds of 'corpse' or death art Virilio discusses and the viewer is what affirms power and a form of scopophilic immortality – they are dead because I belong to the living. The danse macabre exists to affirm belonging with the dead – they are living dead, I am living soon to be dead. From the twentieth century, art's conflation with ideologies driven by war and technologies of mass extermination has somewhat stripped Death of personification, even a form of humanity found in the skeleton or the dancing corpse. Death is the scientist, artist, patron, engineer behind the scenes, the corpse a testament of power alone. My revisiting, along with an increasing number of scholars, of the danse of death for contemporary times must also ask another question – is the twentieth century's supposed obsession with death art conflated with real death changing for the twenty-first century, or, why now? The simple answer, for the purposes of this book, is joy. While not making it explicit, Virilio's examples attest to the space between object and witness, in concentric realms of science, art, war, genocide. The object and the self are as distant as the torturer and tortured. Herb Blau states:

> As for seeing yourself dead, that's the problem of representation which plagues Artaud and deconstructing thought . . . which is the vice of representation in the dominion of death, that death can only be represented. Which is to say it can only be theater, falsifying theater, that repeats it over and over, an interior duplication of the division, the sparagmos, the

originary bloody show – in which we must have thought a little at the very beginning to make a charnel house that seems without end. (1987: 80)

The two major differences between the medieval and Virilio's claims of the twentieth-century danse macabre appear to be the extrication of the viewer from Death and the dead, and that while the latter is in service to power, the former is self-consciously a theatre in which the viewer belongs in *jouissance*. After all, it is a danse, whether with scythe or rose, whether fettered with charnel remnants or cleaned bone-shiny. The danse conjures a troubadour's song, a procession of promise with ambiguous affects or Serres now I am becoming-nothing but still dancing, thinking and conceiving ideas nonetheless. Kristeva exclaims the corpse is true theatre, without masks or make-up, and critically, in Virilio's snuff dance and death art, the corpse is there while I, the witness, am here, and vice versa. This involves a queering of the space and time of life and the time of death, the space of which is unimaginable. Charles Samuelson, along with other posthuman medieval scholars, has emphasized that within much medieval art and literature, there is a 'troubadour queering of time' (2016: 431) found in the refusal of anteriority extricated from interiority, preventing a contemplation of the structure of desire from without (logos) unless also from within (love). Samuelson claims, in his analysis of the thirteenth-century troubadour poem *Flamenca*, that Derrida's concept of différance is appropriate to a medieval sensibility because

> meaning only acquires the illusion of stability via its co-implications with pasts and futures . . . indeed, without rejecting linear time, Derrida refuses to take it for granted . . . a summary of troubadour temporality, this also serves as a reasonable one of *différance*: *différance* is what we could call the *becoming indeterminate* of the present, whereby this 'present' is shown to be sustained by its relationship to a past and a future, neither of which can have existed, or can ever exist, as presents in their own right. (2016: 443, original italics)

Samuelson ultimately utilizes Judith Butler to critique the category of absolute identity as necessary for agency in favour of subversive parody in performativity (2016: 448). He posits différance against Foucault's genealogy of time, which is also, of course, a genealogy of power. Neither is more or less correct or even appropriate, but the importance of the spatialization of spectator-witness and the corpse in Virilio's critiqued art dialectic compared to the constant deferral-inflection of troubadour desire is the importance between a structure of power as different from a structure of desire, and further, a structure of pre-established signifiers of knowledge (of presence and time, object and subject) and structures of potential, unthinkable encounters outside of usual definitions of love. Death as troubadour, whether with lute or scythe, as leading or seducing the dance, is at once unthinkable as troubadour and a most popular motif. Death is the unthinkable future made present and the living dead past made animate.

Testament in bearing witness and testimony to the dead both speak to power. Death speaks to the past but cannot reverse it; we can only memorialize what has passed while never fully apprehending it. Xavier Aldana Reyes states of torture porn films (quoting Agamben):

> It would seem that, as a thanatopolitical scaffold, the *Saw* films, and by extension torture porn might be attempting to reality of the biopolitical body of a contemporary Western subject that has become 'neither a *quaestio facti* (for example a certain biological body) nor *quaestio iuris* (the identification of a certain juridicial rule to be applied) but rather, the site of a sovereign political decision that operates in the absolute distinction of fact and law'. Jigsaw's famous catchphrase 'I want to play a game', would actually ring truer if it read 'I want *you* to play *my* game (and die by *my* rules)'. (66, all original italics)

The inclusion of porn in torture porn may suggest desire, erotica or sex. That flow, whatever it is named, constitutes the 'you' as a 'what', as denying a 'who': the 'what' is the agential singular expressive self, flipped to signified object to expiate power. There can be no transformative element in this 'relation' because it is monodirectional and repetitive by its very structure. Neither element is metamorphozed in this 'game', much like 'games' of biopolitical rhetoric, fascism, war and genocide. Does this form of thanateros belong to a world of eros at all? Covertly does the thanateros of the danse macabre have a political aspect, when everyone must play with Death, everyone will be transformed, while Death does not transform because Death is all manner of desired one to all participants of the dance? Aesthetic seduction by the troubadour Death is a queer relationship with our own inevitable death and a unifying affect of a relationship into which all must enter. The endless occupations of the participants, Bishop, merchant, peasant, maid, crone, seem to show only that signification finally is a unified plane of consistency, that of the dead. While Koutny-Jones (2015) calls the participants of the danse macabre 'Death's victims', how can we be a victim to Death as a personification which affects all? The mode and manner we can be victim of, which is where snuff thanaterotics focuses its attention, can be seen, for example, in the forensic death images of *Polysexuality* (Lotringer 1981) and various uses and repurposing/misuses of 'real' death imagery. More insipid snuff thanateros use as motive the victim's designated subjectification. The only designation Death needs is that one is alive. The very being of life means Death awaits their queer relation, their dance that may take an age or a moment. Small 'd' death is so unrepresentable as to be comfortable with its performative absurdity, a present impossible to conceive, a past where the dead don't lie and our dead future that we know but cannot envisage. Queering time, queering our relationship with the one entity we will all join, Death as a figure literally fucks with time, with life, without power or malice. In this sense, the two danse macabre of medieval and snuff thanaterotics belong to entirely different regimes of expression and affect, and different semiologies.

Enfolded witnesses

The medieval danse macabre deploys the archaic pre-signifying semiologies of dance and gesture, whether courtly or maenadic, in seeking to represent death's ubiquity, its democratic universality. At the same time, the image and reality of death for medieval art and its purposes were not divided (Kinch 2013). The space between witness and image is an enfolded, immersive one, exacerbated by the often (from a hubristically modern perspective) rudimentary or simple nature of the aesthetic in comparison with the irrefutable reality of the actual corpse. Artifice as self aware, because it is naïve, 'cute' or utilized differently from its original purpose as I am doing here with the danse macabre, is effective in including the witness with death. The corpse precludes this inflection by demanding its own othering, whether from our own denial of our deaths or the Man-as-God purpose of the artist-fascist. Kristeva reminds us that the violence of representation is found in the 'delicate alchemy' between artist and world, not in content as much as 'violent transformations of the codes of representation' because the space between art and artist (to which I would add spectator/witness) 'takes place precisely at this interstice between the individual and the world – a privileged space where metaphor, metonymy, and other rhetorical figures come into play' (2002: 122). The space is a gap and voluminous world of teeming affects and expressivities, or what Deleuze and Guattari call interjects and superjects in the event of art (1994). The purpose of dialectic othering involves ossifying the potentials of the gap – signification and meaning must be confirmed. Questions are foreclosed, ambiguities extricated. The danse macabre shows many forms of humans, seeming to attempt to include all. Unlike public executions and other medieval torture porn equivalents, the danse involved everyone, sometimes at once, sometimes one by one, but no one is delivered from the dance. The act of death was very rarely specified, so gendering death, whether by disease or execution, was for other discursive and aesthetic realms. In the dance, there are no sacrifices, of self or other, no victims (unless all victims) no perpetrators, because we are joining with Death, not murdered by Death. While the maiden is more common than the young man, the allegorical purpose of Death and the Maiden is equivalent to Holbein's *The Ambassadors* in that it may represent one subject but its purpose is to remind all of death. We could even include the many paintings of men, especially scholars, haunted by Death in art, whether with scythe or skull. Additionally, in a posthuman turn, we have the so-called 'melancholy death' art tradition, where Death contemplates death, usually a skeleton sighing over a skull or hourglass (popularized in Versalius's *De Humani Corporis Fabrica libri Septem*). The erotic aspect of death and the maiden becomes more fascinating for posthuman and queer studies because death is gendered so ambiguously, and their desiring affects range across a variety of intensities. From many perspectives as inferior or unacknowledged subjects, women fare better in their aesthetic relationships with death than the endless rape representations in art.

Better still, the crone as bringer of death. The figure in 'power' is represented, at once leading the dance and being like the dancers, or as they shall become. When the kind of human, or even the kind of life, you are becomes irrelevant, you have become posthuman. Death is revolting. Taking the dancers away and returning them to the ground, revolution, revoltingness and revolt all at once is found in the too-much but absent signifiers between Death and the dancers and we who see. This uncanny democracy makes Death as a figure and death as a phenomenon strangely alleviating. In current times, on the back of the century of war and genocide, where victims and killability so frequently were represented in opposition to those in power who manipulated death, fascist leaders of all political claims become-Death, the time to both empower and disempower death as figural can offer a joyful respite to the dissymmetry of power. The world of isomorphic binary structural power dissymmetry, where white dominates BIPoC, male dominates female and the gender ambiguous, heterosexual dominates queer, human dominates animal and so forth, puts the latter too often on the side of the dead, and the former become-Death-maker. The dance of death as a jouissant chain of all made equivalent, without signification or subjectification, is enigmatic to rethinking killability. Who leads the dance and how to think the inevitability of death beyond plateaus of power, be they via politics, biotechnology or art? We think of death; we turn to thinking Death. Without catharsis, it is a celebration to be able to delight in macabre, decontextualized images of death's inevitability as something all life shares, in a world where certain lives have burdened too much of their share.

2

Global mourning

Pandemic, trauma and mass death

Mass death has informed many large ethical projects on death and mourning. History seems infinitely repeatable in spite of philosophy's call for it to teach lessons which will somehow prevent the repetition of mass death. The emergence in 2020 of the Covid pandemic shows that the sources of mass death cannot be guaranteed, but the anthropocentric conditions which cause and perpetuate them attest to a prioritization of Western human privilege. This privilege is both banal and malevolently evil, because large-scale conversion of lives to profit functions and hubris props – human and nonhuman – lead to mass deaths. Socio-economic mass death due to Covid failures by various governments (in the case of the UK a form of eugenics of the vulnerable), extermination and genocide of certain human groups internal and external to societies (seen in #metoo and #BLM), invasion of land in the Russian and Israel bombardment of Ukraine and Palestine, and conversion to consumable object in the case of nonhuman animals and ecological resources each show the lines of mournable and unmournable death as changing. Ecofeminism, anti-racist and post-capitalist activists invent activism to convert mourning the entire Earth into changing the way we occupy it. Changing our understanding of death and how we mourn can be a positive catalyst for Earth activism. Death activism is Earth activism: feminist, anti-racist, anti-ableist, queer positive, anti-speciesist.

Trauma as an industry to collective affect

The concept of trauma has become an industry. In psychology, in philosophy, in theoretical and applied manifestations, trauma disperses demands for justice, for mourning, for catharsis. Trauma leaves viscous residue because contemporary capital converts the experience into an energy which must be converted to industry via 'work' – one works on one's trauma, we work on collective trauma, to produce fulfilling outcomes in a fantasy of trauma being somehow beneficial to productive citizenship. The connection between mourning and trauma varies in terms of how tentative it is allowed to be. If mourning is a form of stress, now known as PTSD (a more traditional, long-term result of trauma than mourning in much literature, but also a more reified pathologized subject type), then 'working' through it seems the best outcome. If mourning becomes melancholia, then it is less productive. The plethora of work on trauma makes its definition one that spans the event of trauma as individual, sometimes remembered with clarity or not, right through to collective memory of generations gone. Trauma's affectivity can be acute, chronic or complex like any other pain. Trauma as a spatial and durational phenomenon is amorphous. It is something that happens directly to a subject or indirectly because of violence towards or loss from another. It is collective and subjectified through group dynamics and deeply intimately repressed as so personal revelation may destroy the self. The majority of clinical literature on trauma tends towards resolution as necessary, even while therapies vary radically, not only in technique but also in epistemology. From the work of Freud, psychology constitutes trauma as an event of intense feeling inconvertible to everyday logic, which goes through repression and later the 'cure' in reflection, constituted within a socio-personal structure, or inward facing. Obvious examples are sexual assaults and violence that transgress systematic social taboos. Cultural trauma occurs collectively among people usually of the same self-designation and can occur under a variety of conditions which similarly defy logic, such as war, economic devastation and genocide. Many trauma theorists agree that the single unifying element of trauma is that it be remembered. Alexander et al. state:

> Several definitional accomplishments must be made before an event can qualify as a cultural trauma. It must be remembered, or made to be remembered. Furthermore, the memory must be made culturally relevant, that is, represented as obliterating, damaging, or rendering problematic something sacred – usually a value or outlook felt to be essential for the integrity of the affected society. Finally, the memory must be associated with a strong negative affect, usually disgust, shame, or guilt. (2004: 36)

Yet when writing on how humans perceive death, Freud states: 'So our unconscious does not believe in its own death, it acts as though it were immortal . . . on the other hand, we acknowledge death for foreigners and enemies, and consign them to it just as readily and unhesitatingly as primeval man did' (2005: 190, 191). Trauma threatens to collapse the division between the self and other – the other's death causing personal trauma if beloved or identified as the same group type, society or species. Trauma thins the veil between selves and others while concretizing those divisions which demarcate us from the other-others, the enemy, for anthropocentrism, the animal (hence the frequent claim of trauma as a result of a human 'treated like an animal', a deeply telling and astonishingly confessional interjection). From a posthuman, especially queer feminist, perspective, the divisions between personal and collective trauma begin to dissipate. We can readily say that historically and contemporarily there is, for example, a misogynist or queerphobic war against women and queer folk that designates violence towards majoritarians unthinkable, while violence towards difference is simply not violence because the minoritarian does not count within the scheme of what is an exceptional-because-human agent and what is otherwise, foreign, enemy. But when women become collectives, when queers act together, shame and guilt at not being a majoritarian may be expiated and the trauma may be experienced as a collective. This can be seen in the research currently being done on the connection between the historicity of slavery and the current perpetual threat and actual violence towards Black US persons as a continuum rather than two separate issues of collective/public and personal/private (see, for example, Judith Butler's analyses of the ethico-judicial bind of non-violence as a force, 2020). My aim here is not to investigate or redefine the nature of trauma. I seek to think about how posthuman re-categorization of what constitutes individual and collective groupings, based on alterity, transforms how we understand trauma. As trauma belongs to those left behind, because the dead no longer speak their trauma and we can never access it, from a posthuman perspective we can experience the trauma of the other as a different kind of mourning, and the death of the other as queering how the divide between the living and the dead is demarcated.

This is a ripe time for doing so, as in spite of what distractions the media dangles, the Covid pandemic remains an issue in all countries, exacerbated by varying dissymmetry based on the interrelated ways in which global connectivity means certain countries exploit and extract from others. Plague in its various incarnations, from the story of Oedipus and Thebes (hubris) through to AIDS (homophobia), elucidates corruption in power struggles and oppression of the vulnerable as much as it does new biological phenomenon and threat. The relevance of plague, miasma and trauma was addressed by the New York Theater Group *Theater of War* early during the pandemic, in their rendering of *Oedipus Rex*:

> At the time the play was first performed, the audience would have been reeling in the wake of a pestilence and its economic, political, and social aftermath. Seen through this lens Oedipus the King appears to have been a powerful public health tool for helping Athenians communalize the trauma of the plague, through a story that is as relevant now as it was in its own time. In 2020, Covid-19 challenged Theater of War to go beyond its targeted audiences to respond to a universally shared condition: 'The big difference, obviously, with the pandemic is that it's taken us one step beyond, which is to say now everyone has been impacted by something. It doesn't matter who you are, where you live, everyone has been impacted. Now, some people have borne the brunt of it, and we see the intersection of social and health justice writ large in front of us. We'll continue, obviously, in our performances to foreground that, but everyone has something at stake. So

the beauty of it is the gift of the technology of Zoom met with Athenian drama.' Theater of War's production explicitly appealed to community: while the webinar format in no way reflected the thousands of people in attendance, the performance was followed by a moving discussion with various New Yorkers on the front lines of the pandemic and attended by roughly half of the audience. Panelists included New York City lieutenant paramedic Anthony Almojera, the eloquent vice president of the Uniformed EMS Officers Union (Emergency Medical Services, Local 3621FDNY), who joined directly from his sixteen-hour shift responding to calls in New York City's own plague. Almojera described how the play's references to moaning and wailing invoked for him not just the final cries of the patients but the endless wails of ambulance sirens on city streets. He related for an audience isolated in lockdown the particular pain of entering other people's homes and lives in such dire circumstances: 'I am going into their homes and seeing . . . all the characters that make up their lives. You see a life full, and then you see them as life is leaving them.' Almojera discussed the tremendous toll of endless fruitless attempts to revive Covid-19 victims and of trying vainly to offer comfort while covered head to toe in PPE (personal protective equipment – another of the terms that became all too familiar in those dire weeks). Before the pandemic, he noted, bearing witness at the end of someone's life was a kind of 'blessing', but the need to protect against the virus dehumanized the paramedics, rendering them into 'an apparition' in a mask, all in white, 'almost like a ghost'. Bereaved family members, whom paramedics would ordinarily comfort, had to be kept at a distance as potential patients, forgoing the empathy of shared touch. Even in its virtual format, Almojera's account was indelible and made clear from afar just how much trauma the people of New York were processing. (Fuchs 2021: 60–61)

The gift of trauma

The real of sudden unthinkable death from an invisible source with no knowledge of solution is confounded by the need for virtualizing catharsis and collective trauma sharing and vice versa. Derrida's concept of hauntology in the gift we owe to the dead through memory and bearing witness is in this example at once too real and too far prevented. Layers of PPE and virtualization through either physical distance or the virtual farewells loved ones were forced to use in their goodbyes to the dying make the living victim a mere apparition and giving the gift of death impossible. Derrida states that death is only available for the dying to gift themselves, and death gifts the individual their irreplaceability (1995: 41). The traumatic scenes described above and those globally showed shocking moments of death converted to a theatre where the loved one, being prevented the gift through the witness's fear of and trauma at the threat of Covid, is made the other that dies in place of me; for Derrida this is an impossible rhetoric that in this case makes the loved one the foreigner that Freud claims must die in the unthinkability of our own deaths. Freud claims that the ill relative brings about the most ambivalent feelings of love coupled with a desire for their death, which produces neurosis (2005: 192–193). When the loved one is also the source of that illness and death, within a state of sudden pandemic panic, without possibility of safe mourning, these ambivalences give rise to alternatives to neurosis. A death activist approach to Covid deaths producing neurosis would see also a becoming-with death and simultaneously a becoming-with the virus. D. N. Rodowick states:

> In examining Kant's 1784 essay 'An Answer to the Question: What Is Enlightenment?,' Michel Foucault notes that the task or activity of philosophy turns critically from the investigation of metaphysical systems or the foundations of scientific knowledge to an examination of the present historical moment. The main question of philosophy then becomes how we live or can live our modernity or contemporaneity. If Descartes asks, 'Who am I that thinks,' a unique and individual but also a universal and ahistorical subject, Kant's question 'What are we now, or what are we now becoming?' locates the thinking subject in a precise and unstable historical movement of powerful cultural as well as philosophical change. (2014: 14)

Just as advocates for research into diseases that have 'taken away' loved ones (for example the industrialization of cancer research activism and the ribbon-wearing uniform of various diseases) enter into a becoming with the enemy who 'stole' their loved, the peripheral 'victims' of Covid in the early days, living loved ones and health workers, were forced into a relationship with an other, with invisible but ubiquitous death, with a round spiky reaper. The concept of Covid becomes part of the life of the living. Guilt and shame arrive with a small defeat of that death. For all the world but especially those in the most traumatic moments of early Covid death, becoming-with Covid combined othering and love, war and co-existence, desire for communication with a conceptually abstract death figure, an invisible nature and a corpse visible from behind many layers only.

In the UK people are experiencing death, loss, trauma and PTSD from areas including job role, isolation, lockdown exacerbated experiences of violence and assaults of all kinds, while the recent years of Tory government essentially denied there was such a thing as a pandemic after officially declaring the pandemic 'over', primarily in England, on 4 April 2022 (and holding parties in 2020 and 2021). Meanwhile, Tory peer Michelle Mone allegedly profited £29 million from a £200 million contract for PPE that was faulty and not fit for purpose. The Covid pandemic will remain both active and a cultural traumatic event for a generation, and it is difficult to imagine writing being done without it haunting many contemporary works. For this book, the pandemic, lockdown and the eugenic nature of the death toll and government attitudes offer particular examples of a queer understanding of trauma, mourning, stress and loss. Because the threat of the virus has been announced as over but is not over there is also a clear lack of event in understanding the many traumas induced by Covid as we are required to remember while still under threat. These also resonate with the experiences of the AIDS crisis for victims and loved ones, and for the disabled under current government benefits restrictions. The epidemic of violence towards women all over the world as being declared 'investigated', imagined or over, and the #BLM movement all attest to forms of miasma which power denies still exists, while its effects continue to traumatize minoritarian groups. AIDS and Covid have a rare 'third term' of nature introduced, sometimes as scapegoat, sometimes as weapon, by what all these miasma share as reducible to human against other (human) conflict. Technically, the threat of Covid itself comes from a merged entangled example of nature-culture, a virus borne of human assault upon an environment, a species and individual nonhumans, as emergent via simultaneous biological, ideological, power relation and economic conditions of incarnation. Covid remains antagonistic to human health due to human repudiation of its continued existence as a threat, as if a war were waged and, of course, the humans won. This chapter is not about Covid though. It is about how one 'lives in-with death'. It includes thinking death as immanent while life seems memorialized as something suspended, at least during lockdown. It is about relearning life as if we were dead for a while, while the most vulnerable died in a form of genocide against the elderly, the immunocompromised, the infirm, the extremely vulnerable and those in jobs and socio-economic groups that led to vulnerability. These dead were murdered in a genocide waged by the UK Conservative government against those who simply mattered less, much as welfare cuts waged a genocide in the previous decade. The novelty was that it was the virus killing us, not those creating policy around managing it, so 'nature' was to blame, albeit conveniently nature seemed to choose the minoritarians, of which the government felt least to be viable lives. The trauma of being designated extremely vulnerable was its own kind of isolated posthuman collectivity. The vulnerable were made to feel shame and guilt for being so, as if illness, socio-economic status or job were somehow volitional reasons which welcomed the virus, just as being a woman welcomes rape in misogynist rhetoric. The designations of vulnerability towards Covid involved the entire community of nation-states claiming that because nature had designated to kill certain groups, no taboo of community had been broken. How do these groups, those who survived, those who have lost their beloveds, live within this state? It is a state of living in abidance with death in a way unknown to this particular multi-generational time. Derrida's work on *demeure* approached through the active passivity of passion speaks to the way in which we live within this time of death and mourning. We the vulnerable, are we dead? Deathbound? Dying?

The instant of life

After Blanchot, Derrida claims passion implies finitude 'and a certain neutrality of the "narrative voice," a voice without person, without the narrative voice from which the "I" posits and identifies itself' (2000: 27). Existence within passion occupies the space, according to Derrida, of the middle voice, a voice which speaks to the law by perverting the concept of truth to being fiction. Truth as law is perpetually haunted by the fictive nature of a testimony as an individual's passion while the individual's subjectivity itself is put on hold, without mastery or even subjectivity. This is the abiding self, the self without a home or an abode, the self whose existence is literature because it is fiction haunted by a placelessness and being-less-ness. The very being of testimony is fiction; otherwise, it would be universal law and not testimonial with the potential to be perjury. It is the undecidability of being, of bearing witness, of the collapse of the enunciative function by the attesting non-subject who abides in secret to a testimony which haunts law and life. Derrida quotes Blanchot in speaking of this not-place and the other binaries it collapses:

> In *The Step Beyond* Blanchot associates attestation with the Neuter, the singular place of a passion beyond the opposition of passive and active: 'The Neuter, the gentle prohibition against dying, there where, from threshold to threshold, eye without gaze, silence carries us into the proximity of the distant. Word still to be spoken beyond the living and the dead, *testifying for the absence of attestation*'. (2000: 31, original italics)

Blanchot's *The Instant of My Death* sets the witness who awaits dying within the context of extermination during war: a young man is lined up to be shot, but he is not. In pandemic times and especially for the vulnerable this space is occupied, between living and dying, between waiting and the grace of the death arrived as a strange form of relief, between having no safe abode and abiding with death, between speaking of the death with which one abides and having nothing to say that attests beyond a form of fictive bearing witness. In both Blanchot's example and times of pandemic, as well as other local and global examples of times where the proximity of death for minoritarians is particularly close, death is not avoided. While Blanchot's example is an intimate, personal and individual one, certain subjectification proximity to living with/in death cannot be ignored as the very conditions of life. The intimacy with death leaves life lived as both a triumph and the self as little more than a remainder, a postscript.

The 'I am alive' could be understood as the triumph of life. A fanatical jubilation. That he should have escaped death, whether or not he should have succeeded in the work of infinite mourning that should follow his own death, the survivor would be crying out in this triumphal sentence of libidinal exultation 'I am alive', in the unconscious of the 'unanalyzable feeling'. (Derrida 2000: 96)

The concept of *demourance* leaves the self alive in a way that is not quite living. A living that always abides with death counters the claims by Freud that life is felt exquisitely in the witnessing of the death of the other. The act of othering is critical to designating life as life and death as either a shared dying where those left abide in demourance or death as an evidence of mastery over life through the death of the other. Life and death in the comparison between the death of the other, and the shared death where one escapes, are defined purely by what, or more precisely who, is counted as live able and who killable.

Abiding with death

The severely ableist mentality of many governments during and 'after' Covid perceives deaths as inevitable and as of 'them'. Living within intimate proximity during lockdowns with pandemic death that supposedly threatened all humans created multiple layers of testimony and attestation which chaotically varied in descriptions of 'victims' of Covid who were vulnerable, formulating an almost romantic relationship between Covid death and certain bodies, while ablating the ableism inherent in this depiction by listing exceptions to the 'rules' of who was considered vulnerable and who was not as some faux form of excuse against ableism. For many, living in pandemic times suspends both life and death. It can be claimed that disability itself makes one live in a suspended time, which will be explored in Chapter 5. Life cannot be lived as if it were life before vulnerability: This state is one disabled people know very well – the before and after of disability, if there is such an event, is one of absolute trauma and grief. Global lockdowns forced many to experience certain intensities associated with being disabled. Even the privileged, including those who did and did not flout the recommendations, were made aware of at least the possibility of vulnerability. Defying lockdown expressed a certain will as *pouvoir* that itself verged on a eugenic disclaimer that vulnerability and disability are somehow chosen. This longstanding perception acts to surmount the feeling of de-subjectification that disability, vulnerability and demourance produce. Abiding with death is a threefold experience of awaiting death, abiding with death and living as if one were living as post script. Unlike Freud's melancholia, which is regression into complete narcissism, life as demourance is 'life as the torment of injustice' (Derrida 2000: 89). The torment of injustice is familiar to many minoritarian groups, contemporarily and generationally. Except there is no just or unjust death, just as there is no just or unjust life. To suggest so would be to suggest a logic of life and death. Justice is anthropocentric as is unjust death, so it is only those who cause such deaths that evaluate them based on their own vindications, 'logic' and judiciary ideologies. Just and unjust deaths are reflective, death itself having already occurred is before and beyond these arbitrarily anthropocentric mythologies. Derrida emphasizes and enhances the neither–nor of Blanchot's dead-not-dead young man (who, as a rich, white, young, male would have experienced an 'unjust' death both in social designation and in his strong former sense of a sovereign self). 'Blanchot tirelessly forms according to the model "X without X" ("to live without living", "to die without death", "death without death", "name without name", "unhappiness without unhappiness", "being without being" etc) . . . *Neither-nor*: In this way the witness translates the untranslatable *demourance*' (Derrida 2000: 89) To this I add Blanchot's 'Nor the absence of fear and perhaps already the step beyond' (2000: 9). For what is beyond death? The traditional chronological and utterly reductive narrative of threat-fear-death or threat-fear-survival-jubilation is another anthropocentric and ableist myth. How can we describe those who 'survived' the pandemic, even while it is not over yet despite been announced as such? The vulnerable remain living in a death they have survived. Long Covid symptoms mean more able-bodied people are experiencing disability without definitions that make disability both negotiable clinically and without negotiation in terms of the gap between expression and experience. The neither–nor of demourance shows the poverty of converting vulnerability, disability and living in death to signifying regimes. They are for the living, for subjects. Narratives of existing with disabilities that constitute a living death are the testimonies and fictions of selves without an I. Catherine Malabou states: 'The unthinkable is the metamorphosis that makes an unrecognizable subject emerge from an ontologically and existentially secret place. The unthinkable is a discontinuous – most often sudden – transformation, through which a diseased identity deserts its former reference points – which it no longer recognizes as its own – and fixates upon the undecipherable touchstones of an "other world"' (Malabou 2012: xv). Is this existence in death constitutive of a perpetual mourning? For Freud, mourning is catalysed by the loss of object choice. The self as a fully realized object in the world expressed outwardly as a subject is never anything more than a faith in ego, so it cannot be said that the event which leads to demourance constitutes a mourning per se. The self was never revealed or realized; living in demourance denies the repression of life lived in secret or lifts the veil of the security of life as being realizable. Mourning for a lost love, one has similar residues of faith in another, and the self's perception of that other, but perhaps the loss is more fully realized because the self is haunted by a material absence. Mary Frances O'Conner claims this state feels deeply traumatic to the brain, the neural pathways of which are unable to reroute synaptic trajectories to compensate for a sudden absence of an other (2022). Life during a pandemic for the vulnerable especially, but for all, has been an experience in living in both actual mourning and mourning a life being lived in and with death, an abiding with death. While vaccines and anti-virals mean that the 'not if but when' of humans testing positive for Covid no longer means death, for vulnerable groups this is not the case. The narrative collapses, the 'if-then' of threat-fear-death-or-survival becomes another neither–nor in the undecidability of where, from whom, how one could be infected and what the outcome, long and short, will be.

It is not necessary to see this living with death as qualitatively pessimistic or negative. Like the arbitrary definition of just and unjust death, the emergence of plague and disability is neither just nor unjust; the chaotic traumas which occur are neither just nor unjust. Reflective vindications attempt to make sense of these chaotic turns of events, but nowhere can anthropocentric logic defy them. Can we think a form of living in this demourance with vibrancy? Lykke states:

The short answer to the question of where the mourning 'I' is located in Western philosophy is: nowhere. Therefore, the possibility of it taking up an alternative position to the many philosophical versions of the sovereign 'I' seems to be open. A long philosophical tradition, carried by shifting authoritative voices, reflects on the relation to death of the sovereign 'I', whereas the perspectives of the mourning 'I', lamenting the death of a beloved, have been relegated to the margins of philosophy. A key line of argument of *Vibrant Death* is that this is a serious omission, because a reflection on the positioning of the mourning 'I' can generate important new perspectives. In contrast to the sovereign 'I''s struggles with, and resistance to, the thought of its own death and annihilation, the mourning 'I' is deeply attracted to death in a desiring manner. To the mourning 'I', life appears unliveable without the passed-away loved one, and the 'I''s own death, therefore, stands out as desirable – as a pathway to reconnect with the beloved. What I shall argue, against this background, is that this philosophically different point of departure may enable an alternative relational, transcorporeal, nonexceptionalizing, posthuman feminist and deeply queer approach to death, embracing it as an inevitable aspect of being a vibrant part of the more-than human world. (Lykke 2022: 11–12)

There is a form of trauma inducing mourning for mass death that can particularly benefit from a vibrant approach to mourning – that of activism. This is particularly in the case of activism that seeks liberation of those who suffer the mass death perpetrated by anthropocentric hubris upon the Earth, its environments and each individual nonhuman animal, before and irrelevant of species. There is growing colloquial evidence of the rise in trauma-related symptoms from PTSD to suicide of abolitionist animal rights activists (AnimalsInMind 2018; The Save Movement 2023; Stevenson and Morales 2022; Granovetter 2021; ironically animals are still being tortured in PTSD studies in labs). The status of abolitionist activism, like many other minoritarian activisms including feminism, antiracism and queer rights, is less about positive enforcement of equivalent rights for the oppressed to the dominant and more an embattlement of the self against one's own species. For abolitionist animal rights activists, the onus for animal liberation has very little to do with the absolute alterity of the nonhuman animal and is wholly a combat with anthropocentric dominion, with our 'fellow' 'Man', ultimately with the systematic paradigm of anthropocentrism itself. The nuances of this embattlement will be discussed in Chapter 4, but here I wish to raise the spectre for two reasons. The first is that for many animal rights activists there is a sense of being posthuman in our practice, in that human values and exceptionalism are alien to our understanding of life and death, killability and the freedom of individual organisms to be without having to define their right to being based on anthropocentric definition. It is an anti-death death activism where anthropocentrism claims death doesn't count to the point that death didn't occur. Deleuze states of Spinozan ethics: 'The true city offers citizens the love of freedom instead of the hope of rewards or even the security of possessions' (1988: 26). Is it possible that a posthuman practice of animal rights seeks freedom, a synonym for liberation without mentioning *from* whom the nonhuman is liberated, that is, humans. It is a positive, affirmative liberation beyond reverting to human-on-human argument or anthropocentric rhetoric of hierarchy, species subjectification and equivalence to humans. The Order of Mars is transformed into a Topology of Venus. Abolitionist activism is beyond human argument because in humanist language games the nonhuman as differend can never win. Each act of activism, from boycott to direct action, involves imagining practices beyond human expectations to avoid both capitalist traps of consumerist green-washing to avoiding the law in liberating nonhuman lives from labs, slaughterhouses and transport trucks as a few examples. Abolitionist activists go beyond human exceptionalism, human consumerism, sometimes human law. The third term of nature, what Serres calls biogea, is too often absent in these 'trauma wars' where nature becomes a tool, or weapon, or ideology, between humans. Covid is the evil weapon, animals are the activist-as-terrorist weapon, property turned sentient being. Nature is rarely given its own manifestations without conversion to signification and weaponization. We cry 'kill the virus' with the same gusto as 'kill the animal', and few experience trauma at the confluences of nature as the homogenized other, enemy. Encountering liberation of absolute alterity with no reason divined by anthropocentric fantasies of species, ethology and other humanist knowledges requires a treachery towards humanism in both values and sciences (although Serres reminds us science is always judiciary and in favour of the social contract; 2002: 22). This practical activism can lead some 'humans first' activists and malzoans to make absurd claims, as if the strange biolife of a virus and the demarcated individuality of a curious and expressive pig are conflated as 'all nature' in the abolitionist's mind. Anti-death-making death activism in abolitionism requires practices which can get around those knowledges, rhetorics, laws, ideologies, to be effective, the animal escape routes from humans which Deleuze and Guattari explore in *Kafka*. But these practices involve bearing witness to unutterable suffering and death as do many other activisms. Unlike some social justice activisms, however, abolitionist activism involves bearing witness to mass genocides perceived as both normal and just by humans, something to which most ordinary humans would not bear witness and certainly not regularly. The result is that for even the most ordinary vegan there is knowledge, often with residue from visual testimony, of torture and murder of nonhuman animals that can cause such deep trauma and mourning that it is easy to atrophy, to become catatonic. The 'eureka' moment that occurs when, for example, watching a film such as *Earthlings*, as Will Boisseu coins it (2019: 147), is often simultaneously a moment of deep trauma and impresses upon the activist images which can lead to further trauma. While the suffering of humans in the face of the colossal suffering of animals may seem trite, for activism to continue, trauma needs to be prevented from leading to despair, catatonia, trauma-induced suicide. Hence, the second reason why the spectre of animal rights abolitionist activism is raised here, which is how we can transform risks of catatonic despair into vibrant mourning in order to ensure activism remains active. Obviously, the suffering of an activist bearing witness is inconsequential comparatively, unless it leads to inactive catatonia or, as is more often seen, one of the four silences Lyotard demarcates in *The Differend*, which marks denial of devastating events – repudiation (it did not happen), refusal to speak (I cannot speak for the other, so I say nothing), refusal to testify (I did not see it, so I cannot say anything) and refusal to engage (it is so devastating there is nothing to be said) (1988). Perceiving this form of trauma for activists as inconsequential 'comparatively' can be dangerous as it leads to the 'what about'-ism which makes many activisms competitive rather than communal in fighting kyriarchy. The trauma of bearing witness, which for animal activists is at once banal – available, 'normal' – and devastating, can be transformed to a vibrant mourning through embracing the shattering of self which often accompanies such trauma. The sovereign 'I' is hard to maintain as tenable when that 'I' belongs to a species and a social contract which is perpetrating and normalizing, industrializing and profiting from the horrific acts perpetrated against nonhuman animals every second. The sovereign 'I' designated as the only species of 'I' on this multi-organism shared Earth exacerbates the trauma which occurs from bearing witness to excruciating suffering where perpetrators refuse to recognize any affects that indicate liberty is warranted because those expressions from the other do not conform to anthropocentrically valid modes. The imperialist, masculinist delight in practices such as hunting, meat-eating and other malzoan activities resonates with the xenophobic need for the death of the other, of which Freud writes. Who then wishes to identify as that sovereign 'I' if these are its drives? Most abolitionists begin their activism through awareness they were the perpetrators. Though possibly understood as somewhat luxuriantly narcissistic, this decisive moment of being aware one is a perpetrator and experiencing trauma by bearing witness to suffering is a doubling moment of no longer being the self one was and no longer wanting to be so.

Trauma joy

The first trauma is loss of self, and it is both and neither negative and positive; it is a moment of transformation.

> How should we understand this refusal to accord 'patent' wounds the status of determining causes? And what happens to the 'accidental' element in the constitution of neurotic disturbances? There is a ready answer to these questions: when trauma occurs, it serves as an escape from an internal conflict. The patient takes refuge in neurosis not in order to avoid the war being waged at the front but rather the war raging within himself. (Malabou 2012: 113)

The mourning 'I' which Lykke advocates is the I able to open to the affects of the world, beyond subjectification and species, an I who does not know itself but is supple in experiencing affects coming from alterities beyond anthropocentric conversion to language, logic or the social contract. The mourning I belongs to the natural contract. From a posthuman perspective there are multiple mournings – the actual mourning of each individual nonhuman animals suffering and death, the mourning for the species to which one belongs who shows such indifference and domination to certain lives both human and nonhuman, the mourning for the self who can never return to a state of pre-trauma innocence about what is happening so ubiquitously everywhere in the world (the very mass nature of nonhuman suffering is alone an unbearable weight for many activists, the actual everywhere-all-the-time suffering which can lead to efilism as part of despair activism). Transforming into a mourning I who does not fear death or need the death of the other to experience life is a necessary death that occurs in the demourance of abolitionist activism. An activism borne of life understood as unconditionally shared, mourning must transform into tactics of care and joy in order to be activist, themselves affects which transform conditions for nonhuman animals and all minoritarians. Seeking total liberation while bearing witness makes life seem unliveable for many abolitionists, aid workers and activists. Becoming the mourning-I helps catalyse living the life shared by all life by passing through the sovereign 'I' life as no longer liveable due to its foundation in human exceptionalism and domination. Both the trauma of bearing witness and the trauma of the mass of problems in abolitionist activism can suffocate the self. Life and death can seem simply too much, life as liveable while so much preventable suffering occurs, death as too much due to its scale. The concept of timelines of life and death in relation with activist projects themselves need to transform to prevent the common and understandable phrase that describes activist catatonia: 'I cannot do everything so I shall do nothing'. Individual minutiae of individual lives can beckon the need for care, while large-scale actions occur simultaneously. The hypocritical and speciesist grand exclamations of pseudo-activist marketing such as 'save the whales!' or 'save the tigers for our children to see!' perceive time, action, species and life and death of and for human distortions of chronology, narratives and how activism works on an if-then operation based on the causal will of the individual to make something happen because as a human will alone causes desired outcomes. These fantasies value category, future humans, but attend little to lived life in all its manifestations, and calls for care in activist action. Anthropocentric calls for eco-resolution are reflective of the human who speaks them. There is no trauma except against the ego of the human decrying their or their children's ability to continue to consume/exploit nonhumans. The most difficult question the activist faces – 'what can I do?' is overwhelmingly answered by too much and too little. Both are acts of ethical bearing witness and encountering alterity with radical compassion. Both require different understandings of time, causality, change, tactic. Lykke states as a critical part of becoming a mourning I with vibrancy

> Emerging from these intertwined inspirations, the figuration of vibrant death points towards revitalizations of cosm-ontological understandings of the temporalities and ecologies of the life/death threshold, which are radically different from those dominating Western modernity. Revitalization in this sense implies a rethinking and reimagining of death with a focus on shapeshifting and passing the thresholds of life/death as embedded in non-linear – cyclical as well as Aionic – time, instead of remaining within the mainstream of Western modernity, fixated on chrononormative linear timelines flowing towards final endpoints. Moreover, revitalization in this context means undoing the dichotomous divides between nature/culture, human/nonhuman, mind/matter, living/dead which also haunt dominant Western conceptualizations and imaginings of life/death thresholds. (Lykke 2022: 248)

For victims of trauma, there is, in the many and conflicting definitions, a sense always of the before and after. This is consistent whether trauma exists through devastating events of near-death, disability or bearing witness that catalyses activism. The before and after are singular interstices of multiple trajectories of affects which accidentally encounter each other to become trauma and dissipate in constellations that include joy and mourning as the I is transformed. The after is a perpetual becoming because, of course, there is no 'after' trauma. There is the I that is transformed and continues to be so. Transformation is deeply material and repudiates the Cartesian faith in a mind and a body which experience trauma independently, one receiving symptoms caused by the other in oscillation. Of the neurobiology of trauma, Malabou states: 'Might there be a type of plasticity that, under the effects of a wound, creates a certain form of being by effacing a previously existing identity? Might there be, in the brain, a destructive plasticity – the dark double of the positive and constructive plasticity that moulds neuronal connections? Might such plasticity make form through the annihilation of form?' (Malabou 2012: xv). Questions arise: How can we be vibrant within the mourning I, the post-traumatic I? How can symptoms become acts of radical compassion in excess of and beyond humanist ideas of reclaiming or curing the self with the belief there is an ability to reverse time and return to the sovereign I? And would we want to anyway? Is the question even relevant considering there is no reversal? If we are post-trauma, we have an opportunity to enter a becoming posthuman. We are anti-'death of the other' activists, but our sovereign I is lost, so we are also death activists bearing witness to our own dead selves and living nonetheless. No cure can reverse time. Activism makes the mourned dead expressive and the post-trauma dead self thrive.

3

The denial of desire
Suicide and the right to death

Concepts of rights regarding human subjects – those recognized and registered as worthy of life – often invoke terms such as *free will* and *liberty*. Interpretations of 'will' include ego (psychoanalysis), volition without meaning (existentialism), force/puissance (Nietzsche), mediated relational expressivity (Spinoza) and the will of a general consensus that humans have a desire to persist in living. Moral philosophy, usually an advocate of euthanasia, retains the idea that embracing death should come only after a 'good' life (good usually meaning long) or as an evasion of torture or illness-induced suffering. Currently, the majority of countries which allow voluntary assisted suicide have many conditions, such as a requirement of an expected life of less than six months due to terminal illness, mental competency and the ability of the patient to be able to administer the suicide drug themselves so as to deliver any blame from a 'murderer'. Refusing treatment can also be made available, which can sometimes lead to a more painful, though considered passive, death. Some rare cases of assisted suicide for conditions such as depression are increasingly visible. In general, there is always a demand for a reason or vindication for death that outweighs the demand society makes on us to live our lives no matter what. Usually, that demand, even in the case of depression, must be understood as physiological, beyond our control as embodied subjects (reinforcing the prejudice that mental illness is not illness), rather than an actual will to die as an active desire which is prioritized over the default expectation of the will to live. Palliative care seeks to make the 'good' death, a better way of dying, an easing into the inevitable that can no longer be denied. The increasingly popular use of and training in 'death doula' practice reflects demand for good death. The ill become consumers of death technologies, customers in their own death but, like all other consumer actions, only if they can afford it, financially or with mental 'capacity' externally weighed. Generally, caution against legislating in favour of assisted dying cites external causes symptomatic of social inequality that are the impetuses of the desire to die, so a too liberal attitude to assisted suicide would lead to increased injustice in who was dying and why (see, for example, the conclusion to Woods 2006 and current disability discourse around euthanasia and eugenics). This valid suspicion of motive for the desire to die resonates with Spinoza's invalidation of suicide. Sanja Ivic discusses Spinoza with Kant on the impossibility of resolving suicide with human will. Ivic demarcates two elements of Spinoza's ethics which speak to the impossibility of self-destruction, the external cause element and the not-the-same-subject element: '"External cause" argument (E3P4) and "Not in the same subject" (E3P5) argument are premises of Spinoza's argument for the impossibility of self destruction: E3P4: "Nothing can be destroyed except through an external cause." E3P5: "Things that can destroy each other cannot exist in the same subject"' (2007: 134). The problematic notion of an individual being a singular consistent essence or *conatus* (will as endeavour) is where Spinoza's ethics fail human subjectivity. Queering death implies an interpretation in which conatus is much more about a corpo-affective material vitality than 'will' in a restricted human sense, and this way of understanding conatus makes fleshy, corpo-affective desires for dying as conative as desires for living.

The phantasy of the subject being both singular and consistent, demarcated from other entities and so responsible ethically for behaviour towards these others, but not towards any alterity in and of the self, is not one that sits easily within the context of either being as a form of becoming, where multiple intensities which are rarely consistent are what collate into a tactical self, or with semiocapitalism, where the self is alienated from the self and trained to seek fulfilment externally to chase the idea of full integration as a self-knowing self. Where the self as integrated whole is presumed before the introduction of an impulse to not be, the question of being and not-being seems clear. But where we acknowledge the messy and metamorphic multiplicity of selves that is the self, in its various relations with the self and others, the idea of externally acting upon the self seems likely, even inevitable. We are not the same subject as ourselves, so acting upon ourselves is not improbable. This reduces the importance of the external cause logic that underpins many arguments which approve and disapprove of euthanasia. For the former, terminal sickness or suffering is an external cause which somehow alienates the body from its own subjectivity. In a Cartesian turn, this sickness is more often approved if it is entirely corporeal, while gaining approval for mental illness- or suffering-induced assisted suicide is still rare. In the case of the latter, the prevention of seeking death due to external causes such as prejudice, poverty and non-terminal disability configures external cause as a eugenics machine, rightly to be critically examined and usually reflectively turned on the societies which lead to these external sufferings. The self, even while contemplating the end of self, is rarely in canonical philosophy given self to self when the will to live is overtaken by the will to die. Here we turn to Kant, who similarly saw the will to live as default and the will to die as absence or cruelty to self. Kant sees the attitude one has towards self as a universal attitude towards humanity, in his five principles indicting suicide, as irrational. Suicide as an act is a means, not an end, for Kant. Like Spinoza, Kant sees the desire for death as coming only from external causes, be it external to logical will or external to the body (1949: 56–58). Suicide prevents individuals from assessing the effect of their act after the act; it reduces 'men [sic]' to 'beasts [sic]' and shows a contempt for humanity in general. From a post-structuralist and anti-anthropocentric perspective, the problems in embracing humans as benevolent are clear, but to stay with Kant a moment, it is the continuing idea of the integration of self which Spinoza also presumes (but not consistently elsewhere in the *Ethics*) that means the self cannot have oppositional or conflicting internal life which is stronger than the will for persistent living. This seems out of step with almost everything that comes after – psychoanalysis, world wars, recognition of minoritarian selves (human and nonhuman), poststructural dismantling of the 'subject' and of logic. Kant and Spinoza are helpful in the way they show what is presumed within a subject, as opposed to what constitutes the lived reality of being a self/selves. Especially in Kant, there is a strong, though arbitrary, moral tone which designates life as good and suicide as a necessarily debasing act. Edwards writes:

> In reply to Kant, it must also be emphasized that a great many cases in which people have committed or have attempted to commit suicide do not at all resemble debasements of the kind just described. If I commit suicide I may do so freely. I am not necessarily the victim of the stronger will of someone else. Nor am I indifferent to my own feelings or my own dignity; but on the contrary I may compassionately decide to terminate what I regard as my pointless (or even perhaps degrading) suffering. In such circumstances I have not become a thing, and I have not at all debased myself. (2007)

Contemporary areas of thought that embrace suicide openly, such as the Mark Fisher-inspired new nihilism, retain the difficult moral dilemma of suicide being somehow inherently 'bad' when it does not have an external cause, but embracing the badness seems to be a reason for many of the (mainly white, male) proponents of the movement to celebrate it (although Fisher himself saw nihilism as neither negative nor having a moral value). Thus, we see even in pro-suicide realms, there is the 'good' suicide affiliated with a life well lived and the 'bad' suicide celebrating nihilism, and all seem to have to come from 'somewhere'. It is rare to find discussions in philosophy about those who simply wish to cease, without necessary suffering or sadness beyond that life is just not for them. It is in literature where positive attitudes to suicide can be found. It is relatively easy to argue against canonical philosophy's denial of death wishes without 'external causes' in terms of the division of labour between philosophy and literature when contemplating the distinctions between the mourning 'I' and the sovereign 'I'. While deathboundness without 'external causes' is taboo in philosophy, it does flourish in literature – among others in the literature on love-death (e.g. see Lykke 2022). The will of romantic poets to 'die young' could perhaps also be considered as an effect of queer desires for death. In relation to what Lykke calls 'love-death' literature (2022), 'lost love' still belongs to the 'external cause' regime. Nevertheless, from Orpheus to Werther to Karenina, literary/poetic descriptions indulge passionately in the protagonists' fleshy desires for death in ways which go far beyond a mere pinpointing of the 'rationale' in the shape of an 'external cause'. The fact that Werther, for example, had to be banned in several countries in order to stop the 'suicide contagion' from spreading is also interesting in relation to the ways in which queer deathboundness, on the one hand, has been tabooed since the beginning of modernity but, on the other hand, figures as a well-recognized literary trope in mainstream bourgeois literature, and, additionally, in sociological terms, conceived as a societally 'dangerous' agency, a virally infective desire, undermining modernity from within. This chapter will explore how we can navigate a suicide activism for all, which gives individuals access to their own lives *and* deaths, and why our liberty still denies us our own death as an easy and peaceful event.

Suicide from outside

A century after Spinoza, Hume critiqued the default philosophical logic of human life at any cost. In 'On Suicide' Hume denied that preserving life was essential to God's will by counterarguing that welcoming natural death, through illness or accident, was part of this belief, so avoiding death was as contrary to God as preserving life. While Spinoza has been embraced in posthuman theory as a vitalistic philosopher, his use of 'God' is now variously and tactically understood as a sense of 'spirit' or lifeforce, a part of the belonging all lives, known and unknown, human and nonhuman, have with cosmic interconnectivity. The posthuman understanding of God does not alter the argument of Hume or Spinoza. Both show fidelity to the unknowability of life. In Spinoza, this unknowability is a critical part of both being a life and an ethical encountering. In Hume, knowledge leads to melancholy. Lemmens states: 'In *The Tractatus* . . . Spinoza enigmatically identifies the highest good man can attain as "the knowledge of the union that the mind has with the whole of nature (TIE, 13)"' (2005: 49). In *The Tractatus*, Spinoza seeks joy in living, which would offer a vitalistic alternative to the futility of life; it is found in union with the unknowable infinite substance of God that is the whole interconnectivity of nature. He describes this joy in a way that is akin to affect, which is why many posthuman theorists of affect now turn to Spinoza and affect theory against the more oppressive and exhaustive concept of knowledge as enlightenment. Joy and the meaning of life are found in, to put it reductively, feeling. In contemporary philosophy, affect describes expression-experience openness to alterity, the embrace of metamorphosis and the infinite interconnectivity between intensities, be they situations, organisms or those which the self encounters within the self. For death activism within this book, affect belongs to the Order of Venus, or Love, because it does not seek knowledge; its constituting clinamen is supple connectivity. However, to understand love as inherently aligned with such concepts as positive life or benevolent good does not exclude certain phenomena which logic and knowledge would place on the side of malevolence and the bad. Spinoza speaks of expansive and diminishing affects, which he describes in *The Ethics* as joy and pain. The multiplicity of any organism's capacity for mingled affects within, following Deleuze and Guattari's concept of molecularity, means that joy and pain as expressions and affects are always co-present – within an organism, within relations between organisms, environments and affective expressions. The issue for current understandings of suicide arises when we automatically place our 'knowledge' of the concept of suicide on the side of pain. Accessing the definition of suicide through the Order of Mars, or War, according to Serres, means we close off the phenomenon to becoming a judicial 'truth' where the motive for designating suicide as always bad or wrong is not acknowledged as the reason for its designation – usually, suicide has been designated wrong for religious and now legal reasons with a variety of interpretations, most often reducible to denying an individual control over their own life or death in favour of the church or state, of capital labour or obedience. Hume critiques this Martian definition:

> Do you imagine that I repine at Providence, or curse my creation, because I go out of life, and put a period to a being which, were it to continue, would render me miserable? Far be such sentiments from me. I am only convinced of a matter of fact which you yourself acknowledge possible, that human life may be unhappy; and that my existence, if further prolonged, would become ineligible; but I thank providence, both for the good which I have

already enjoyed, and of the power, with which I am endowed for escaping the ills that threaten me. (2005: 5)

Hume calls all edicts against suicide versions of superstition, which have their source in motive, be it religious or capital. Hume also shows the absurdity of Kant's claim that suicide closes off the ability to know if life can get better, which is made compulsory for human logic to pursue by Kant's edict. For Hume, the joy of having been is not erased by suicide. To the contrary, it evinces the variability of the self to experience mingled and diverse affects, showing awareness that sometimes the saturation of simply not wishing to be, which also comes from as many diverse minglings, is compelling in a positive, logical way. If we think of suicide as simply an expression by an organism, there is no reason to align it with good or bad. Regarding Western institutional prevention of suicide, most are clear in their motive. For the church, why would someone who believes in an eternal afterlife not wish to die? For the State, especially the neocapitalist state that denies welfare, bodies must persist until they are utilized; then they are left to die unless wealthy, for the family, brutally. It is those left behind who lament suicide, not the dead. Minoritarian bodies in current Western conditions are literally left to die rather than allowed access to either life or death, good or bad, though being left to die through the 'food or fuel or medicine' welfare cuts as seen in the UK in the last decade is inarguably a bad death. The Martian Order belonging to the hierarchical state, which ignores its vulnerable and poor, would describe death by starvation or freezing as a form of suicide, just as they would claim drug-related deaths, eating disorders, obesity and even disability lead to a form of volitionally chosen death. These are not suicides; they are examples of when the affects of a wealth-driven state deny expressing opportunities of liberty and joy to those in need of them. These states deny the 'God' of Spinoza by denying the connectivity of all organisms and communities and the ethics of these connections and the encounters they produce. These are murders by bad ethics. Suicide is the active taking of one's own life, under one's own choice, a deathbound drive which is vitalistic, queer to the default notion that life endured counts as living at all costs. While the concepts of free will, choice and the ability to decide with clarity will always be philosophically murky areas, there is no denying that certain lives simply do not wish to persist, for as many reasons as other lives wish to persist.

Suicide activism?

Can we speak of a joyful suicide? Of suicide activism? Perhaps it is easier to begin with that to which suicide doesn't belong. In 'Betrayal: The Thanatocracy', Serres identifies ours as a society of death, implicit in a Martian society of war, combining the power to know with the power to destroy, or own, and pleasure in that destruction that overpowers any pleasure in living. We live, he claims, trained into a horror of life:

> It becomes culturally natural that knowing requires dying. That knowing requires smashing the object to pieces. Hence the iron law of all education: It is hammering. No, the education of children was not within the power of Jupiter or Quirinus, the priests or the producers but in the hands of the soldier rabble . . . you all rest easy: The solution is Utopian. The soldier rabble don't even need to be on the watch. Look well around you who, yes, who, well who loves life? We are all suicidal. Seek one just man in this shuddering Sodom, on the eve of the raining down of the tar pitch, a just man who loves life unconditionally. (2011: 11–12)

Our love of signification, of triumphant identity, extravasates our bodies from their expressions and capacity for affects. Does Martian suicide even belong to death anymore? We are all suicid*al* but that is an intensity impulse, not an affective expression. It is a form of constant malaise, an atrophy symptomatized by what Berardi calls 'an epidemic of unhappiness' (2015: 165) born of semiocapitalism, where 'the only social categories remaining are winners and losers' (2015: 51). How can we love life under these conditions by which our being emerges? We emerge within death, or at least on the battlefield of Mars, where if we lose, we are dead, and if we win, at what cost and with what pleasure? This is a reductive and cynical attitude towards life, but it is how semiocapitalism works, so the question becomes how we define joy under these conditions. The situationist art book *I Want to Be a Suicide*

Bomber by Sherif Xenoph Ibn El (aka the Deleuzian queer theory scholar Zafer Aracagok) is a litany list of all the reasons one would want to die and take victims with oneself, and each is a decidedly Western, neocapitalist frustration that cites the many promises of satisfactions of 'life' shown up as mere conflicts between winners and losers. These include quotes from Freud, Plath, Cixous, Pasolini, Genet and forty other songwriters, poets and philosophers, all of whom critique how desire has been robbed of our bodies by the thanatocracy of winners and losers, of promised fulfilment when we never lacked in the first place. Troubling the idea that the suicide bomber act is an Islamic drive of fundamentalist phantasies of eternity, it shows how capitalist, heteronormative familial and other structuring beliefs create a competitive territory of absence before our voluminous desiring bodies emerge into the world. We have lost the will to want (as fluid drive, not of owning objects), so all we want, as Aracagok and Serres claim, is to die, perhaps taking others with us not as victims but so we won't feel so alone. Wanting to die as a perpetual state is not suicide; it is a symptom of contemporary life. It is encountering life as a simulacrum, units of knowledge for accumulation, measures of success or failure, diminished compassion and empathy in a world becoming increasingly horrific. But this is only one attitude to take towards both life as thanatocracy and suicide as a perpetual affect. Can rethinking suicide also help rethink living and life?

A deathbound society makes life radical, surely? Very little has been written on posthuman understandings of suicide, possibly due to the posthuman being a vitalistic reclamation of ways of living differently. If our society is deathbound, or in the practice of making-dead those deemed never worthy of social life and a nourished physical life, then a pro-suicide concept would seem to side with semiocapitalist and fascist regimes that place certain bodies low on the hierarchy of social stratification or refuse to recognize these bodies except occasionally as statistics. That certain bodies barely register as life means theirs is a non-lamentable death, and for this reason, persisting in life is a radical act. Two questions arise from this idea: first, what of the privileged? Could suicide – at least in discussion if not reality – foster a form of deprivileging certain subjectification? Second, is persisting in life as an act of defiance a romanticization of either social or medical pathologies that does not smoothly encounter the lived existence of certain selves? The first question is more philosophical because it can involve actual or metaphorical suicide. Deleuze and Guattari's call to becoming is antagonistic to much contemporary ideology around difference and inclusion. They remind us that signification reads the body based on the biunivocalization of pre-ordained options (1987). Who we are is a coalescence of a selection of isomorphic binaries – white/Black, male/female and so forth. The final designation of how our subjects are read based on these pre-signifiers inserts us into a stratum within the social hierarchy of subjectivities, our subjectification in comparison to others. Just as the Order of Mars reduces all to winners and losers, signification hinges upon the dominant and the Other – white is not in opposition to Black but the failure to be white, male is not in opposition to female, but the failure to be male, humans is not in opposition to animals, but everything which does not conform to anthropocentric patterns of dominion is designated animal, historically including women and non-white persons. Corporeally, Deleuze and Guattari tell us that signification and thereby subjectification occur through the legibility of the plane of the face, whose template is the face of Christ. That face remains the face of what is now the almost mythologized 'white, Western, able-bodied, hetnorm, straight, rich male' which forms the basis of inclusivity policies and trainings and is also the reason why the current move to the Right among media and various global conservative nationalist groups is bent on 'reclaiming' this subject who has become the 'victim' of the 'witch hunt' of 'woke' culture. The shared concern of both inclusivity and the 'war on woke' is the continued demand for legible subjectivity. Via Serres, this would mean that all acknowledgement of any other would be played out on the field of Mars, a field of War, where knowing leads to a dissymmetrical dialectic of encounter as power over another, not as mutual mediation. Identifying not *that* lives are, but living being conditional on *what* lives are is signification as death, and all life is excluded before it emerges. Serres states:

> The Order of reasons is repetitive. The knowledge linked up in this way, infinitely iterative, is but a science of death. A science of dead things and a strategy of the kill. The order of reasons is martial. The world is in order, for this mathematical physics, where the stoics meet Plato, up the way, and Descartes, down, and order reigns amidst the heaps of corpses. The law is

the same throughout. They are thanatocratic. There is nothing to know, to discover, to invent, in all this repetition. It, falls, *in the parallel of identity*. Nothing new in the reign of the same. . . . The law is the plague. Reason is the fall. The reiterated cause is death. Repetition is redundancy. And *identity is death*. (2000: 109, my emphases)

Expanding this into entire groups, societies and global life and living literally becomes a perpetual battle. But against Durkheim (2006), suicide is of the organism struggling between emerging via the signifying Order of Mars and their own impulse to life and/including connections with other lives. Not, as Durkheim argues, because the organism as a hermeneutic individual is incapable of integration into society. Contemporary culture's continued obsession with signification, even in defence of difference and inclusion, makes living for its own sake and on its own terms impossible. In many ways, it makes being born, or at least born into life, unthinkable. While I do not claim phantasies of free will and free living of one's life demand, one knows the existential conundrum 'who am I', being told who we are and then being integrated or not based on these significations to which we do not subscribe means that the 'me' who is designated as 'this identity' is alien to one another, so we are already in a state of what Lacan would call *spaltung* and Deleuze and Guattari would call schizophrenia. But Lacan blames spaltung on the individual and sees it as a psychological symptom, while Deleuze and Guattari see schizophrenia as both a symptom of capitalism (or what I will here tactically describe as hyper-signification semiocapitalism) and a way out. Deleuze and Guattari identify eight aspects or principles of signifying regimes. These are worth citing in full:

The signifying regime of the sign is defined by eight aspects or principles: (1) The sign refers to another sign, ad infinitum; (2) the sign is brought back by other signs and never ceases to return (the circularity of the deterritorialized sign; (3) the sign jumps from circle to circle and constantly displaces the centre at the same time as it ties into it (the metaphor or hysteria of signs); (4) The expansion of the circles is assured by interpretations that impart signified and reimport signifier (the interpretosis of the priest); (5) the infinite set of signs refers to a supreme signifier presenting itself both the lack and excess (the despotic signifier, the limit of the systems deterritorialization; (6) the form of the signifier has a substance, or the signifier has a body, namely the Face (the principle of faciality traits, which constitute a reterritorialization; (7) the system's line of flight is assigned a negative value, condemned as that which exceeds the signifying regime's power of deterritorialization (the principle of the scapegoat); (8) the regime is one of universal deception, in its jumps, in the regulated circles, in the seer's regulation of interpretations, in the publicness of the facialized centre, and in the treatment of the line of flight. (1987: 117)

These eight aspects work in concurrent and inextricable coordination, and the power of each tightens the power of all. When setting out so clearly these eight techniques of subjectification in our signifying regime, the actual stranglehold the regime has on subjects evinces the ways in which the regime makes it unachievable to live. At the least, a new terminology of living is required. It also makes it easier to see the vitalism and vibrancy found in active deathbound suicidality, as it is for poets and artists. For the majoritarian, it is of benefit to belong to the regime; for the minoritarian, it is not; for the nonhuman animal, it is so impossible that it leads to nonhuman daily death by the billions. Yet curiously, white men still commit suicide more frequently than any other demographic (which I will discuss in the next section), so what is meant by life here are minoritarians yet-to-be-born, already dead, or do we live a form of suicide by submitting to the signifying regime and could this help suggest that suicide activism is a way out of a situation that can barely be described as a life lived with creative freedom? There is an outside, though access to outside the regime is conditional and risky. Art, activism and practices of revolt attempt to access the outside but must work within inescapable conditions – revolt *against*, transgression *of*, as has been critiqued by Foucault among others. Revolting and escaping are incited by, but also enslaved again through, these eight aspects, which I will truncate to (1) referral, (2) circularity, (3) metaphor hysteria, (4) interpretosis, (5) despotic limit, (6) faciality, (7) scapegoat and (8) deception. The majoritarian benefits in performing the self within these aspects. But it is always a highly regulated performance, and if the majoritarian is also in the position of interpretosis priest, designator of the scapegoat and benefits from deception, then there is paradoxically more room for him to deviate. Contemporary attempts to integrate equality as diversity and inclusivity demand that alterity selves become subjectified and stratified along the eight aspects, which can then lead them to being included or scapegoated by the majoritarian priest. In a Foucauldian turn to manufacture and refinement of self to self, one is made victim of one's own alterity as both performance and failing when attempting to be recognized. Further, the valid desire for visibility and recognition comes through faciality, through designations of gender, race and other signifiers based on referral to and divergence from the Christ face/majoritarian white male. Should we attempt the despotic limit – despotic because capitalism's ability to subsume imagination and convert it to currency is infinitely malleable – we risk occupying the outside, or we risk actual death, the ignored or the sacrificed scapegoat. All these strivings, all these attempts to connect with our communities of all organisms, must happen in current conditions through these eight regime tenets. For minoritarians and especially for nonhumans, to belong is both exhaustingly difficult and involves a displacement of any singularity of self in exchange for a majoritarian-recognized licit version of difference, which is no difference at all, just tokenistic inclusion, isomorphically inferior, referral to the same.

Suicide and techniques of work

Concurrent with diversity and inclusivity programmes are trainings on and calls for 'deprivileging'. Deprivileging is considered a postmodern management theory (see Gebhardt and Thatchenkery, for example). Deprivileging involves those in positions of power to acknowledge, account for and actively unravel the privilege into which they were born or have managed to slide. Privilege does not bring reward so much as it brings ease, just as suffering is not relieved by wealth or liberty so much as by a state with the absence of suffering. Postmodern management theory attempts to resolve post-thought with neocapitalism. Deprivileging has a more curious potential, one which may explain the persistent resistance to it. Deprivileging involves the death of the eight registers of the majoritarian signifying regime. In turn, it leads to the death of many individuals: some the death of their whole, others a piecemeal death, where whiteness or heterosexuality or wealth or able-bodiedness is emphasized so as to access the most power. Deprivileging requires a certain grace in setting aside any privilege to open the way for alterity to flourish. If we seek social diversity and inclusivity that does not demand the description of signifiers, we do not add to those described; we destroy the describing system, the Order of Mars. Yet the Order of Venus, openness to love for alterity itself, will require the death of the privileged self, to whatever degree this is accessible. At the very least, activism involves a self-made social suicide of the privileged self. Resistance to this form of suicide is the content of the 'war on woke'. From one perspective, the suicide of the privileged subject towards becoming a mediative self is the very least vitalistic, difference-affirming activism required. But what of the minoritarian or minoritarian aspects? Being 'included' on the oppressor's terms, both exhausting and impossible, a loser's game, means death already. Sekowski and Lester emphasize the role of self-criticism in suicide among young people (2022), showing when criticism is not turned towards the system but the self, metaphoric and actual suicide entails. Baumeister similarly studies suicide as an escape from the self (1990), but what is the self under the eight conditions of the regime, and who is this self about which we are speaking? There is the socially dead, unrecognized or victimized or forced to enact majoritarianism, slid into the Christ face as Deleuze and Guattari tell us: 'there is no exterior, there are no people on the outside. There are only people who should be like us and whose crime it is not to be' (1987: 178). The minoritarian too can choose social suicide by becoming-clandestine because any regime of signs always includes others within the assemblage which are operating, whether they are recognized or not. Many groups seek this form of activism, a presence that is presence without clear recognition, where the force of acts and affects is prioritized over the validation of a certain group. Much art, especially art collectives, eschew the artist for the movement. Velocity, trajectory, dissipative affects constitute the becoming of selves and artworks as forms of revolt. The subject does not exist. Seeking existence is admonished for suicide for the sake of affects which dent and reorient the regime. This form of minoritarian suicide has also been named domestic terrorism, where the clandestine nature of esoteric groups and abolitionist animal rights rescuers are placed in the same category as suicide murderers and fascists. Activism often involves a form of social suicide. Being minoritarian can lead to the more finite version of becoming-clandestine, actual suicide. Deleuze and Guattari criticize the masochist and the drug addict who take their body without organs – the reorganized body in service to its own new circulation of intensities rather than those organized by the signifying regime – to its limit and end in accidental suicide. They claim taking the Body without Organs too far can lead to being killed or to catastrophe (1987: 161). But are these really catastrophic? If Deleuze and Guattari call for becomings-woman and -animal as if these states of intensity are pleasurable in their non-recognition by signifying regimes, they fetishize to an extent. Why is the suicide a fetishization too far? If this world, and this life, is not for us, majoritarian or minoritarian, is their criticism of suicide so dissimilar to a society that makes suicide available only through hazardous and risky means? Is not suicide, not-being, the most clandestine, most anticapitalist option of all?

In order not to be

Before I conclude with opening the possibility of not-being as a form of queer death activism, it is important to mention that at no point am I offering a romanticization of 'reasons' for death. While it is almost impossible to find writing which advocates for suicide, and writing about suicide can lead to 'suicide contagion', clinical psychologists agree that on the whole there are two psychical states which lead to attempted and completed suicides – unbearable pain or suffering and a feeling of hopelessness that things will never change (see Lester, 2022 Joiner, 2005, among others). Terms attached to suicide such as 'prevention' and 'crisis' which frequent clinical and theoretical discussions on the topic insinuate a linearity that may not benefit a suicidal self's state but tend to benefit the clinical apprehension of the cause–effect aspect only. There is a persistent sense that suicide always has an external cause (both outside of the body and outside of a state of 'good' mental health or a 'stable' psyche). The reasons given for a persistently suicidal person's feeling are both atemporal and immanent – a feeling of perpetual nowness with no past or future and a sense of pain which itself has neither beginning nor end but is its own state of being, or integral to the being of the person. This is easy to understand with terminal illness or disability; however, it is also the case that the expectation, even demand, for a life-loving psyche is simply not practical for all selves. To suggest that life is experienced as absolutely prioritized over any level of another form of being – including not being – is spoken from the mouth of privilege where living is easy and counts as the only form of how life is lived. Default pleasure, joy or even suffering are all assumed as necessary conditions of living. Pleasure, joy and suffering can also be the life of death, an ecstasy with validity and a care for life through its extinguishment. For many, whether privileged or not, and without the necessary need for an external 'cause' (as seen through persistency in suicide attempts under different conditions), not being is the state of being that is most desired. This is a phenomenon that is still utterly taboo, difficult to speak about, difficult to write about. It is the queer closet of life, of death studies, of care theory. One can desire death and be healthy, mentally as 'sound' as one needs to be. For the suicidal, living becomes a state of 'passing', concealing a deep desiring identity which is jubilant and filled with expressivity and affect; only these are for death. The suicidal is queer against life, but exists with authenticity and validity independent of pathology. For many suicidal selves, our lives are 'managed' in the most neocapital way as to be sustained at any cost. Yet care for the living is at an all time low, and lack of care for the deathbound means horrific failed suicide attempts leave lives in unlivable states of damage when all that was desired is a good death on one's own terms of being deathbound. The hypocrisy of taboo around becoming-dead is startling. Famous artistic suicides (Gilles Deleuze's defenestration, Virginia Woolf, Sylvia Plath, even Mark Fisher's 'good negative') have been active positive acts, final passions of passionate lives where both positive and negative have been indivisible intensities that were overwhelming or quietened, who knows and what is the purpose of knowing? Current suicide care as 'management' of life, 'management' of energy is insipid in its value of the demand to live without compassion for, or even recognition (without pathologization) of, the desire to die. As queer as deathbound desire is, it remains concealed in the closet to the point of imperceptibility – no one *wants* to die exclaims the smug life whether they are living or simply persisting. Life management does not explain deathbound desire. Beyond the death drive, there is a desire for a state of suspended perpetual peace, a posthuman being that is not being but that, like posthumanism, decries the world as it is and chooses not to occupy it, where the self is inextricable from the world but seeks another world, hence another self. Our clinical obsession with reasons is yet to explain sufficiently why some of us simply seek death no matter how our circumstances change. Pharmacology for depression, when successful, often leads to successful suicides. Is the famous 'cry for help' coined in 1961 by Faber and Shneidman a cry for ourselves or for society? Certainly, for many activists, there is the risk of the wall being hit, where the anthropocene seems so resistant to difference, ethics and alterity that life within that system seems untenable. Yet this is another 'reason'. And this is why I wish to suggest suicide can be seen as a queer death, even tentatively a queer form of death activism.

Clinical psychology seeks to homogenize or at the very least categorize/subjectify suicidal persons. While studies have been done on the high rate of white male suicide, and comparative studies have been done between the suicide notes of women and men (Lester and Yang 1990), suicidality needs a queer lens for two reasons. LGBTQIA+ people have an inordinately high rate of suicide. The three most frequent clinical assessment models for LGBTQIA+ suicide risk and reasons are the diathesis-stress model, which suggests physiological predisposition to depression in LGBTQIA+ persons (a form of minoritarian pathologization that deserves its own Foucauldian critique); the differential-susceptibility model that places suicidality on environmental factors, especially family and early-life bullying; and the minority stress theory, which would most align with Deleuze and Guattari's emphasis that in a signifying regime, liberty for minoritarians is limited. The minority stress theory does retain the onus upon an individual's own mental health as the ultimate pivot for suicide ideation or completion (yet another 'labouring job' at which we are either successful or unsuccessful, rather than a final, passionate, corporeally affective and effervescent experience). The external cause aspect of LGBTQIA+ suicide attempts and completion is a question of the homophobic regimes of global societies, and the tendency to pathologize is not of benefit to these persons, so I am not here wishing to address these particular theories as to 'why'. But we owe it to queer theory to acknowledge that our community's high rate means there is something that allies queer suicide with suicide being queer. If we return to the key aspects of queer theory (rather than LGBTQIA+ identity), we embrace metamorphosis, mutable identity, expressivity and affect, velocity and intensity as elements of ourselves and those with which we connect, in the abstract and the material. The question that turns back on the questioner. The category with no definition. The voluminously present unknowable. Queer non-identity belongs to the world outside of identity equalling death that Serres maligns. I argue that the reductive nature of suicidality being chemical, or environmental or any 'factor' which reduces it to a causal narrative of pathologization underestimates the potential for suicidality to not be a destructive or negative impulse/symptom of a cause, but a state of intensity which can and does persist in some persons who simply do not wish to be in the state we currently identify as living in this world at this time. It is a repudiation of life as compulsory, just as queer theory repudiates the patterns and narratives of compulsory heteronormativity. The high rate of continued attempts evinces a wishing to be that belongs to an immanent state, which could even validate the constant suffering/no future elements of clinical suicidal definitions, but are these states necessarily curable? Is suicidality an illness that can be cured? Possibly for some, but just as queer desire is as infinite as those organisms who express it, would it be a form of compassion for both self and others to accept that for certain persons, life is simply not for them; that there is no desire for living, or life drive, that it is atrophy in the face of being forced to live (the face of the signifying regime, the priest or the psychiatrist no less) that causes as much if not all pain? Is there a living deathbound desire that thrives towards the absence of existence? Is that necessarily the opposite of life, when semiocapitalism turns much life to living-dead status? Is there a different way to talk about and with suicidality that is merciful instead of pathological? Is suicide a form of self-love, belonging to the order of Venus, a 'to be born' (a phrase from Irigaray but here used alternately to her intent)? Contemplating contemporary theories of self-care/compassion rather than self-destruction/annihilation or, worse still, forced management to live – can suicide be gracious/compassionate to oneself? We must open a space of expression for sought suicide. Better still, a space for expression *and* access to a swift, compassionate end to life for those who seek a becoming-absent. Luce Irigaray states:

> What appears to us in the present is no longer hidden by what has been said about it; we are now facing what is still to be experienced and said. And this compels us to resort to a quite different language which lets the other be without bending it to our saying. A language which lets the presence be without intending to define it *a priori*. A language which allows any 'to be' to appear without our knowledge of it . . . this seems to be impossible for us. However not to attain this other way of using language amounts to using word(s) as an instrument of death and not of life. And yet we cannot abandon we cannot content ourselves as speaking being with such a destiny. It is thus incumbent on us to give another function to the word, especially as far as living beings are concerned. Instead of designating and apprehending them through a name, we must make room around them to give them a place for their own words. (2017: 66–67)

Irigaray is adamantly *not* speaking of suicide here. But the work is titled *To Be Born*. The suicidal person is yet to be born into a self who is able to speak as a person seeking or even a being-in/with death. We are the failed living, the isomorphically non-thriving, in need of cure. Deathbound desire is a successful drive. The living are the failed dying (even though we are always all dying). We can thrive in running towards death, just as living does not mean thriving, and aversion to death can lead to all manner of Poe-esque paranoias. Critics default to vulnerability, as if every suicidal person has a secret homicidal person waiting to exploit their suicidality, or myriad people ready to claim someone was suicidal for their own nefarious murderous reasons. I am not suggesting we hand out free samples of pentobarbital. I seek a way to queer our communications around suicidality, to make a space for the queer ways in which being-with-death can make some of us 'live' differently and desire to live not at all. Suicidality is unique to each individual, so it is a queer way of being in the world, and like queer history, demands its subjects remain silent, clandestine, practising desire in secret. We must allow suicidality to be born, with mercy, compassion and grace, and also in community and with curiosity, so that vulnerability and vibrancy are understood as part of the same death-desiring self, not reduced to a victim of circumstance. There may be reasons, there may not, but validating either is not for the external priest of interpretosis. Lykke's devastatingly beautiful ficto-theory on the right of every critter to have a vibrant life, which always includes a vibrant death, is worth citing in full, as she writes of her becoming-deathbound in a state of perpetual mourning for her beloved:

> I consider life and death, ontologically, to be a flat continuum of inhuman zoe dynamics. However, continuum or not, death is also a threshold. My beloved's moment of death taught me about the decisiveness of that threshold. Her final exhalation was a radically transformative moment, transmuting a human subject into inhuman otherness. I have speculated intensely on the wall of silence which separates the mourning 'I' from the dead beloved. What is behind it? I know that until I go there myself, I must stay with speculations and intuitions. My beloved is gone as the subject she was. She is something radically different now – an instantaneous spectral presence, a vibrant, inhuman zoe existence, ashes mixed with algae sand, as well as minute chimera living on in other bodies . . . I have longed intensely to co-become with her new assemblages. I have imagined how, through my own death, I will become-one with the algae sand with which her ashes are mixed. I have longed for this merging: 'Going to the underworld and staying there forever!,' as I wrote in the Overture to Vibrant Death. (2022: 236)I have longed to die since my beloved died, several years ago now. I have written poems and philosophical reflections about the love-death of the mourning 'I', who is becoming-one with her dead beloved and her new assemblages. I have fantasized about different ways to die, imagining Virginia Woolf's suicide by walking into the river Ouse with her pockets filled with stones as well as my friend Berit's story about her recent experience of almost dying from blood poisoning, experiencing a sliding away towards death, while her dead beloved life partner came to hold her. I have concentrated intensely on the threshold between life and death – this threshold that is so decisive, even though, along the lines of Braidotti's immanence philosophical, posthuman death theory. (2006, 2013)

Lykke's ability to utilize poetic enchanted and enchanting language to speak with suicidality beyond a pathologized subjectivity, even beyond the 'reason' of her beloved's death, takes this desire outside the prosaic limits of life as always benevolent or even better than death. It demarcates ideation, which sometimes converts to completion and sometimes does not in its queer impulses, as belonging to the realm of lyrical prose, of the Underworld, the outside. The very language of suicide does not belong to our signifying regime. If we listen to and care for suicidality, we can nurture the life that seeks vibrant death. With care, absent of violence, especially the violence of the options the suicidal have to die – with suffering, with failure, sometimes with assistance that leads to criminalization of the merciful – we can nourish ourselves if we find ourselves the death-desiring, and others who listen will nourish us simply by learning our language, a language that does not belong to the compulsion to live. We must accept that for some of us, the persistence of life is unbearable, and a vibrant death is how we see our perfected becoming. This may be one of the most difficult and unpalatable messages of this book. It is easy to accept the metaphoric suicide of the privileged subject as necessary for a more ethical world where love of power is exchanged for queer becomings together. To listen to those who dwell with death is less familiar. But the continued attempts and suffering of the suicidal means at the very least it is time to listen differently, with artistic language and with grace. And then who can tell what a suicide activism may create?

4

Abolitionism

Mass death and the nonhuman animal

I start this chapter by exploring two quotes which have both been mis-ascribed and circulated continually in popular culture. Both quotes are relevant because they address the economy of grief and death, but also may provide an entre nous to the possibility of joy in activism spurned by deep mourning for a certain kind of death based on alterity and unknowability. The first quote has been utilized by everyone from Queen Elizabeth II (who used it in her post-9/11 speech) to Nick Cave (who claimed it in a blog) but which comes from the British psychiatrist Colin Murray Parkes. He states:

> The pain of grief is just as much part of life as the joy of love: it is perhaps the price we pay for love, the cost of commitment. To ignore this fact, or to pretend that it is not so, is to put on emotional blinkers which leave us unprepared for the losses that will inevitably occur in our own lives and unprepared to bereavement little help others cope with losses in theirs. (2009: 39)

The second quote, beloved of acolytes of the negative ethics of Mark Fisher and Slavoj Zizek but likely from Frederic Jameson, is 'Someone once said that it is easier to imagine the end of the world than to imagine the end of capitalism.

We can now revise that and witness the attempt to imagine capitalism by way of imagining the end of the world' (Jameson 2003: 76). It may seem counter to my project of anthropocene dismantling to begin a chapter on nonhuman animals with two theorists whose interest in nonhumans is not in evidence and whose belonging to institutions of psychiatry and Marxism, respectively, leaves little room for alterity within and for experiences of grief. What both quotes show is that within the very premise of a perceived binary is placed its antagonist as the structuring possibility of its affects – without the knowledge of loss there is no love, and critically without love there is no grief. Without the seeming impossibility of an all-annihilating apocalypse, there is no capitalism, because capitalism feeds us fantasies of an apocalypse to incite our perpetual hunger for consumption, abstract accumulation and the de-materialization of the Earth. In a way, the latter could cynically be mapped onto the former – capitalism, especially semiocapitalism, has overlayed love with consumerist abstract desire (for 'things', for accumulation, for acceleration), and grief has been overlayed with the end of the world (so that the only reason for grief is it reminds us of our own end; it is not, technically, grief for an other but a narcissistic self-reflection/fear). And yet, just as these two quotes show the condition of possibility of one term found in another, just as this book discusses the condition of life found in death and vice versa, there is an enigmatic draw to these quotes which creates a different way of understanding animal activism, reading the quotes in a deliberate deviated way to their purpose, turning each as a lament into a call to action.

Imagining worlds: Endings and beginnings

I will begin with the second quote, Jameson's 'Someone once said that it is easier to imagine the end of the world than to imagine the end of capitalism. We can now revise that and witness the attempt to imagine capitalism by way of imagining the end of the world.' This is because Jameson's quote is observational, while Parkes's will be used in the context of this chapter as activation. It is difficult to weigh up whether Jameson's statement is a statement on grief as exhilerating or on the inspirations that can be taken when we give up on fighting the perpetual mutability of neo-capitalism and start imagining new possible worlds. The latter, presumably, is what is called for in his claim and that of the end of the world being an exhilarating starting anew, breaking historical repetitions, prioritizing imagination over the ironically atrophied ossification of the world through capitalism, even while capitalism itself is endlessly permeable and adaptive. Is capitalism the end of the world? Of only this world? This chapter is about the devastating reality of the status but, more importantly, lived experiences, of nonhuman animals in this world. As I have written elsewhere (2020), nonhuman animals already embody the reality of capitalism *as* apocalypse. Each species and genus but always, most critically, each animal life exists via a structural emergence as a node within anthropocentric extractionism – the world perceived and exploited as resource alone. One way of defining and understanding neocapitalism and semiocapitalism is by defining them through this apprehension of the world. Resource and extraction vary depending on each emergence of life, but the prioritizing of 'use' over sharing the Earth and allowing the other to be with their own space and liberty is the fulcrum of this definition. In reference to semiocapitalism, this is particularly in evidence when we think about the invocation of words such as species and their use. Species at this time is less related to natural history and biology than anthropo-fetishism and biotechnology, both always also inextricable from wealth accumulation. There are obvious examples: certain species are bred to be murdered for 'food' and milk and wool extraction, such as pigs, cows and sheep, camels, chickens and goats, among others. These species make up the huge majority of the Earth's nonhuman mammals. The 2018 Proceedings of the National Academy of Sciences (Yinon M. Bar-On, Rob Phillips and Ron Milo, 2018) claimed that 70 per cent of all birds are farmed poultry, 60 per cent of all mammals on Earth are livestock, mostly cattle and pigs, 36 per cent are human and 4 per cent are wild animals. In Great Britain in 2022 over three million animals were used in vivisection (https://www.understandinganimalresearch.org.uk/what-is-animal-research/numbers-animals) and in the United States each year (as of 2020) over 110 million animals are killed in laboratories, from schools to commercial research laboratories (https://www.peta.org/issues/animals-used-for-experimentation/animals-used-experimentation-factsheets/animal

-experiments-overview/). Like the so-called agricultural species versus domestic pets or exotic wildlife, the species in labs are relegated to greater (usually apes, baboons but also dogs and cats) and lesser (rats and mice, reptiles and amphibians, and water fleas). Any attempt to address species hierarchy is essential, but focus must not be removed from the absolutely unique singular experience of an individual organism and their existence as being bred to be utilized, plundered, incarcerated, raped, tortured and murdered. Nonhuman animals in 'entertainment' are often 'wild' animals, domesticated through tormenting and violent training, to allow humans to indulge their scopophilia. There are more tigers in captivity than the wild. Zoos, circuses and other exploitative practices raise a very difficult question about capitalism and the end of worlds – is it better for an animal to go extinct than have a species continue if that continuation is an incarcerated, deprived, diminished capacity for liberty and self-expression?

Humans lament species extinction, without acknowledging for whom an exotic species exists. An individual animal may or may not lament the disappearance of their own species, but this does not balance the suffering and continual holocaust of existing as a perpetuation for the sake of human pleasure in novelty, even while environments are destroyed so agricultural animals are forced to graze on wild lands to nurture their own deaths. These overlapping cycles of being born into the end of the world for individuals and species of nonhuman animals all come down to the value of the nonhuman for the human. Nonhuman animals on the Earth at this time are variously experiencing what Charles Patterson calls the 'eternal treblinka' (2002) of human treatment of animals. Nonhuman animals coalesce all the suffering and oppression experienced by humans considered other. Patterson explores equivalences with Europe and slave transport, the United States and slavery, with women and sexual exploitation, with the exploitation of children and with the Holocaust. Elements which de-individualize single lives such as herding and factory farming join many oppressed groups with common practices against animals (2002: 54), from live transportation to use-value rhetoric around certain groups or species being homogenously stupid, dangerous or ripe for commercialization (2002: 73). Many others have made these equivalency comparisons, notably in the arenas of ecofeminism and afroveganism. All share attention to equivalences not in order to assert the hierarchy which warns against unethical treatment of animals in order to prevent the cruel treatment of humans (as does, for example, criminal profiling) but to show that human structuration of power in its intimate inflection with capitalism creates fatal world-endings for billions of lives for whom 'life' is a tentative existence defined by a necropolitical agenda of high disposability, extractability and killability. In this sense, one crucial way of imagining the end of capitalism is imagining the end of the world that these individual animals encounter as the tenets of their existence. Ending these various practices ends the conversion of life to extractible resource. Ending the fatalism of a life born to death – the end of the world as the very condition of the world and life into which these nonhuman animals are born (usually bred) – is a way of imagining the end of capitalism. This purely through opening the potential of a life born as a life unto itself lived on its own conditions, without a need for vindication, use, resource or utility. This would lead to a conclusion that animal activism, which refuses all animal exploitation – abolitionism – is not an act of war between humans, as it is currently structured by the media and in many senses necessarily through demands and petitioning for changes to law. Instead, or in addition, animal activism is a Venusian order, an order of love, because it embraces, indeed demands, the end of the world, which is a world only for humans, by turning to the unknowable other and seeking nothing except liberty for that other. Abolition is an act of love that exchanges conditional 'life' born purposefully for suffering and death with life as an unknowable, imperceptible force opened to its own unfurling. False rhetoric, which names abolitionist activists as terrorists (e.g. see the *Prevent* act, UK Government 2018, revised 2020) simply because we consider nonhumans lives over property, carries insinuations of violence. In most cases this violence is the ideological conversion of 'property' 'stolen' as 'theft' to an individual's life understood as belonging to itself as a life. Abolitionists call it liberation of the nonhuman animal towards their own life, the government names it theft away from the human. As death studies shows us, the killable are not endowed with 'life' and certainly property is not deemed to have a life.

The act of love which comes with the end of capitalism, where anthropocentric property ceases to be understood as such, has far-reaching consequences.

Not simply for nonhuman animals liberated from their suffering, but for more abstract Earth elements, such as geography where nation-states and borders that produce fascism, toxic patriotism and war have the very idea of ownership contested. One's 'property' is a declaration of war on both the Earth and against those who would care for each patch of Earth, each environment and ecological area. In theory we have eradicated human slavery (which of course in practicality is simply not so). The very idea of owning 'everything but human' nonhuman animals and Earth denies the living, vital, joyful singularity and connective relationality of these events, just as semiocapitalism converts our own lives into significations and subjectifications. The end of the world, the end of neocapitalism as resource plundering for wealth accumulation and semiocapitalism as the reduction of all materiality to empty signs of exchange, can be brought about with the act of love which is abolitionist activism's refusal to comprehend property where there is life. In a breathtaking essay on nonhuman animals who self liberate, Rachel McCrystal bears witness to the hypocrisy that underlies the anthropocentric ideology that animals aren't lives but property. She states:

> Those who profit off of animal agriculture know the power of individual farmed animals and their acts of rebellion. There is a reason why they are hidden from the public behind deceptive marketing campaigns, lobbying efforts, and locked gates. There is a reason why rebellion is bred out of domestic farmed animals. The owners of farming corporations large and small know that to hide and obfuscate individual animals is just as much a foundation to their business as physical exploitation and harm. (2023: 203)

McCrystal discusses individual animals who both self liberate and liberate other animals incidentally or deliberately. The awareness they open to the public who consume them confronts humans with the reminder of life within the object designated 'food' or 'test item' or 'produce item' is ignited by their rebellion against being an object, against incarceration, against fear and towards escape routes, acts of individual creativity borne of drive to thrive, terror, desperation and resistance (all theoretical and anthropocentric emotions, we can never know the drive of the nonhuman but their corporeo-affective resistance is all too clear in cries and writhings). McCrystal discusses the heartbreaking insidious deliberate breeding of nonhuman animals based on docility, as if breeding the resistance out of an animal can breed out their impulse to strive or thrive or, indeed, live. McCrystal acknowledges that making a poster child out of individual animals to show their agency is problematic, for isn't the most meek, least resilient, still in need, perhaps in greatest need, of liberation as an act of love? Her essay shows the designation of a life as an object is both a deliberate sublimation and a denial of the individual experiences of each individual organism's thriving, which we can never know. Violence, the Order of Mars, may praise the heroic escape artist, the animal who breaks free because to show active forceful agency aligns with anthropocentric ideals of selfhood and victory, winners and losers, the deserving and undeserving. The Order of Venus remembers those docile animals may sometimes (most often) need assistance, without condition or proof they desire to thrive. Venusian activism also celebrates those animals who self- and companion-animal liberate, in the basic act of understanding no individual animal need fulfil a human template of agency to deserve life and acknowledging we can never perceive how a nonhuman animal thinks their own thriving. As an act of absolute love, we are compelled to love unconditionally without demand for purpose or reason, we cannot seek to extract a subjectivity, because that is simply a different form of semiocapitalism and use. It is enough that animals are; it is irrelevant who (formerly what, be it species, genus or individual) they are. In the same volume as McCrystal's essay, Krista Hiddema emphasizes the problems when territories of war effect abolitionist activism. Reduced to their basic binaries, on one side there is effective altruism (EA), which is aligned with more traditional animal rights based on quantitative, usually utilitarian measures and methodologies and, by implication, 'logic' and analytic philosophy. On the other is grassroots, one-by-one animal liberation, direct action and principles of care that use all kinds of awareness to change laws, raise consciousness via social media and stealthier, often designated illegal, activisms, focussing on both quantitative and qualitative, individual animal lives and experiences driven by an ethos of care and love, which is (often in a denigrative or diminishing way) relegated to 'emotion'. Unsurprisingly, the former is usually dominated by men, the latter by feminist and queer activists. Problematic is the anthropocentric perpetuation of the antagonism between each as a Martian structure of war. Just as activism finds itself grappling with both using the master's tools *and* finding clandestine ways to create new tools of both destruction and creation, so too abolition needs both sets of practices, a multi-trajectory act of dismantling *and* creating, of forming the end of worlds and the beginnings of new worlds simultaneously. Hiddema states:

> The EA dominance in the AAM must change, and it must start with funders. The power of money must be harnessed to power love. Emotions and love are often the place where the spark of change begins. They are a springboard that connects us and inspires grass-roots advocacy, integrity, political action, and changes that people make every day in their everyday lives. Human history is littered with the tragedies caused by leaders who believed in numbers. We cannot continue to make this mistake for animals. If we are to truly transform how animals are viewed and treated, it must start with compassion, respect, understanding, open-hearted listening, and humility. It must start with love. (2023: 188)

While love does not exclude logic, logocentric activists have a tendency to exclude love, because they play/fight on the anthropocentric field of war against malzoans, where the third excluded term is the nonhuman animal themselves, Serres's biogea:

> The game with two players that fascinates the masses and opposes only humans, the Master against the Slave, the left versus the right, Republicans against Democrats, this ideology against that one, the greens versus the blues . . ., this game begins to disappear when a Third party intervenes. And what a Third party! The world itself. Here quicksand, tomorrow the climate. This is what I call 'Biogea', an archaic and new country, inert and alive, water, air, fire, the earth, the flora and fauna and all the living species. . . . International institutions in vain perpetuated those two player games which remain blind or harmful to the world. Who will have the audacity to found an institution where Biogea will finally be represented and have the right to speak? (2014: 30–31, 32)

Serres emphasizes that the end of semiocapitalism hearkens listening to the Earth, to biogea, whose language we do not speak and with whom we can only experience encounters inconvertible to anthropocentric (or capitalist) meaning. This does not mean biogea does not speak. Animal rescuers hear the nonhuman animal speak perpetually, in their silence and trauma, their squeals, their escape, their pure alterity. In this sense, Serres shares with us a concept of the other of the natural order, who also belongs to the order of Venus because our relation is far too complex to be reducible to dialectic opposition. It is a relation of clinamen turbulence, of empathic affect, of a de-structured 'logic' of love, because it is logical that we cannot convert what is best for a nonhuman animal other to anthropocentric understanding. Biogea resonates with Lyotard's idea of the differend. The differend is also an excluded third other. Lyotard speaks of this excluded third other using the example of the concentration camp victim, specifically related to the Nuremberg trials. The death of the other, the annihilation of those victims who also suffered through until their murders, means that they cannot speak at their own murder trials. Yet the denial of the event of murder is described by Lyotard with the four silences: the 'it did not happen', or 'I did not see it happen', or 'it is none of my business' and 'I cannot speak for the other so I will not bear witness'. For the nonhuman other, the banal everyday evil of malzoanism could be translated as follows: 'it is normal that it happens', 'I refuse to watch it happen' (the 'happy farmed animal' excuse), 'I am not a vegan/animal liberation subject-type' and 'we don't know how animals think/feel (malevolently or benevolently) so it can't be apprehended'. Lyotard mentions treatment and suffering of nonhuman animals a number of times in *The Differend*, not to emphasize the reduction of holocaust victims, but to show the need for obligation to the other without condition or empathic equivalency (or even presence). The differend is the one who cannot speak because they cannot be heard – because they are dead or because they are othered, so their speech is not perceived. If they can speak and be heard, they cannot be a victim, because they are alive and able to testify. This shows that within the territory of Mars, within dialectics of logic, the third term, the other, oppressed, tortured, murdered, can never win. And yet we have an obligation to the other, be they incarcerated, murdered or simply because they are other. This obligation circumvents all four forms of silence. Obligation refuses any understanding of the obligation to ethics based on the blindness that comes from putting oneself in the place of the other (thereby measuring obligation based only on subjectivity and equivalence). Lyotard states:

> [170] Instead, obligation should be described as a scandal for the one who is obligated: deprived of the 'free' use of oneself, abandoned by one's narcissistic image, opposed in this, inhibited in that, worried over not being able to be oneself without further ado. – But these are phenomenological or psychoanalytic descriptions of a dispossessed or cloven consciousness. Which are far too human and humanist. They maintain the self even in the very acknowledgement of its dispersion. Could we begin with the dispersion, without any nostalgia for the self? And think therefore the splitting of the self apart from any finality, if it is true that finality is still the action of a self which is exerted upon an object beforehand and from a distance, even if this action momentarily cleaves that self? Of course the idea of a splitting would also have to be abandoned then, since it presupposes a beautiful totality: the result. (1988: 109–110)

There is no being an activist. There is only activism. Therefore, there is no being a right or a wrong kind of activism. There are only the affects one produces, one being an amorphous term for an act of activism which may involve an individual or many or any combination of teeming molecules of activist impetuses. Lyotard explicitly states that one must die to oneself to be in obligation. He also points to the 'in perpetuity' of obligation. Result insinuates finitude, self-congratulation, narcissistic advocacy. Lyotard emphatically expresses that in order to show obligation to the other, without condition, one must *die to oneself*. Obligation without condition is love. Love involves, as its very first premise, death of the self. Without this, the other remains an object, activism remains results based ordered by anthropocentric logic and with finitude and the terrain is one of war – between different kinds of activist selves, between abolitionists and malzoans, between humans and other humans: for Lyotard language games, for Serres war games. The language of love is an entirely different game, an entirely alien relation – without war, without opposition, without self, without other. This is 'perfect' activism. I use this jarring word inspired by bell hooks on love:

> Taught to believe that this understanding of what it means to be perfect was always out of human reach, that we were, of necessity, essentially human because we were not perfect but were always bound by the mystery of the

body, by our limitations, this call to know a perfect love disturbed me [here she speaks of the first epistle of John]. It seemed a worthy call, but impossible. That is, until I looked for a deeper, more complex understanding of the word 'perfect' and found a definition emphasising the will to 'refine'. Suddenly my passage was illuminated. Love as a process that has been refined, alchemically altered as it moves from state to state, is the perfect love that can cast out fear. As we love, fear necessarily leaves. Contrary to the notion that one must work to attain perfection, this outcome does not have to be struggled for – it just happens. It is the gift perfect love offers. (2001: 92–93)

Does this mean not only is there not being an activist but there is no activism, there is only love? Love for the other is no longer love for the other because the self is not maintained as a subject; it is a becoming-love conduit to liberate the other's expressions of life? Refinement seeks no result. It seeks the adaptability, listens to the untranslatable call for obligation. To love the nonhuman other involves death of self and life of the previously uncounted as living coming into presence. Undifferentiated, our own becomings liberated from the fear of loss of subject, loss of self, the joy in death of self towards love make the end of the world for us filled with infinite potential for states of love, ways of loving, grand and small, intimate and abstract. Activism is nothing but tactics of love, and love is everything beyond dialectics, opposition, semiosis and war. It is the end of capitalism as the beginning of the world.

Beyond an economy of love and grief

And now I return to the first quote introduced in this chapter, Parkes's:

> The pain of grief is just as much part of life as the joy of love: it is perhaps the price we pay for love, the cost of commitment. To ignore this fact, or to pretend that it is not so, is to put on emotional blinkers which leave us unprepared for the losses that will inevitably occur in our own lives and unprepared to bereavement little help others cope with losses in theirs. (2009: 39)

As introduced in Chapter 2, an increasing amount of work is being published on animal activists and trauma, which is to be expected in regard to activists being in conflict with many of our own species while witnessing acts that are both as bad or worse than violences of war or genocide and seen as utterly banal or inevitable. Interestingly, most work to date on trauma and animal mass murder has focussed on slaughterhouse workers and the psychological effects of the 'job', which overwhelmingly affects lower economic groups, women and BIPoC folk. The focus of trauma and psychological assistance creates a lament for the worker, technically the murderer or processor of the corpse. The nonhuman victim remains the third or absent term. New work on trauma in activists is called 'trans-species trauma' and seeks to 'depathologize the stereotypic characterization of animal activists as angry extremists and instead view them as integral voices within a system in search of healing' (Granovetter 2021: 660) She continues:

> Activists encountering ecological degradation and injustices against animals face unique trauma, resulting in novel terminology to describe the adverse effects. Jones (2007) identifies earth and animal activists as 'a category of activists who are at particular risk of trauma' and identifies these forms of activism as ones that entail 'inherent physical and emotional risks' (p. 19). She coined the term 'aftershock' to give language to the 'reverberations of traumatic events endured by activists' (p. 24). By employing novel terminology, she seeks to capture nuances that extend beyond diagnosis. Similarly, Mann (2018) designates a new concept, 'vystopia', to describe the existential despair experienced specifically by vegans as they come to terms with the massive scale of violence, secrecy, and denial surrounding animal agriculture and exploitation. Similar to Jones (2007), Mann (2018) suggests that trauma may arise in the symptomology of activism. (Granovetter 2021: 662)

Many welfare and abolitionist activist groups have shared various studies on individual and collective trauma on behalf of direct action activists as well as those who have born witness to the treatment of nonhuman animals through visual media and other indirect exposures. Psychologically, there is a resistance to categorize abolitionist activists with other forms of human PTSD studies because of the deep sense of betrayal from our own species as well as trauma being a shared and displaced experience – trauma *with* other activists and *for* or on behalf of the victim – rather than an inward psychological experience.

Recall that trauma is a socially mediated attribution, and it becomes frozen, persistently reexperienced and emptied of speech in part because it is excluded from social discourse. As the culture fails to mourn nonhumans deemed commodities, activist grief becomes encoded as trauma to the extent that it is embedded in a defended, psychically frozen collective. Activists who choose to bear witness, and suffer trauma as a consequence, illuminate a darkened corner of collective awareness. When the deep multispecies pain of activist encounters is culturally validated, activist trauma can relax into grief. As forerunners of a paradigm shift that acknowledges human continuity and kinship with nonhuman animals, they model what is necessary for collective healing: the willingness to suffer (Granovetter 2021: 675).

While the trauma of animal activists is a critical area of study, what Granovetter shows is that a disjunct between species and lives, unconditionally, without attesting first to categories of species and bearing witness purely to the suffering and murder and attempted liberation of individual lives, requires a willingness to suffer: the price of love is grief. Granovetter, after Melanie Joy (2018), emphasizes that when acknowledged, trauma can relax into grief. These affects are independent from, and both theorists suggest require a forsaking of, the individual subjectivity of 'the activist' (removing the 'I' that begins each of the four silences). The specificity of each trauma experienced by a nonhuman animal is neither colonized nor appropriated by the activist. Ours is a unique trauma which is shared, without the desire to 'restore' our identities or psyches. What is needed is to 'restore' (a misnomer because there has never been an entirely benevolent Earth ecology) the relationships humans have with nonhumans and the Earth, more correctly a reimagining after the end of this anthropocentric world, towards a new ecology of love to replace the semioeconomy of exploitation. While very few writers on activism and PTSD use the word 'love' for nonhuman animals (always ironically invoking the spectre of the 'animal lover' who eats meat and drinks milk), I claim that abolitionist activists love in a way that is amorphously unconditional and does not belong to a diachronic system. Most activists do not register species, breed, categorization of nonhuman animals. Battles are chosen based on circumstance and a faith in perceived need. So that activists may even 'hate' or be phobic of certain species in that illogical visceral way that phobias work. But in spite of this, the cry for help heard through bearing witness is unconditional. Surely this is love? Without proof, evidence of worth, hierarchies or personal fetishism of species, abolitionist activists convert their love to grief (perhaps now indistinguishable or reversible) and use that to act to liberate. PTSD and trauma in activists do not request sympathy or assistance for the activist, but for the forgotten third term, the differend, the nonhuman animal. Similarly, studies of trauma in animals is irrelevant, because this is another way to make animals prove their validity against their value, so the millions of horrific psychological and nociception experiments on animals carried out in the name of proving validity are counter-hypothetical and hypocritical, designed against the unconditionality of embrace of alterity that defines trans-species and ecosophical love. The idea that grief is a form of relaxation suggests the hope that grief laments a loss which has passed (the end of animal agriculture, murder, enslavement and so on) and that trauma is preventing effective abolitionist activism because it ossifies individuals becoming incapable of action, always backward facing, returning to flashbacks and experiencing, in repeated liberation acts, a cyclical momentum which never seems to evolve. Trauma is a 'what has been done to me', grief is a 'what can I do for the other bearing witness to what has been done to the other'. In modern pop psychology parlance, the concept of gaslighting is common among domestic violence or even state and national politics, and most often women, BIPoC, queer, disabled and poor people are the victims. Of course, capitalism as an ideological system is the ultimate gaslighter. For activists being gaslit about the purpose of activism is a constant atrophying technique, exacerbated by the twofold strategy of being named terrorists by governments and working within industries and physical structures such as windowless slaughterhouses and high-security vivisection labs which deliberately conceal the acts of devastation that occur within. Being gaslit is at its simplest being made to feel insane against one's own knowledge of truth. For activists to continue our work, perhaps welcoming being insane is a way to overcome the traumatizing affects of malzoan gaslighting. Because we do the activism anyway, so we have diminished the importance of the individual integrated 'sane' psyche, and fighting for the unknowable other, we have diminished the value of the subject as human, even before its various combinations of subjectivization. Are abolitionist activists schizo, multi species and individual aware? Are we dead to the world? We are certainly made to feel thus. And perhaps this is a critical part of living in ecosophical love, fighting for the other. A life that converts trauma to grief is the price of love being grief, and grief is the laminar flow which converts to activism. Unlike the grieving individual of Parkes, who has lost and can contemplate a past which has passed, abolitionist activists live in grief, life as grief. Vitalistic understandings of grief and mourning are all the more important in these circumstances. Abolitionist activism requires the death of a self, death to unquestioned adherence to one's own species, possibly to any acknowledgement of species, joy in grief, impetus in trauma. It is a form of death activism, because within the amorphous love is always joy, vitality, thriving, coming not from success and satisfaction (though seeing a rescue animal express unto itself is undeniably thrilling), but from the gracious obligation to love.

Artistry in mourning: Lament as activism

Love, like activism, is not a singular consistency. Like activism, which bases its actions on the Spinozist aspiration to do one's (collective and individual) best to open space for the other to express their own capacity for joy, love relies on the commitment to creating that opening for the other without guarantee that practices are known in advance to be right or wrong, flawed or meticulously designed. Like love, activism is messy, metamorphic, constantly attentive and attendant. Serres states: 'There are indeed no stabilities except in a universe in which everything flows, unstable' (2000: 31). Serres discusses Epicurus as delivering the Greeks from the *foedera fati*, or the fated appeasement of the gods by sacrifice of innocents, usually in the name of war in the case of Iphigenia or nation-state dominance in the case of the Theban miasma. The foedera fati is an operation of the Order of Mars, defeating the enemy, defeating the inclement weather, defeating the curse, the idea of restoration through violence, combat with gods, nature, in adherence to faith in fate. In welcoming and celebrating

Epicurus's embrace of chaos, which also includes atheism and a refusal in the closed futurity concept of fate that denies chaos and deifies control, Serres sees actions of *foedera naturae*, of the Order of Venus, of love. 'To take on alone the fire of the heavens, not to displace it by unleashing violence on the nearest bystander, the virgin Iphigenia, but to advance, unarmed, before it deciphering lucidly what is happening: this is precisely conduct contrary to all religions, to the terrifying constitution of the sacred' (2000: 118). Bataille claims: 'The sacrificer needs the sacrifice in order to separate himself from the world of things and the victim could not be separated from it in turn if the sacrifice was not already separated in advance' (Bataille 1992: 44). Most importantly, 'this is a monologue and the victim can neither understand nor reply' (Bataille 1992: 44). The scared sacrifice still separates human from world, appeasing what looks like a pantheon: gods of science, development, food, entertainment, but which are actually a monotheistic violent appeasement of the god Anthropos because our fate is perceived as dominion. Against this Serres utilises the Order of Venus, of love, stating:

> And by [Epicurus'] courageous action, heroic above heroes, Epicurus brings about the birth of Venus, from the agitated waters. To know the *foedus*, love and friendship. The contract of nature, *foedera naturae*. Finally definitive, and the gods are outside of the world, as the ancient reiteration of sacrificial crisis is brought to a close. . . . Now, delivered from violence, freed from our dependence on a sacred space and time which has no relationship to us, our feet finally set on the high place protected from the sea, fortified by the science of the wise against the initiatives of Mars, we can bring things forth as objects, outside of the mechanisms regulating our unregulated violence . . . the sacred is formed by this repetitive and catastrophic dynamic. Epicurus the hero willingly takes the place of the virgin. Unarmed he disarms the process, founds a new history, an objective science. One can now see how Venus replaces Mars. *Foedus* is in short, a political constitution. (2000: 118, 119)

For Serres, science here does not refer to the perception of objective knowledge of the world by humans. This he critiques elsewhere, stating, 'And this relation between convention and fact, unique in human history . . . has not been given a judicial name. It is as if the verdicts of humans coincide with those of objects. This never happens except in miracles and sciences' (2002: 22). In the example of Epicurus, Serres defines science against the fatalistic faith humans have in their own perceived guarantee of understanding the world and its future based on edicts from 'above'. This faith is easily translatable from Olympian gods to the gods of anthropocentrism, namely, power and capitalism, but also hubris and fatalistic belief in dominion. There is a science to activism, which is why in-fighting within abolitionists is so detrimental, as they return to anthropocentric understandings of focus on the right and wrong way to do things.

The science of activism is a foedera naturae which accepts chaos and the constant turbulence of nature and relations between organisms collectively. Activism must tactically apprehend the other as an object/subject unique emergence in need of care in a variety of very different and unique ways. When done via foedera naturae, the Order of Venus, activism comes to the other seeking knowledge insofar as science can assist the other's capacity to thrive. The use value of the sacrifice is absent. The other no longer belongs to capital, and the activist is ready to replace the victim with their own subjectivity, unravelled self and, most importantly, activist body. Science in service to anthropocentrism seeks to defeat death heroically, and the sacrifice is usually the nonhuman other. Vivisection laboratories and journal articles which utilize animal testing even use the word 'sacrifice' rather than the more correct 'tortured' and 'murdered' to align their operations as somehow heroic against the God Thanatos or perhaps more correctly the Keres/Fates. The anthropocentric war against ageing, disease and death has left billions of unnecessary 'sacrificial' nonhuman victims in its wake, just as the profit of animal exploitation and consumption has become a new god of 'wellness', 'health' or nutrition. Activism as love does not know its fate. We ride the turbulent clinamen of need, we adapt science used for exploitation into that of ecological nurturing, we place ourselves as or in front of the victim to ward off the spectre of the gods rising again. Critically, *we disprove through activism as love the perceived fated inevitability and 'necessity' of nonhuman animal exploitation and death.* The dialectic structure which underpins anthropocentric animal exploitation insinuates 'this is their fate as animals'.

Foedera Naturae transforms the dialectic to chaos, their to our and fate to love. Death is the only inevitable, Thanatos the god of nonviolent death, a minor deity, a quiet ending not to be defeated as death is a simple part of nature.

Lament remains an integral part of activism. It is often the initial catalyst for the conversion from war to love in relations with nonhuman animals. How can the creative act of lament as activism jam capitalism, how can love jam capital desiring machines and end the end of the world? Of Hellenic tragedy and the lament, Casey Dué states:

> Lamentation and funeral ritual are both incorporated into and transformed by tragedy, as Charles Segal has shown: 'All of the three extant tragedians incorporate within their plays the rites of lamentation that we know from archaic poetry and from other premodern societies. All draw heavily on the function of song in an oral culture to give ritualized expression to intense emotion and to provide comfort, solace, and security amid anxiety, confusion, and loss. By absorbing the cries of grief into the lyricism of a choral lament, the tragic poet is able to identify the emotional experience of suffering with the musical and rhythmic impulse of dance and song' [Segal 1993: 16] Segal argues that while tragedy is heavily indebted to earlier poetic forms of commemoration and expression of suffering, it is also 'radically new' in that it transforms whatever it uses and synthesizes genres and rituals in new ways. Formal laments for the dead in the Greek tradition generally conform to a three-part pattern, which consists of a direct address, a narrative of the past or future, and then a renewed address accompanied by reproach and lamentation. In tragedy, these three elements are both combined and isolated from one another in countless ways to express immeasurable sorrow. Any one of the three parts may evoke the genre, emotions, and rituals of lament, thereby contributing to the overall atmosphere of sorrow and evoking the pity of the audience. Just as lamentation in tragedy is generally separated from the rites of an actual funeral, so also the poetic structure, traditional themes, and language of lament can be manipulated and employed with great effect in nonritual contexts. (2006: 10)

Activism is, after Serres, scientific (without being judiciary or driven by anthropocentric motive), but also, like benevolent eco-sciences, artistic. And, like activism, the art of lament is one which involves thinking, expressing and acting differently with the intellect, the flesh, with movement and creativity. Activism as a creative lament is an appealing concept because it encourages the death of the self as subject without replacing the subject with absence (atrophy, compassion fatigue) or its own sacrifice or martyrdom (or any other saviour complex so rife in contemporary allyship activism of all kinds). We can mourn, but we can still do. Lament activism disrupts semiocapitalism by belonging to the fluid, feminist, strange collective space of the *chora*, antagonistic to the polished hero. Characteristics of activism follow many of those of lament, including use of gesture, dance and song, which are equivalent to care, nurturing, speaking and listening in a non-anthropocentric way to the nonhuman other. Especially in reference to the specific needs of each unique rescue or liberated nonhuman animal, our inability to receive consent on the terms of these animals means our approach is sometimes retreat, our intervention is often provision of food and warmth and wound care, then absence. No demands of reciprocity can be expected in acts of love. And there is no measuring reciprocity anyway, because these others have their own expressivity inscrutable to humans, in spite of the violent attempts by ethology to translate them. Activist love makes no demands and acknowledges its own fallibility in not knowing in advance what is 'right' or 'good', what will 'work' or 'not'. We ride the flow, we listen and respond in asemiotic ways. Guattari states: 'In primitive societies, one expresses oneself as much by speech as by gestures, dances, rituals, or signs marked on the body. In industrialised societies, this richness of expression is attenuated; all *énoncés* have to be translatable to the language that encodes dominant meanings' (1996: 149). Primitive for the Hellenic tragedians was clearly women, boys, national others; all the while in the background, the actions of animals were converted to omens and portents and their bodies slaughtered en masse as sacrifices to guarantee the future or appease higher authorities, a perpetual translation and economics of restoration of the control of fate by the hero, as individual or nation. Lament mourned the hero, the nation and the dead. Dué writes:

> But whereas the majority of the laments of tragedy are a special combination of lament for the dead and lament for the hero, the laments of captive women span all three categories. Captive women lament their fallen city as much as they lament their husbands, brothers, and sons. The spectacle of Troy and its sack dominates the odes that Trojan women sing. (2006: 11)

Abolitionist activists lament the suffering and death of nonhuman animals in their billions, so 'the dead' is relevant to lament as it is an overwhelming number. We also lament the individual to whom we bear witness, because thinking only through species or statistics risks forgetting the immeasurable suffering of an individual cow or pig or rat to whom no one listens. And we lament as ecological mourning, the loss of the Earth. The rhizomatic reach of abolitionist activism is not ideologically specialized or exclusionary. We do what we can, but we think cosmically of the multiple connectivities which lead to the suffering of individuals. And in spite of the deep cynicism mourning the billions of animals can pique towards humans, most abolitionists are still deeply concerned with intersectional oppression of humans, not as extricated from, but part of the lament for the Earth and its occupants. While many humans eat meat while lamenting loss of exotic species, is not lamenting the exoticism of each individual nonhuman animal a better way to be an effective and affective animal activist? Is extinction of the wild an escape route and the rewilding of agricultural animals a liberation from lament/by lament? The longstanding opposition between the ecofeminist 'emotional' activist and the logocentric analytic philosopher animal rights theorist is comingled in lament. Both lament human treatment of animals. Both can find emotive and corporeal affects through activism, and this activism requires logics of care, sciences of nurturing, especially in relation with attention to ecosystems affected by the dissymmetry in certain species within different environments and the overall relations between every organism and their location, human and nonhuman animal, plant, bacteria and all of the Earth's kingdom.

Among our love as lament, and the transformation of lament to love, we must remember, and I hope this has been clear throughout this chapter, that abolitionist activism is *never about humans*. It exists because of what humans do, and the violence and suffering is fought by both humans and nonhuman animals, in myriad asemitoic ways. But I speak here of humans converting our wars into love, our sacrifices into agents who have their own desires and capacities for joy, our lament into activism, only insofar as the effects of these paradigmatic shifts nurture the other, the nonhuman animal. For just as apocalypse literature and film premised on the 'what if something treated us as we treat animals' trope is as horrific as it is banal in reference to everyday global human practices, so too we must acknowledge that if our suffering as activists needs to transform into something that propels action for good, *we cannot imagine the unbearable suffering of the nonhuman individual animal at every moment.* I do not claim all animals suffer all the time. But billions do. And then they are murdered, which in many ways could be construed as merciful if the murder was not so violent. All without our need to inflict this upon them. Because we refuse to allow the human subjectivity which sustains the concept of dominion to die. Even though it would open the world to ourselves also in unthinkable ways. Our effects upon ecologies and environments cause sufferings we cannot predict and disequilibriums that effect all occupants of the Kingdom Earth. Without knowing the other, we must always actively acknowledge (lament) and prioritize (mourn) their suffering and deaths. The gestural, sung ritual of lament is a style of activism deeply attentive to *foedera naturae*, to love. And here I will end with Irigaray's touching words on how we can love the other:

> In order to be able to welcome the other, a certain fullness must be restored, which escapes the control of a will. Time is indispensable for such a reconstitution which will permit the memory of oneself, of the other, of their difference and of their approach. The other cannot be kept, sheltered thanks to a simple decision, Irreducible to us, we cannot apprehend the other in order to find a dwelling for them. This place of hospitality for the other becomes built as much as, if not more than, we build it deliberately. Made of our flesh, of our heart, and not only of words, it demands that we accept that it takes place without our unilaterally overseeing its construction. It is in secret that it unfolds without any mastery by our seeing, by our domination through language. Remaining hidden, the other can be safeguarded. And it is certainly not when unveiling that we can

protect what the other is as other nor prepare the path going to meet with them. (2002: 144)

Relation with the other as love, like lament, is a dance, a song of silence and whispers, through a veil of imperceptibility, involving flesh and heart, indivisible from thought and action, invoking affect. Because we are dancing in our lament but also always dancing *with* the other, whose consent we cannot receive, and whose responses we must allow without interpretation, feeling expression with affect, affect with expression, not only the way of love but the way of ethical encounter. As I have quoted elsewhere and often, Serres sees the coalescence of grace, stepping aside and dance as part of *foedera naturae*:

> whoever is nothing, whoever has nothing, passes and steps aside. From a bit of force, from any force, from anything, from any decision, from any determination. . . . Grace is nothing, it is nothing but stepping aside. Not to touch the ground with one's force, not to leave any trace of one's weight, to leave no mark, to leave nothing, to yield, to step aside . . . to dance is only to make room, to think is only to step aside and make room, give up one's place. (1997: 47)

Abolitionist activism is death activism. Against the killability and unmournable death of the nonhuman animal, we bear witness that they exist, they are, exploited, tortured and killed and we mourn them. We transform our mourning into the activism of lament that leads to lobbying, liberation and indirect and direct action. Without prescription or structuration, we love unconditionally and die to anthropocentrism in order to listen to the untranslatable other. To gift ourselves to care and nurturing, through logic, compassion and risk, we die to ourselves, acknowledging the subject lives within a territory of opposition, of war, of mastery, of conflict. Upon dying to subjectivity, we are born to the Order of Venus and to love. We lament while we love, we mourn while we love, but the death in the activism is what makes us creative, subtle, gracious, becoming-host, the very least of our obligation to nonhuman animals.

5

Capital zombies, death and disability

This chapter argues that for many bodies, we exist in a zombie state. Different bodies perform their zombification differently, and individuals are made-zombie in multiple ways. Zombie culture has become a critical part of performance art in death studies as a critique of colonialism and the genesis of the term and as a navigation of terminal illness and living 'beyond' diagnosis. On the other side, culture 'wars' have led to resistance to social change such as decolonizing knowledge or genderqueer subjectivity, showing the atrophy of style in anthropocentric knowledge that suggests dominant ideology is its own form of zombie, in its need to feed off alterity in order to diminish it. Zombies are everywhere, whether as enslaved labourers or identities converted from material flesh to social media simulacrum. This chapter navigates the body in neo-capitalism as a form of useful corpse, in docile self-regulation. It engages contemporary critical disability studies to ask whether we – the well and the sick, the normal and the pathological – are already dead, what prevents us from knowing and how our somnambulistic state predicts the imperative to work for bodies, whether they are living or dying. The duration of what living and dying means under these conditions provokes a challenge to the clarity of the terms. How can posthuman activism inject life into simulacrum, queer the zombie for the chronically ill and disabled, and should it at all?

Martin O'Brien coined the concept of 'zombie time'. O'Brien, a performance artist with cystic fibrosis, given a limited lifespan he has far exceeded, states:

Death did not come for me. In attempting to understand what it means to live longer than expected, I formulated the notion of zombie time. This is the temporal experience of living on when death was supposed to happen. I have previously written about zombie time as being: '[. . .] a different relationship to death and life [. . .] It's a form of enduring life when death is no longer the certainty it once was. It is no longer linear, it's full of breaks and ambushes. In zombie time, you keep moving but not towards anything, just for the sake of moving. No goals, only desires. No plans, only reactions. The only constant is the presence of death but not in the way it once was, for the zombie knows death and breathes in death. Death is in me, instead of somewhere else'. (O'Brien and Bouchard 2019: 263; O'Brien 2019)

Berardi discusses the succinct inextricability of zombification and capitalism in tracing suicide as a means of liberation for the original Haitian zombie. Rahul Gairola critiques the Western appropriation of the figure of the zombie (or originally zonbi) as a monster, returning sympathy to this creature as a victim, focussing instead on the Afrofuturistic reimagining of the duppy. The otherworldly duppies are

queer phantom figures, and supernatural landscapes in which histories of colonialism and queer sexuality mediate movements between the terrestrial and spiritual realms. The supernatural and the sexual become vehicles for one another in facilitating and complicating postcolonial, queer of color sexualities of the women protagonists. . . . Given the immeasurable sorrow wrought by the middle passage and maritime capitalism on the African diaspora, it appears fitting that haunting figures would linger amongst the living. (Gairola 2017: 19)

Gairola and Berardi, as explorers of Afrofuturism's liberatory techniques and semiocapitalism's enslaving techniques, respectively, both see death as a means by which being the zombie is finally exhausted and escaped. For Afrofuturism, semiocapitalism and chronic terminal illness as lived by O'Brien, the zombie is not a state in the future to fear or an external other monster which poses a threat, but the very existence by which white Western wellness and work enthral the subject. Postcolonial theory continues to negotiate the haunted heritage of zombification, just as globalization sees this heritage unfurling in real time through transformed but no less enslaving means of racism, coerced obedience and fear under oppressive white regimes, overtly and covertly violent in perpetuating the figure of Anthropos as default white, just as he is male, logocentric (which Derrida ties inextricably to ethnocentrism), able bodied and heteronormative. The post-1960s zombie is somewhat of a different creature altogether, zombies which are 'rewilded' through not being enslaved by masters but their own appetites – zombies who constantly crave human flesh, the Haitian producer now the insatiable consumer, all caused by an invisible 'Master' of Anthropos as the slave owner, the weapon of war experiment gone wrong, the toxic fallout or the technological advance which reanimates the dead. The third form of zombie is that which O'Brien develops. The disabled body in neo-capitalism, especially an increasingly welfare-less world, is the body which doesn't work in every sense of the word. Neither producer because disabled nor consumer because forced into disability poverty, the sovereign subjectivity of chronic disability spoils the logocentrism which sees the body as the wilful expression (*potestas*, not *potentia*) of the mind. Chronically ill, and dying diagnoses, posit a body which is neither dead nor alive in a sense that conforms with linear chronological and deeply heteronormative narratives of birth, marriage, reproduction, death, all the while working to be productive and buying pleasure to be consumer. What all share, the Haitian zombie, the chronically and terminally ill, the capitalist worker prevented from escaping, is the strange seeming oxymoron of denial of access to the freedom of death. Thus, for the purposes of this chapter, the zombie, though manifested through nuanced histories and specificities of power, shares throughout its many incarnations, enslavement to a life not belonging to itself and the impossibility of death as liberty. I use the pronoun 'it' because the zombie in all incarnations is an 'it' owned by another in its legal, medical or aesthetic incarnation, never fully articulated as an 'I' or a 'they' as an acknowledgement of belonging and sentience and reciprocity of sentiment. Ghosts may haunt us, but the zombie is the self we are, haunted by the self we could have been under different circumstances, emergent through different qualities in different territories of (de- or a-)signification.

I begin with O'Brien because his artwork, written and performed, shows an ambivalent relationship with life lived technically not as human life but as waiting or within a coming death that holds the seduction of freedom from pain, tedium, striving without the promise of recovery. In this state of existence O'Brien's notion of zombie time also describes the way in which many disabled sufferers of chronic, but not necessarily speedily terminal, illness exist, especially those who covet death in nations where assisted suicide remains illegal. In Chapter 3, I discussed the suicide that needs no vindication. This chapter includes attending to the enigma of the suicide that technically may be called something other than suicide, perhaps an acceleration or ending of zombie time, currently known as assisted suicide. In many cases this form of zombie existence, which for very different reasons and under different piques of intensity to that of the suicidal, has become intolerable for the disabled person and society, the latter seeking to forget the inadequate or unproductive flesh which simply refuses to die, the former having to develop a new relationship with their own pain, diminished or altering abilities and what it means to live when life expects the fulfilment of a performance of a certain level of wellness, exacerbated by the industrialization of wellness as an expression of the sovereign subject's willingness to be healthy, as if disability is a result of agency or effort. I emphasize that when using the term *disabled* here I am specifically writing about those forms of disability that may be degenerative or slowly terminal or lifelong conditions which reduce capacities coupled with levels of chronic pain. These will be unique to individuals just as each diagnosis is unique in symptom intensity. As some arbitrary examples, autoimmune diseases such as severe rheumatoid arthritis, ankylosing spondylitis, multiple sclerosis and even diabetes and cystic fibrosis, both of which are currently under reclassification as potentially autoimmune, could be included in relevant forms of degenerative disability. Each person's story, like their disability, will be uniquely experienced and expressed, so my tactical use of examples is neither exclusionary nor exhaustive. Many other degenerative diseases would also be included but the pathologization of the individual-become-their-disease is not valid. What matters is that certain disabilities make life increasingly difficult to untenable, and disabled people come to occupy this zombie time, being expected to live 'well' or 'normally' but prevented from the ability to die, and under current healthcare conditions in most nations, radically undernourished in the areas of assistance and care, from access to drugs and therapies, to being denied liveable or even any payment to survive. In many cases the disabled who are unable to work yet, even if they wished, are also unable to legally die and are being annihilated in their thousands through a form of eugenics by just letting us starve, freeze or otherwise perish, because under semiocapitalism we 'fail to thrive' and so leaving us on the mountainside removes the culpability of murder, though it is so by any other name. What also makes the chronically ill degenerative disabled belong to zombie time is our failure to fit into the beloved, deeply capitalist hero narrative of, for example, cancer, where we 'fight' and 'win' and 'beat' the disease because 'fuck cancer'. Illness is structured upon the territory of War, the Order of Mars, and if we don't win, we are to blame. This suggests all illness is perceived as winnable. The shame which accompanied cancer only a few decades ago is now the shame of the degenerative or chronically ill – either get better or hurry up and die seems to be the pervasive personal, political and governmental enunciation related to the disabled living zombie time. Because we are neither killed nor cured, there is no imminent endpoint, no happy or sad ending, no narrative at all. We are just occupying a space of corporeal enslavement between a particular kind of body and a particular kind of society, both of which have very unique and often difficult demands. That is not to say being disabled in this way is simply suffering under the mastery of a body that causes one pain, the 'my body does this to me' of Scarry's tortured body (1985).

Living in pain is in itself a form of queer existence, as O'Brien emphasises, devoid of the narratives and smooth events of both heteronormativity and heterotemporality, punctuated by dazzling creative agony and ossified atrophy of being less-than-nothing all without easy applications of qualities of good and bad, even though we have good and bad days (the latter often bring the greatest creativity, the former make us sick with their normativity). What I seek to explore here and in this first section of the chapter is the inapprehensibility of the zombie body, a body that does not belong to capital time, a body that is neither fully alive nor fully dead only insofar as it shows all bodies occupy aberrant versions of a life being lived. The productive body of the worker, the most directly insulted body in the face of what I will call this form of disabled body – 'the body that wouldn't die!' (because we are monsters who belong to schlocky B-Movies, society doesn't believe in us, so let's be unbelievable) – is also a zombie body. Life is precious; Berardi cites the Foxconn corporation's official statement on suicide prevention in their workers, when they decide to no longer offer insurance payouts to the families of workers who commit suicide (2015: 180). Precious to whom? The worker's 'life' is precious because the work is precious. The life – what does that mean for a worker? A zombie life, measured by productivity. Subjectivity, in posthuman terms when measured by the ordinary simulacrum of social media and descriptors of career, status and net worth, is a zombie life when no signified can be found beneath the signifiers, within the flesh. But is this just a phantasy of depth, of interiority? Is zombie life what defines life now, against some pastoral myth of a true life well lived? All these words are subsumed by posthuman critiques of what anthropocentrism has transformed from myth or post-death Elysium to achievable capitalist neo-fantasy (externalized from the daydream to life as a lived dream). A 'true' or 'authentic' 'life' 'well' lived seems to sum up the virtualization of life as 'seeming', when the question for all is 'what is produced?' Authenticity is saleability, wellness is volition and self-management, life is a gift to be lived at any cost and to be packaged so that others may seek to live the same. Zombie life spans all forms of life, from the mega-rich who exchange the empty signifiers of labels and zeros to the bedroom influencer refining what life means via likes. While denigrated as zombies, unproductive, different, unpalatable, perhaps the lives which fail to fulfil semiocapital zombification are better described as weird life, weird because they make living strange, and the concept of life itself is weird, in not really counting either as alive or as dead. In queer culture, authentic usually insinuates living one's life against expectations of what is validated as an arbitrarily moral evaluation of a good, normal productive life. Can chronic degenerative disability be both zombie time and queer authentication of life being the accident of nature that is entirely independent from a priori also being precious or good? When subjectivity itself is labour, and time is utilized in cultivating the self, then zombie time is queer time, devoid of both labour and self, aspiring neither to good nor to productive life, but mainly survival and often not even that. Far from performance art experimentation and playing with privilege, chronic degenerative disability plays with being a body without organs as absolutely necessity.

While no body is normal, our bodies are queer whether we like it or not. Agency is irrelevant. Degenerative disabled, chronically ill life is a strange negotiation of queer relations between medical professionals, relations of intensities with various corporeal nociception, capacities limited and extended and changed, and a self that has such diminished ego due to desires that exceed the self's ego defined as the titular illness. This occupation of various miasma reflects that of the well, self-stylized semiocapital self. For medical, think social signifiers, for pain think external validation, for capacities think productivity ingenuity. We may all occupy zombie time. Does disability, or the horrific history of Haitian zombification for decolonization, or violence and diminishment and murder for women and queer people currently being considered illegal and highly killable make us monsters more aware of the weirdness of our zombie existence, so that we navigate with different escape routes and a more voluminous fleshliness? Because we won't die, and we cannot live as the 'normal', are we the baroque undead?

The art of (maybe) dying and zombie time

'So the power to define life and death relies on a fragile system of standards, discourses and practices relevant both to medical expertise and to the capacity to play with legal boundaries' (Paltrinieri 2015: 36). For those with degenerative disabling diseases neither the law nor medicine is able to define zombie time with words more meaningful than extrication to an object for speculative cure, most often formed as 'coping', and the legal proviso, in those countries which still refuse euthanasia, that 'what if' is a viable possibility, primarily 'what if you regret dying' (a bizarre post-mortem capacity for contemplation) and 'what if there is a cure'. In the majority of legal cases, it is often another form of extrication to an object, usually by the family, which leads to charges or blame. One's own life, as stated many times in this book, never belongs to one's self. For the degenerative disabled occupying zombie time, our status in and as capital is the ultimate vocabulary in capital-speak – 'management' of the disease, 'coping mechanisms' for getting through the day, 'access' to medical treatments, 'organization' of appointments and myriad other novel phrases which insinuate inclusivity is not attention to difference, but one's disease becoming one's job, usually a second job. Within semiocapitalism, we can only dream of the exoticization of being pathologized as freak. Now it is work, and our outcomes of pain or degeneration constructed as a result of our 'work' ethic, while both popular media and medical journals are peppered with feel-good success stories of individual's 'overcoming' their disease through sport or hobbies, often with added financial gain. No longer the teratological aberration, as long as one is good at one's job of being disabled, one is included, albeit reduced to a decorporealized metaphor for transcendence. In the case of many degenerative disabling illnesses, there is a clear insinuation the cause is psychosomatic (see, e.g., Dickson, Toft and O'Carroll 2009; Moretti et al. 2012; Friedman 1972; Andersson et al 2015; Dube et al. 2009, as just a few of thousands of examples) and often patients are gendered and racialized in a way that insipidly suggests bad management. I am not an immunologist, and the questions as to whether certain contemporary ideas around childhood trauma and inherited trauma can switch on genetic propensities to disabling disease are ones that need not be addressed in this context. However, it is worth mentioning there is some kind of blame associated with a developed rather than congenital disease. Nonetheless, almost all disability follows the course of management of life as correlative with worthiness of suffering. I have focussed on degenerative and particularly autoimmune disability as an example of the kind of disability which occupies zombie time, but it cannot be emphasized enough that every disability is utterly singular, and homogenization is the very crux of comparative narratives of striving, which lead to shaming and blaming disabled individuals for their relationship with the semiocapitalist 'employment' by their disability as being a success story or not. We are not comrades in disability under semiocapitalism; we are competitors. The disabled occupying zombie time are a nagging reminder that disability as work is what, in disability studies after Lauren Berlant (2011), has been called 'cruel optimism'. Diachronic divisions dismember existing in zombie time: the cruel optimism of enforced striving against irrefutable suffering; the demand to live juxtaposed with the demand to die; and overarching all the very concept of psychosomaticism which, even in cases of disability which are not medically designated to a form of modern or genetic hysteria, are still measured by the mental 'wellness' of the disabled individual.

Making the diachronism of psychosomaticism redundant may be a way to transform living, being, expressing and being affected as a degenerative disabled body become an art. No matter how benevolent or banal the concept of psychosomatic illness has become in embracing a supposedly post-Cartesian understanding of embodied selfhood, for the disabled there is still a deeply embedded sense that somewhere and somehow we have volition which we have failed to control in the measurement of our suffering. Hero stories in their cruel optimism are spectacles for the able, to alleviate being haunted by the being of disabled persons and their own potential for disability as much as a fall from grace as from health or able-bodied capacity. Overcoming or managing disability is just another form of semiocapitalist competitive job: when Bessel van der Kolk claims *The Body Keeps the Score* (2014), we are confronted as to whether we are accumulating enough points to win or lose. The psyche is phantasized as ultimately controlling the flesh. Being liberated from feeling at fault for one's disabilities can create a catharsis of alleviation and empathy for we disabled. At the same time, reducing the complexities of the physiological, corporeal, psychosomatic, economic and socio-judicial intersectional aspects of what it feels and means to emerge with disability in the world, including the personal private world, to an interior versus exterior, mind versus body and trauma versus nature economy of blame is pop psychology at a reductive and harmful level, which threatens also to reify into inarguable science (as did, for example, the war on opioids where all people in need of pain relief are addicts, or the autism/MMR jab). No matter how far feminism, queer theory and even postcolonial theory has come, it seems there is still a jarring chasm in the space between, within the term *psychosomatic* for disability. Visibility, representation, retelling histories may all continue to be relevant and coveted, but when these occur, capitalism will seek to extract some form of moral psychosomatic paradigm from each example of disability to make sense of cause, severity and duration of disease. I will remain focussed generally on the autoimmune category as a single example for two reasons: the first is diseases which belong in this category are often degenerative and highly likely to be somehow contextualized as to both cause and severity by the psychosomatic argument ignited by works such as Van Der Kolk's, and secondly, because I speak from an embodied perspective, not as an authoritative voice but simply as one example of how it feels to be expressed as and through this body with these symptoms that deeply challenge the value of living over the grace of death. My use is tactical and should in no way be taken as a template for either disability studies or personal experience. What I aim to do in this section is challenge the formerly malignant but now claimed benign relegation of disability to the psychosomatic. In order to deliver certain disabilities' relation with life and death – the 'zombie time' disabilities – I seek to imagine new vernaculars to navigate expressing as these bodies beyond psychosomaticism and its deep connections with semiocapitalist understandings of disability. Elizabeth Wilson states:

> Following Brauer and Freud, feminists have tended to retreat from the biology of hysteria and theorise hysteria as primarily ideational. It has been almost universally agreed amongst feminist commentators that what is most interesting politically and what is most important theoretically is the complex condensation and displacement of ideational content that motivates hysterical attacks. The way these contorted ideational structures are then converted into bodily symptoms has attracted less attention than one might expect. Oddly enough, it is the very mechanism of conversion (of psyche into soma) that has been the least explored aspect of conversion hysteria. We may be well equipped to answer why hysterics convert but we appear to be collectively mute in response to the question of how they convert. Breuer and Freud's often quoted axiom that 'hysterics mainly suffer from reminiscences' (1895: 7) has been deployed perhaps too partially. Hysterics do indeed suffer from reminiscences; they also suffer from bodily symptoms: they are paralysed, blinded, in physical pain, they cough incessantly, they have difficulty breathing. Perhaps the most obvious aspect of hysteria – the physical disability – has been attenuated in feminist accounts of hysterical symptomology. (2004: 5)

Wilson's interest in the neurobiology of hysteria and attention to corporeal symptoms reverse and somewhat fill the chasm between psyche and soma, showing the texture and function of the space between, the 'how', as the ignored third term, the very space which dispels opposition or dialectic relationality between flesh and self. In contemporary popular science this has also become a common turn, famously in books such as Kolk's *The Body Keeps the Score* and Lucia Osborne-Crowley's *My Body Keeps Your Secrets*, both of which discuss inherited trauma, childhood stress and raised cortisol levels, which lead to autoimmune diseases and degenerative disability. The psychoanalytic, phenomenological and popular reversing of psyche to soma, which attempts to explore and even alleviate shame and agency in being a disabled body, illuminates the feedback paradox of the relation between psyche and soma, a kind of chicken–egg idea that childhood or even DNA imprints of trauma lead to neuro and biological changes which manifest as disability, while attending to the serious psychological damage of Wilson's critique of feminist psychoanalysis's ignoring of physical suffering and the visceral embodiment of hysteria. Put simply, reconfiguring the most basic psychosomaticism of psychical damage causing physical damage, these different challenges to the dialectic show that whether or not there is a trace and following, possible eradication of physical symptom from psychical trauma, the trauma of the physicality of pain and disability has its own impact on the psyche. It is the latter I am most interested in. The former, the idea disability has a cause, a psychical origin, belongs in the realm of knowledge as exhaustive, to the Order of Mars, the battlefield which promises a victor and a defeated. Certainly, in certain circumstances, disability may be cured or bettered, but for we of zombie time, there is a need to think and live in a way ascendent from the perpetual feedback loop of mind affecting body affecting mind. Semiocapitalism's wellness help for us simply affirms its blame on us.

What would happen if the zombie didn't belong to or was enslaved by either the master capitalism, the master medicine, the master law or even the master disease as externalized from 'who we are' as instead *how* we are. Can we shift the empty, ossified, eternally hungry zombie, hungry for answers, hungry for cure, hungry for able-bodiedness, always waiting, waiting, waiting in the zombie waiting room, into a baroque, multi-folded and enfolding invagination of pain and creativity and desire for death and converter of agony to something else? There is no vocabulary for the how of how it feels to be disabled. Denied expression beyond hero stories or symptom source, degenerative disabled zombie-time occupants are queer in our simultaneous silence and speechlessness. If we speak, we must confess, to medicine, to the analyst, to the law. The options for confession seem to be blame, shame or work. Instead, degenerative disability can create us as mystical forces within zombie time. Turning to Bergson on the force of affect, the how of sense, he states:

> To the multiplicity of systems contending with one another, armed with different concepts, would succeed the unity of a doctrine capable of reconciling all thinkers in the same perception – a perception which moreover would grow ever larger, thanks to the combined effort of philosophers in a common direction. It will be said that this enlarging is impossible. How can one ask the eyes of the body, or those of the mind, to see more than they see? Our attention can increase precision, clarify and intensify; it cannot bring forth in the field of perception what was not there in the first place. That's the objection. It is refuted in my opinion by experience. For hundreds of years, in fact, there have been men whose function has been precisely to see and to make us see what we do not naturally perceive. They are the artists. What is the aim of art if not to show us, in nature and in the mind, outside of us and within us, things which did not explicitly strike our senses and our consciousness? The poet and the novelist who express a mood certainly do not create it out of nothing; they would not be understood by us if we did not observe within ourselves, up to a certain point, what they say about others. As they speak, shades of emotion and thought appear to us which might long since have been brought out in us but which remained invisible; just like the photographic image which has not yet been plunged into the bath where it will be revealed. The poet is this revealing agent. But nowhere is the function of the artist shown as clearly as in that art which gives the most important place to imitation, I mean painting. The great painters are men who possess a certain vision of things which has or will become the vision of all men. (1992: 135)

Pathology and psychoanalysis seek unity in exhaustive knowledge to attain a phantasy of reset, a return to unsullied Anthropos. Sovereign subjectivity is well and able. It knows aspiration to eternity even while accepting death's inevitability. All bodies are bombarded with sensations in excess of their agency. We repress, we convert, we call them symptoms. When it sometimes feels like all that one is, is symptoms, disability can no longer tolerate the signifier of the name of a disease to sum these senses up, to ameliorate them. We are a cosmos of symptoms that can never be translated to language, to be confessed or converted. We are the persistent photograph before the developing bath which realizes form and representation, because even with diagnosis, even with treatment, the perpetual sensorial visions reveal the infinity of the flesh's potential as neither good nor evil, but nature's exquisite configurations of the messy involutions and convolutions of being organic matter. Anthropos calls this a failure, medicine calls it a puzzle, society calls it an aberration. When living in zombie time, when there is actually nothing one can do, the expression and experience become creative, in solitude, in quiet, without the need for a hero story that expresses the creativity into an externalized representative object. Zombie time is a novel space of imagination, delivered from mastery towards a becoming-otherwise that is neither dead nor really living (however, to claim this creativity does not diminish quality of life is fetishistic and cruel optimism). The energies are ecstatic; otherwise, we would not be lumps of nociception and delirium, so we produce, excessively, just like the mucous O'Brien's CF body produces. What we produce may not be aligned with wellness, but it does not diminish the vibrancy of the body of zombie time. Colebrook states, 'Bergson defines mysticism as the creative spirit liberated from practical affairs and inertia, and it is because of its mystical component that Christianity had the potential to remain active, not simply resting with a negation of the world but proceeding to bring forth a new world of life's own creativity, a creativity feeling itself in its own creative joy' (2014: 105). Bergson critiques the material as that which attempts to collide jubilant or ecstatic effort with the manifestation of life, divesting anthropocentric phantasies of agency in creativity as fulfilling any criteria of newness and dynamism. I once again emphasize that we bodies in zombie time, just as we have little qualitative differentiation between living and dying, also do not experience affects of joy as delight over suffering. Joy in this sense can be understood as pique, as excess beyond words and certainly the rhythms of incessant pain waves, or coughing phlegm, or minute full body spasms which share more in common with ecstasy beyond good and evil than with transcendence. It is precisely because we are within the flesh so absolutely while being attentive (albeit in an altered consciousness) that we degenerative dying are the zombies who are too much.

A critical aspect of degenerative zombie-time illness is often chronic pain. I define pain here as more extensive than the deep neural expression of nociception, including the associated pain of attempting to act with limited capacity, or the pain from constant symptoms such as coughing. The variety of pains which zombie-time lives experience are sometimes useful, sometimes useless, often showing as defunct the general theory of pain as a self-preserving necessity of a healthy body. I will not explore the neural specifics of pain here because the relevance of biochemical and neurophysiological definitions of pain are less relevant than the refined, myriad and enfleshed actuality of a pained body, where one's own body causes one pain from a source that also comes from one's own body. Awareness of the multiplicity of consciousnesses of one's own flesh when living in pain, often feeling like living as pain, evinces how expansive is the thousand tiny sentiences of a body operating against itself, as a singular expression far beyond a simple mind–body divide. Pain is not always a condition of or contributing factor to the deathbound aspects which zombie-time duration may experience, but when it is, it can be an important factor in the decision to accelerate or desire for relief that leads to the cessation of life, the deciding moment of death activism. While this could be then considered a 'cause' for suicide, consistent with Chapter 3, there is a confounding and absolute lack of logic in an inner experience of disease and chronic pain that no amount of pain clinic sessions, management, analysis, therapy, physiotherapy or explication from experts can access. The experience of the body in pain, but here the *body that pains itself* is beyond epistemology, beyond genealogy, beyond all horizons of signification. Deleuze and Guattari speak of the masochist who desires pain. How is desire configured in a body, becoming a Body without Organs due to the multiple intensities of various pains, when the pain is not desired, but which constitutes the body so severely that a desire for relief is as fluid and impossible as the cessation of desire itself, except through actual death?

Pain can be converted to cause, but then we can answer the cause of 'what' in what causes disease, sometimes at least. We cannot answer the why of disease. It belongs to the random chaos of nature that capitalism seeks to answer and the answer to which usually falls to the chronically ill. Endless suggestions from armchair experts as to 'try yoga/drink vinegar/pray/think positive' are not so different to clinical consultancy in the curious volition attributed to the zombie for neither living normally nor dying pathologically. Our persistence is a philosophical question equivalent to those larger unanswerable metaphysical questions of 'who are we/why are we here?' and this question is one that O'Brien, myself and many other degeneratively disabled people ask ourselves, without moral conditioning, but perhaps with a certain frustration of the peculiar duration of zombie time, especially when it hurts: not 'why am I here?' but 'why am I *still* here?' Pain is unsignifiable, like (the purpose of) life (and all those other existential, transcendental and usually highly anthropocentric questions) is unsignifiable. Chronic pain is an Artaudian Body without Organs or unsignifiable waves of intensities. While Deleuze and Guattari discuss the masochist in their two examples of the Body without Organs (the other being the junkie who has their own relevance in the current so-called 'opioid wars' in relation with degenerative illness, chronic pain and disability), the pain of degenerative 'deathening' has a physiological and nosological source (diagnosed but often not) but no subjective source and yet semiocapitalism interrogates the sick, medically, personally, politically, as if one will be revealed in the subject. 'You don't look sick' or 'where did it come from' are all manifestations of 'why are you sick?' Reed et al. (2022) claim their study of identity and chronic pain is the first, and they describe their foci in studying ninety-eight participants as involving 'issues related to identity and death anxiety were associated with pain catastrophizing, pain acceptance, and pain-related disability, above and beyond pain severity, fear-avoidance, and age' (2022: 35). The adherence to signification of identity which the study places on sufferers of chronic pain is astonishing:

> Indeed, identity is considered to be one of the major existential buffers designed to minimize death-related anxiety, and empirical research

shows that when reminded of death, individuals are more likely to validate their own identity-related worldviews. However, chronic pain may alter one's identity by affecting their current self-perceptions and their future objectives, preventing individuals from engaging in identity-related behaviors. In other words, chronic pain may conflict with one's goals. (2022: 36)

The comparative study Reed et al. use is from PTSD, so the enfleshed aspect of pain as an asignifiable distribution of extra-linguistic excessive intensities is re-anchored to a perceived origin event rather than embracing the lack of causality which the embodiment of being 'sick' involves. No origin event, be it a gene fault, an inherited trauma fault or any other kind of reason, rationalizes the flesh of the body in pain or degenerating, even though the very title 'degenerative' involves the phantasy of a perfected template of the original Adam/Anthropos fallen. Interesting, however, is the result which the study shows in the transformation from self as stable subject, or noun, to the self as better adept at 'coping' when transformed into goal orientation:

As expected, our study found that a stable sense of identity (self-concept clarity) was related to pain catastrophizing and acceptance. Paralleling ABDT and the inability to engage worldview defense mechanisms, the existential concern of 'Who am I?' plays a central role with individuals in chronic pain. It is possible that pain severity, instead of prompting explicit thoughts of one's mortality (evidenced by a non-significant correlation between pain severity and death anxiety), is rather associated with motivating goal cognitions, reminders of one's limitations, and one's thwarted roles in society (e.g., not being able to participate in community events). This idea is congruent with the significant correlations between existential anxiety and self-concept and pain-related disability in the present study. An individual may have an affective and cognitive response to limitations related to chronic pain, prompting them to pursue meaningful goals (or not). However, because causality was not assessed, it may be that acceptance of pain helps individuals have a more stable sense of self, and/or pain catastrophizing results in one's sense of self becoming disrupted. Further research is needed to assess these possibilities. In addition, the non-significant relationship between self-concept clarity and pain-related disability, after accounting for other variables, suggests that the relationship between identity and pain-related disability may involve specific cognitions and emotions that were not assessed in the present research. (2022: 51)

The role of catastrophizing in chronic illness underestimates that it is a condition of capitalism leading to what Berardi (2015: 217) calls the spasm, the double experience shock of acceleration and exhaustion by which semiocapitalism produces its subjects in perpetual anxiety. The spasm is precisely the perpetual catastrophizing that constitutes the working zombie who must produce. This because, instead of constitution via enunciations of what can I do, capital zombies are enunciated by statements of what if: 'what if I lose my job?' 'What if I can't pay for food or fuel?' And enunciations ascend classes to 'what if I can't buy the newest or best tech/car/house' to the billionaires', 'what if I can't own the world/live forever?' Somewhat perverting Reed's outcomes, the chronically ill, the deathbound, the zombie-time durational apparently respond well to goals. In capitalist translation this could be seen as productivity, but as we already know, governments do not see the disabled as productive but reliant, even while demanding they appear productive. Interpreted a different way, a life in tiny goals, especially useless goals from useless bodies, becoming-artist as O'Brien, or super-masochist as Bob Flanagan, or millions of other examples of the artistry of being chronically ill and disabled as simply persisting, this is a life in verbing, not as noun, consistent with life as becoming. Especially if death is seen as imminent and moreso, deliverance, it may be a sought goal – the peaceful becoming, the pain-free euthanasia or assisted suicide. Reed et al. emphasize that current thinking in psychomedical studies of pain show the acceptance of death leads to a concretization of beliefs. I violently disagree. What they define as a reification of beliefs insinuates that death awareness is always death anxiety, which is a considerable and frankly offensive homogenization of chronic pain bodies. Death awareness does not necessarily cause a negative feedback loop of death anxiety as they claim. Death awareness causes a quickening of intensities that psychiatry may translate as anxiety and suffering, but their clear aversion to contemplating death as something more than inherently anxious or morbid or generally unacceptable elucidates their own 'healthy' relationship with death as fostering anxiety, just as the capital zombie is no more or less the zombie of death duration, just occupied by different qualities of intensity. Ultimately, and strangely, they suggest a new form of identity that does not include pain can only be understood as an advocation of repression and/or general distain for the 'normal' population over the persistence of pain, and especially the visual or verbal enunciation of pain, in the disabled and chronically ill.

We live in the zombie time, hour by hour, day by day, with goals perhaps, but always tempered by temporariness:

> Temporariness can, I think, offer an interesting set of possibilities especially in light of the work of disability activists and scholars to refigure the term 'able-bodiedness' into 'temporarily able-bodiedness' to underscore the inherent temporariness to all embodiment. Thus, explaining the functioning of temporariness in fat temporality is not itself a full critique. When entrenched in a socially marginalizing phenomenology of temporariness, however, what kinds of anticipation can one experience if they are not in the right time ? If one's body is constructed as 'to be changed' and as not legitimate in the present, then it affects one's daily projects of embodied care in particular (i.e., food, rest, activity, relationships, etc.). (Rodier 2018: 139)

In his seminal work on crip theory, Robert McRuer shows suspicion at the straightening up of crip people, through bio political intervention and also accessibilities discourse, stating: 'sooner or later, if we live long enough, we will all become normate' (2006: 198). McRuer aligns crip discourse on accessibility as a form of incorporation with the resolving of the 'queer' problem, how to make queer mainstream, normal and incorporated. I would add both are tolerated in the same way as the living productive zombie worker, as the breeding (especially white) woman. Deviation from incorporation discourse in semiocapitalism has replaced normalization discourse because being productive and sellable is more important than being normal. The most emphatic problem seen in McRuer's statement for the chronically ill degeneratively dying is that we will never live long enough to become normate but we also won't die fast enough to stop being a problem. We are the queer living dead. O'Brien cites Parsons in his own work on zombie time, in zombie queer context:

> In his 1951 publication *The Social System* Talcott Parsons outlined a theory he had been developing since the late 1930s. The text draws attention to 'medicine as a professional institution engaged in the social control and rectification of a form of deviance and disequilibrium in society: illness' (Carol Thomas 2007: 16). Parsons' theory rests on the notion that 'healthy' people are able to fulfil societal obligations, such as work, whereas sick people are not and thus sickness functions as a form of social deviance, 'their incapacity undermines the social structure' (ibid.: 17). He outlined what he saw as the sick role. This, as he understands it, is a 'legitimate status allowing for the suspension of the ill person's normal social roles' (ibid.: 17). Parsons argues that if someone is ill their social deviance is accepted if they take on the sick role. Parsons notes that 'the sick role is also an institutionalized role, which [. . .] involves a relative legitimacy, that is so long as there is an implied "agreement" to "pay the price" in accepting certain disabilities and the obligation to get well' (1951: 211, italics in original). This is a position that has certain obligations attached to it but, in turn, allows the sick person legitimacy. (O'Brien 2019: 260)

Georges Canguilhem, in his historical and contemporary discussion of the genesis and meaning of pathology juxtaposed against the 'normal', affirms this idea of quantitative excess as detrimental in his exploration of the earlier physiologist Auguste Comte's reading of Broussais. According to the 'Broussais Principle', pathology of the body was measured rather than identified, as a result of degrees of physiological normalcy. Independent and unique pathology and nosology did not exist in the theories of Comte and his contemporaries. Like pleasure and its existence not as some 'thing' but as a degree of what was already present, actual human physiology was incapable of anything it did not already present, only of excesses or serious diminution of the 'normal' (temperate) condition. (This resonates with new age wellness claims that there is no such thing as disease, only dis-ease.) Canguilhem offers as example another Broussaisian, Bichat, thus:

> Bichat's hostility toward all metrical designs in biology was paradoxically allied with his assertion that diseases must be explained in terms of the

definitely quantitative variations of their properties, with the tissues which make up the organs serving as a scale. 'To analyse precisely the properties of living bodies; to show that every physiological phenomena is, in the final analysis, related to these properties considered in their natural state and that every pathological phenomena derives from their increase, decrease or alteration, that every therapeutic phenomenon has as its principle the return to the natural type from which they had deviated; to determine precisely the cases where each one comes into play . . . this is the general idea of this work.' (Canguilhem 1989: 61–62, quotes Bichat 1801: xix)

Canguilhem uses this prevalent model of pathology as affected normalcy as an introduction against which he later argues. However, his desire to locate a drive within medicine to cure begins with the exposure of medicine as wanting to reform. Medicine's drive to return to 'normalcy' sick states of being holds up as desirable a single example of that which the discourse deems acceptable as a state of being. Canguilhem evinces the alignment of early physiology with theories of pleasure located around a return to a 'normal' equilibrium and a healthy state. Pathology is inextricable from physiology in the same way that pleasure is inextricable from the flesh in traditional discourse, most particularly in Foucault's analysis from the Greeks to the Victorians. The study of pathology and physiology and the study of pleasure's relationship to the body both focus on quantifiable measures but without the potential for transformation that a focus on quantity (to do with time) rather than quality (to do with space and the object in space) could offer. Physiology and pathology work within a system that requires time only within *a* space, and time, especially not zombie time, the durationality of an endless illness, is unthinkable. Because the degree of variation in physiology and pathology is not one that evolves forward but one that works within a rigid measurable space and simply traverses backwards and forwards along that measure, the subject moving in time can never exceed the limits or borders of the measurable space. It is never an 'unknowable' or limitless space. Quantitative measure not only eradicates any ability to theorize illness beyond deviance as independent but also retains, in both discourses, an adamant beneficial 'state' of normalcy which claims not to be driven by a moral or subjective code but a physiological (and hence supposedly 'truthful') system of temperance. Illness comes to refer not simply to a 'wrong' state of being, but rather to an extreme version of something found within normalcy. Canguilhem states:

> To define the abnormal as too much or too little is to recognise the normative character of the so-called normal state. This normal or physiological state is no longer simply a disposition which can be revealed and explained as fact, but a manifestation of an attachment of some value. When Bégin defines the normal state as one where 'the organs function with all the regularity and uniformity of which they are capable', we cannot fail to recognise that, despite Broussais's horror of all ontology, *an ideal of perfection soars over this attempt at a positive definition*. (Canguilhem 1989: 56–57, original italics)

Perfection, both in medicine and in the history of desire, is not something to aspire towards or aim to attain, as it is in certain other discourses. Unlike the case in religion or athletics, the perfect state in medicine and desire is something *necessary* rather than optional, something which is forced upon the subject as the subject's own responsibility rather than a goal admittedly set up by the given discourse towards which the subject looks for guidance. Perfection masquerades as the minimum necessary state for corporeal well-being, and the term *normal* in both medicine and desire is a degree zero level of being. Because normal is degree zero rather than a 'thing', it can claim no value judgement. It does not suggest a super-human in morals or flesh; it instead demands a regulation of subjectivity that is compulsory for the good of the subject, not the good of the discourse that prescribes it. A level state of being is demanded of the subject and a point of beneficial equilibrium both in pleasure and in the physiological flesh is necessary rather than suggested. The bound continuum of normalcy and health clearly exhibits how easily the point of 'normal' could alter through time, but precisely where the alteration passes from normal to pathological or excessive is unclear. In this sense, the ill body and many incarnations of the disabled body need to 'work' on their illness as if it were a job and an economic balance, and normalcy or the myth of health is the promotion to the next level. Even worse, all the jobs are in management. Excess is retained from the nineteenth century in both traditional and alternative medicine. In O'Brien's and Flanagan's case of cystic fibrosis, it is the 'deviate' gene leading to the 'excess' mucous which will not only kill them but which becomes unpalatable while they (refuse to) die. For severe autoimmune diseases it is the excess of inflammation which affects all organs and disables, then kills. The ways in which HIV has become part of zombie time shows most emphatically the linking of excess associated with morality, both in the devastating delay of treatment which led to mass death, but also AIDS being the most morally evaluated of diseases, where the tipping point from HIV to AIDS is also that from temperance to excess in homophobic imagination. Just as the poor are relegated to being 'excessively lazy' in spite of the intense labour of surviving, the disabled and chronically ill existing in zombie time are considered both excessively alive ('but you don't look sick'/'you look well today'/'do yoga/meditation/exercise') and excessively dead ('you've lived past your date'/the unspoken 'when will you die' which often denies many forms of welfare support). All the while the 'healthy' are simply better performers, because it would be difficult to imagine anyone with access to healthcare not going through life without sometimes needing to manage that health, the zombie worker of capital also the zombie worker of their own wellness because, as Canguilhem states, normal is that of which we are capable, not uniform universal measure, a very Spinozist sounding idea. In these ways the relationship the chronically ill have with our consultants, doctors and other interpreters correlates with the analysand and the analyst, the schizophrenic and the psychiatrist. Do we believe the specialist who gives us x many years? What does that mean in illnesses without the fast action of, for example, aggressive cancer? Zombie time makes peace of the indeterminability of no kill or cure, but those outside that time struggle to do so. This reflects the way euthanasia is denied to many because of what external persons want, rather than the patient.

Zombie time is a queer time, and a time of death activism. At any point, the duration may turn to a desire for death as the most comforting embrace, a form of deliverance and salvation beyond the capacity of an anthropocentric understanding which takes as its first tenet avoidance of death as constituting life. Being told one has time to live does not, in practicality, deviate one from any other life, because death comes as part of chaos, and chaos comes as part of our bodies, our birth, all repudiative of and disinterested in the narrativization of life lived in human time, populated with heteronormative human events of capital-zombification – birth, marriage, reproduction, death/work, eat, 'play' (healthily, productively), sleep, repeat. The zombie-time sick body is a Body without Organs and a body that shows Bergson's idea that possibility is not about the historicity of the future but the chaos of the present opening infinite possibilities. In the introduction to Berardi's *Futurability*, he cites Bergson's 'Le possible et le réel', where Bergson names possibility the 'pre-existence in the form of an idea' (in Berardi 2019: 2), continuing 'disorder is simply an order we do not seek' (in Berardi 2019: 3). In the dialectic between patient and clinician, ordering the disorder can be helpful, it can be tactically useful in imagining various and variations of trajectories of possibilities. It can even be comforting on dark days where the pathological label excuses the disruptive painful intensities of the flesh. But the diagnosis is not the future. Death in zombie time both is and is not the future. The dying have to think possibility of death with (at least) two prongs of futurity, the dead/not dead, and the many other imaginings of futurity, from the banal to the floridly dreamed. Interestingly, it is then to the BwO that Berardi turns to illustrate the shift from possibility to actuality as an expression of chaos (2019: 5). There is no necessary romanticization of the sick or disabled body in navigating our possibilities as BwOs because all bodies are indeterminacies and multidimensionalities. The sick body seems to have both its time and its multidimensionality reduced, for the former possibility is no possibility other than 'early' death, for the latter nothing more than symptoms and suffering within binaries of good/bad, well/ill and pleasure/pain or working/not working. The very excess by which we are defined shows chronically ill bodies are productive, too productive of abject excesses. We also produce absolutely alternate ways to exist within a body which is often intolerable, often calm, like being untethered in an unpredictable sea where consciousness is the vessel but the flesh is the entire ocean. In this experience, death can be many possibilities based on the intensities and expressions which produce its event horizon. Death is death, certainly, but that finitude and cessation as a possibility has as many dimensions for the chronically ill as our own pain and sensation, inconvertible to language.

Ethical understanding of disability and illnesses which include chronic pain belongs to death activism by forsaking a healthful understanding of death as only one comprehension of death's possibilities. So too, zombie time is proliferatively asemiotic time, the oceanic time beyond language that jams capital zombie-worker time. We are the living-dead, or the dead-living, word order is exchangeable, the existing, animated oxymoron continues nonetheless. Currently, not fitting into productive time often ends in accelerated death, not from disease, but societal neglect, and those deaths are the organizing deaths of capitalism, not the disorganized chaos of the death of disease. The chronically ill have to formulate artistry to experience duration. Living in these bodies requires imagination, often deathbound with joy, or lifebound with exhaustion, challenging myriad binaries of the normal and the pathological, life and death. Diagnosis, drugs, treatment can all ameliorate pain and other symptoms, but the only experience of chronic illness comes from its durational sensation, the rest are words, critical and clinical. Zombie-time demands an urgent rethinking of euthanasia laws as the very foundation of agency for disabled and chronically ill people, where current laws in seeking to prevent the worst case scenario 'what ifs' about supposed nefarious relatives or bystanders still give agency only to those healthy others, not the occupant of zombie time. We are the living-dead, but many of us can still utter in various ways, and our relationship to death shows it is not only one form of possibility but within itself offers a thousand tiny possibilities of affects towards futurity.

6

The unspeakable death (that is not death)

The apocalypse, the end of days, the catastrophic moment where human life ends, where the end of the 'world' translates to the end of humans, seems the least palatable of 'activisms':

> We can characterize this turning point in the following way: up until these last few years, man had the power to give himself death individually and alone; now, it is humanity as a whole that has acquired, marvellously and appallingly. this power. It can do this. However. what it can do. it cannot master with certainty. so that it comes back to each of us to anxiously ask, Where do we stand? What is going to happen? Is there a solution? (Blanchot 1997: 102)

Ecological activism, even what centric governments consider eco-terrorisms (which usually are not deathbound), most often found on the left, and far-right radicals, all seem to share a fear of a certain kind of species apocalypse: for the left ecologist such as Extinction Rebellion, the end of humans due to the destruction of the Earth; for the far right, the end of what they term humans as a minor subset of human life, but what refers to able bodied, trad-male, heterosexual and critically white human bodies. There are a number of other apocalypse anxieties, including those which seek to preserve other species in order to retain an ecological balance to in turn preserve environments conducive to their maintenance, or that sickening buzzword 'sustainability', of human life accustomed to a certain standard of living. What is shared, whether the anxiety and the solution focus on fascist or so-called ecological concerns, is the primary idol of the human, be it as the prime mover of all valuable and valid Earth life, or a caretaker of our own future, or an existential reason for why life would exist at all. The end of the world and the end of humans are often spoken as interchangeable. Twilight of the gods is now twilight of the humans. When we imagine or fear the end of the world, what is meant is the end of humans, reducible ultimately to our own individual ends (which we strangely hope will be before, at and after the apocalypse – avoidance, sacrifice, survival). There is something almost endearingly 'retro' romantic in the return to the idea that nature will rise up and destroy us, a vivid phantasy of the reversal of the Anthropocene. This was in evidence during the Covid pandemic and in times of climate crisis, as if nature is a monolithic sentient entity reversing the battlefield in the Order of Mars. Even the fear of nuclear annihilation speaks of 'the bomb' as if a nuclear apocalypse can be blamed on the effects of a series of warheads of which we have no authorship. The continued Martian structure of antagonism from without propels us towards the apocalypse via affects of our own doing, a moebius reflex of our own expressions as a species, while we fear these as extricated from our ecological manipulations. Human fascination with death, coming via an/one/the apocalypse, continues to exhibit an obsession with event over duration as a perpetual delay or repressive apparatus in order to feed the capitalist immediacy of unsatisfying pleasure loops of desire and capture of the object or (unsatisfying) satisfaction, a dialectic of now without immanence, a tiny futurity. At the same time, imagining total, unifying apocalypse helps alleviate awareness and acceptance of individual death in a similar way to other death alleviators, such as belief in an afterlife, or absolute faith in medicine, or transhumanist faith in technology, or generational faith in reproduction as immortality. Fearing an apocalypse is far more glamorous and romantic than one's own quiet, inevitable, frequently ignoble corporeally messy and painful death. Similarly, coveting a shocking, stunning, exhilarating singular event alleviates the care and duration which surrounds many ordinary experiences of dying as duration. Our deaths are easier to think as if they were a film, and the shared mass event allows us to think we are succumbing with all others (ameliorating the guilt of dying as a failure to thrive, because semiocapitalism sees death as failure at one's job of living) while insinuating we may survive, thereby proving our right to live and superiority over those who do not, deeply reminiscent of the smug West's belief that Western ease of living compared to other global areas is deserved rather than one of accidentally being born into the West, similar to being born into money, or white skin, or able-bodiedness. In every apocalypse story there is the insidious faith that extinction is something individually, or racially, or wealth-based, or technologically survivable if only we work hard enough. The apocalypse, in definition and in survivability, becomes a disappointment. In 'The Apocalypse Is Disappointing', Blanchot states:

> What does the problematic event teach us? This: that insofar as it puts into question the human species in its totality, it is also because of this event that the idea of totality arises visibly and for the first time on our horizon – a sun, though we know not whether it is rising or setting; also, that this totality is in our possession, but as a negative power. This singularly confirms the preface to [Hegel's] the *Phenomenology of Spirit*: the power of understanding is an absolute power of negation; understanding knows only through the force of separation, that is, of destruction – analysis, fission – and at the same time knows only the destructible and is certain only of what could be destroyed. Through understanding, we know very precisely what must be done in order for the final annihilation to occur, but we do not know which resources to solicit to prevent it from occurring. What understanding gives us is the knowledge of catastrophe, and what it predicts, foresees, and grasps, by means of decisive anticipation, is the possibility of the end. Thus man is held to the whole first of all by the force of understanding, and understanding is held to the whole by negation. Whence the insecurity of all knowledge – of a knowledge that bears on the whole. But let us reflect a little further. The problematic event about which we should rejoice because it confirms us in our relations to totality – it is true, only in a negative way – and also in our power over the whole – a power, it is true, only of destruction – why does it disappoint us? It is indeed a power, but one in relation to which we remain at a loss. A power that is not in our power, that only points to a possibility without mastery, a probability

– which is, let us say, probable-improbable – that would be our power, a power in us and power over us, only if we dominated it with certainty. But for the moment we are just as incapable of mastering it as we are of wanting it, and for an obvious reason: we are not in control of ourselves because this humanity capable of being totally destroyed does not yet exist as a whole. (Blanchot 1997: 105–106)

Totality of event is denied by the denial of totality as a species. Even in apocalypse the killability of some over others remains in the minds of people, be it prioritizing one's own family or nation or race. Majoritarian prejudice is not annihilated with the world's annihilation. And rarely is the fate of nonhuman animals included in the anxiety over and mourning at the thought of a world-ending event by extinction catastrophists. This apocalypse preamble is here by way not of introducing a chapter on the apocalypse, which, as Blanchot claims, is indeed disappointing, if not boring. What Blanchot suggests emphasizes a tendency in human extinction anxieties to think in terms of totality of time (one event, one mass death), while denying a totality of 'victims' by prioritizing some over others as counting as potential victims to be preserved or reasons for an apocalypse to be prevented.

What I call the least palatable activism, the cessation of human reproduction, is an activism that welcomes human extinction, but refuses both the phantasy of the totality of the event and the residual maintenance of the killability ideologies which privilege certain victims over other lives in either being saved or fear of being lost. This activism, which shares aspects with antinatalism and movements such as the Voluntary Human Extinction Movement (VHEMT) (but not efilism), is itself met with many presumptions that concretize anthropocentric tendencies. These presumptions is what led my most recent book (2020) to be met with hate and rape and death threats. It clearly touches upon the very limit of what humans can tolerate as ethical Earth relationality. I list these as a reflection on what inspired many of the content of the threats (even though these reasons were not present in my work, they were the default insinuations towards which anthropocentric thinking leapt) and also in order to reiterate what a call for human extinction is *not*.

When death is not (really) death

Human extinction activism is *not*:

1. Violent – When discussing the very potential of not reproducing, an anthropocentric loop is completed in popular imaginings of what this means. Rather than configure not reproducing as a wilful act of force (that is, an affective expression within the world), for women/domestic familial/bloodlines it is configured as lack (childless not childfree, met with lament and mourning) and for men/state/race it is 'extinction equals annihilation'. I mention this as a popular response through both personal and philosophical trajectories. When my previous *The Ahuman Manifesto* was published in 2020 the large majority of hate mails and death threats received centred around my antinatalism, specifically my responsibility to continue the white race as a white woman strangely juxtaposed with the condemnation that I want everyone here now to die. The racism and violent patriotism (these were, after all, often very detailed death threats) with which a call to an absenting of humans technically without death is a strange paradox. To not exist through antinatalism does not involve death or dying, except, according to these threats, the dying of a race, nation-state or other ultimately arbitrary division of the species human by melanin, relatively recent history and the often violence-associated significations and values these uphold in the name of power alone. The recoil from less militant but not less generically affected respondents was similarly violent in that it assumed in order for humans to cease, violence must be involved, especially in the context that when humans have historically been forced to cease, the violence of genocide, eugenics, forced reproductive selective control and other manipulations which always make human absenting conditional on which type of human has been integral. Both responses are to a violence of signification of *who dies*. Antinatalism in its most basic (and only) definition is the cessation of reproduction. As a relatively utopian idea, the enforcement of antinatalism remains in the realm of dystopian artworlds of fiction and film, because how do we enforce the cessation of human reproduction without violence? This default question masks the persistence in the attribution of violence to human actions which are taken as natural or biological. We rarely see publications or

popular meditations on the two violences of forcing a life into being without consent or of what forcing eight billion-and-counting human lives and their consumptive practices onto an Earth without the consent of other Earth lives does to those other lives. The violence of bringing into being has emerged as a new intensity of Schopenhauer's logic of consent:

> The most traditional justification of antinatalism is that human life is bad and that creating more of it is, from a rational viewpoint, dubious. Arthur Schopenhauer expressed this view succinctly in his 1851 Studies in Pessimism: 'If children were brought into the world by an act of pure reason alone, would the human race continue to exist? Would not a man rather have so much sympathy with the coming generation as to spare it the burden of existence, or at any rate not take it upon himself to impose that burden upon it in cold blood? (Schopenhauer 2007: 8).' (Häyry and Sukenick 2023: 8)

Attribution of violence is not a necessary part of antinatalism. It is ascribed perhaps because of novelty or of any anthropocentric idea having a residual violent imposition. But antinatalism is beyond anthropocentrism and is entirely amoral, as there is no eugenic selection involved. Meanwhile, Phillipp Schönegger claims that antinatalists fulfil the three 'dark triad' criteria of Machiavellianism, psychopathology and narcissism. A priori indiscernibility between antinatalism and a general tenebrous dark pessimism seems inevitable as a reaction to antinatalism. Prioritizing the deeply neocapital sense that more is always better, and trying again, whether it be with breeding happy/genius/ perfect children or species (including our own) is worth more than nurturing the lives here, once again elucidates that there is an arbitrary connection between a moral good and the vague concept of 'life' (not individual existences so much as imagined future existences) as opposed to 'death' (not actual threat or occurrence of death of existing lives, but species discontinuation as an actual death). The potential and imaginative spark of how to live and co-exist in a world and nurture the lives here, needing nothing more, especially not acknowledging lives which don't exist and never will (a double negative that conceptually shows its own redundancy), conceals something insipidly narcissistic about the conceptual importance of the continuation of 'me' in individual and nation-state anthropocentric identity which has very little to do with a celebration and care of life as it is lived, and more to do with the enamouring fantasy of an insipid fascist prioritization of one form of defined human subjectivity over another nation/race/species. Contemplating this critique of antinatalism leads down the route of analysing the critics far more than imagining the opening of the world and does very little for the purpose of contemplating what the cessation of humans would mean for life on Earth.

2. Eugenic – Killability and the necropolitics justifiably demarcate the tendencies in the death humans impose on one another as asymmetrical and in conflict with an individual's capacity to fulfil sovereign subjectivity. Mbembe, summarizing Hegel, states: 'In other words, the human being truly becomes a subject – that is, separated from the animal – in the struggle and the work through which he or she confronts death (understood as the violence of negativity). It is through this confrontation with death that he or she is cast into the incessant movement of history' (2003: 14). History and futurity co-emerge in ethical considerations of the annihilations of peoples. Those people have variously, according to Mbembe and after Hegel, been denied the human agency which allows them contemplation of their own subjectivity against the 'animal' subjectivity of existence because humans contemplate their own death and struggle against it. My reduced version of Hegel's demarcation of the animal/nature and the human/subject after Mbembe sets apart (as addressable unto itself) the question of the critical nature of acknowledging, addressing and accounting for the history of genocide, racially, disablist and other prejudice motivated mass murders, including the prevention of reproduction of certain groups of peoples, as an issue which is not part of the same struggle to think a new ecological ethics where futurity for past horrors has the wrong righted by the perpetuation of the oppressed groups. These entirely independent conceptual and material contemplations of how we may ensure the other thrives are mapped upon each other for nationalist and racial motives, in a way resonant with the 'humans first' arguments outlined in the abolitionism of Chapter 4. It is critical to remind ourselves that currently extractionist capital does overwhelmingly negatively impact the quality of life for many traditionally deprived peoples while propping up both Western consumerism and the 2 (or increasingly 1) per cent in a continuation

of aligning certain peoples with animals and nature, now from evolutionary status to resource accessibility. While ecological concerns and historical eugenic oppression remained interwoven, they are not interchangeable. Righting a wrong through 'replacement humans' is an impossible attitude to fully address the violent horrors humans impose upon one another and has little to do with immanent thriving and liberty. Liberty through equal capital, when that capital is a Western version of excess, misjudges what liberty means for individuals and groups of people. Currently, the capacity for liberty, and what liberty means for unique individuals, is still constituted and defined by majoritarianism, so how we think of immanent expression of agency is very different to white, nationalist, colonialist expression of sovereign subjectivity. Suffice to mention here that while both death of all nation, state and border is an aim of death activism, accountability and acknowledgement of histories remain – death activism is not ahistorical, but it is deterritorializing: a topology of understanding, exploring tenets of definitions of liberty and equality so as all the Earth's occupants transform their relations and content.

3. Fast – Speed culture and anthropocentric being enamoured by disaster and apocalypse have meant that antinatalism becomes synonymous with a mass extinction single and unexpected, ferocious event. Perhaps due to the difficulty of extricating violence from extinction in anthropocentric thinking, perhaps because we humans like to think we are important enough not only to perpetuate our genes but also to witness the end of the world in our own lifetimes, extinction often invokes singular and sudden. The cessation of humans, which anyone who decides that the Earth has been exhausted by humans decides upon when choosing not to reproduce, is considered a private matter (although women are still made to account as to why), but to suggest we should all cease reproducing contracts the durational quality of slow extinction into the shock of confronting loss of *us* as a species in popular consciousness, primarily because representations of human extinction cling to images and narratives of violent occupation, invasion, disaster and mass annihilation as all, once again, playing out on the Order of Mars field of violence. There is another way to understand human extinction as a slow, considered, careful and highly scientific and artistic existence unto non-existence whereby no one is harmed or killed. Covertly, to care for the

eight billion now has proven to be far more impractical than we are able, a situation which reflects anti-choice activism which cares for clusters of cells until they exit the uterus. Larger questions of how we experience time – deep time, meditative durationality, the slowness of attentive care, the differential speeds of grace contingent to who, human or animal, is in need – are also questions which jam speed-capital's replacement culture, accelerationism, accumulationism, consumer culture, inattentive culture and throw away (again of human and nonhuman peoples) culture. Even popular ecological movements use urgency to leap to an imagined future generation, coupling a meaningful call to action with an overwhelming urgency that can often lead to catatonia. An antinatalist movement such as VHEMT reminds us there is no enforcement or time limit. The movement is needed urgently, but to cease reproduction does not necessitate murdering the eight billion here. While I seek a more ubiquitous need for not reproducing to be a global concern, rather than one belonging to each neo liberal private individual, ineffectual in the face of both an enormous growing population and an enormous consumption dissymmetry, both death activism's antinatalism and VHEMT remind us we are not contemplating extinction as a cataclysmic event. The relationship between antinatalism and duration is an area outside of the remit of this book, but our experience of duration in time of ecological crisis is a consideration which can change many of the presumptions that default antinatalism to an Order of Mars rather than a practice of care, of long and metamorphic Order of Venus, which death activism advocates.

4. Martian – Salient to apocalypse enamourment from without, and to that without being variously aliens (invasion), nature (disaster) or human other (totalitarianism), a call for human extinction is imagined as forcefully imposed. Aspects of this imposition include a sense that no normal human would advocate the end of the human species, that human extinction would always be a result of horrific violence, treachery against one's race/species, right down to a quiet notion of a moral judgement against the species that carries a smugness which reflects the antinatalist's will rather than the ethical affects of what a world with diminished and eventually no humans could express itself as becoming. Colebrook states of disaster narratives in general, and *Heart of Darkness/Apocalypse Now* in particular:

> What is lost and mourned is our illusion of moral grandeur. There is neither voice, face, nor vision attributed to them. *Heart of Darkness* and *Apocalypse Now* are about the end of the world insofar as they confront the end of the grand lie of civilization. They are also texts that produce the end of the world as the end of us, or – more accurately – the end of us as the end of the world. (2023: 18)

In Colebrook's title, *Who Would You Kill to Save the World?* she exposes the sense that the world is us, we never really mean the Earth and all its occupants who, even at eight billion, far outnumber us in diversity and species even before individuals. She also re-emphasizes the default of ending the world to killing, that without us the world has surely ended. This illuminates the anthropocentric imagination that positions *both* ending the world and saving the world are strategies which form and occupy a Martian terrain of war, violence and conflict. Yet even were we to be required to kill to save whichever world is being defended, antinatalism still does not need real-life, real-time killing in order to allow Earth life to flourish in whichever ways it goes. Antinatalism kills the idea of the value of the species human, it kills a concept, an arbitrary and, based on our track record, frankly pretty accurate notion that humans are bad for the world. In this sense we must 'kill' the concept of a species, not any individual, to save the world. This concept-killing/not-actual-killing would nonetheless be a long, slow, variable experience in Earth time of dying out duration, rather than a spectacular battle with a sudden outcome. Not reproducing in itself is neither moral nor immoral, nothing is harmed as an exterior entity (the question of psychological harm in not breeding versus harm in bringing a life into being is a more interiorly existentialist and anthropomorphically narcissistic one beyond the remit of ecological considerations). Colebrook sums up:

> [Plato suggests] we must not simply watch the world unfold but become aware of ourselves as auteurs. Kant argues that practically we must view nature as if it were created in harmony with our sense of order and virtue and yet recognize that this transcendental order is not nature's own but an effect of our powers of synthesis. Nietzsche defined the fall, and perhaps origin, of humanity by way of its relation to theatrical viewing: the ancient

Greeks were once capable of viewing life in its full intensity, enjoying the festive cruelty of existence. With morality, order, and language, the Dionysian force of life was increasingly subjected to systematization, not encountered in its complexity but judged by way of a 'higher world' that rendered this world guilty. (2023: 89)

Again, Anthropos shows his Apollonian superiority in designating the world beneath the human and in need of the human, which then relegates contemporary natalists as against humans, or having a superior smugness. This oscillating dialectic is an entirely different territory to that which seeks and sees synthesis as a power/force beyond Anthropos, beyond Martian, synthesis as reciprocity, involving all the senses, quietude and care which the amorphous amoral unconditional inevitable relationality of love necessitates. Rethinking the not-actually-death death of the species human as a reterritorialized Topology of Venus simultaneously alters nature delivered from an us/them, to be defeated or saved, including all the human, nonhuman and ecological relations within.

Human extinction activism *is*: care/ful/ing, inclusive (all reproduction is nationalism), slow, Venusian, a death activism that does not actually involve death.

Will to traversal: Against kith and kin

Deleuze and Guattari state:

Becoming produces nothing by filiation; all filiation is imaginary. Becoming is always of a different order than filiation. It concerns alliance. If evolution includes any veritable becomings, it is in the domain of *symbioses* that bring into play beings of totally different scales and kingdoms, with no possible filiation . . . like hybrids, which are in themselves sterile, born of a sexual union that will not reproduce itself, but which begins over again every time, gaining that much more ground. Unnatural participations or nuptials are the true nature spanning the kingdoms of nature. (Deleuze and Guattari 1987: 238, 241)

Deleuze and Guattari's primary tenets of becoming, which invoke Spinoza and the ethical dimension of becoming, affirm that relations of filiation are at best, always imagined. While it would be foolish to claim genetics do not play various roles in disease, the relation between psychological-somatic aspects of passing down or passing through behaviours remains in fascinating contestation, and problematically retains a Cartesian split between physiology and psychology, thought and behaviour. Any evidence as to both the cultural spectre of the biological need to reproduce and the connection between genetically related persons remains between science and superstition. Each seems implemented as evidence of the need for reproduction and the psychical connection between familial relatives as a tool to excuse or vindicate events and behaviours, both benign and malignant. It is just as easy to find relatives who loathe their offspring and parents and people who do not wish to reproduce, even though these are all underrepresented, represented as part of a narrative drama, or a perceived misanthropic failure to be often highly gendered nurturing mothers and patriarchal fathers. Animal studies ethics, including analytic philosophy's animal rights argument, as well as arguments for procreation, historically veer towards verisimilitude of phantasies of genetic connectivity, from Peter Singer's Great Ape project to heartwarming stories of long lost relatives. These are not being judged as bad or good, simply used to show that what Anthropos seeks to vindicate as 'ethical' encounter continues to be founded upon a superstition of likeness. Deleuze and Guattari's emphasis that nature is both unnatural and inherently interkingdom, rather than species discrete or specific in evolutionary deviation, opposes the verisimilitude argument for ethical consideration while simultaneously exposing the hypocrisy humans use in claiming something is 'natural' when we so often mean we have no argument for it, so we default to big 'N' Nature as an inevitable a priori unsullied by anthropocentric ideology. This is so of the need to breed as much as it is the need to protect those humans and animals who look like us and to impose oppression upon the 'unnaturals' of Anthropos, historically homosexuals, gender non-conforming people, the disabled and the classification of BIPoC as fauna.

Taking nature as defined by Deleuze and Guattari as interkingdom symbioses and as unnatural due to species indiscretion advocates for deep ecosophy and questions the blood ties which are happily critiqued in the horrors of 'blood and soil' fascist ideology but have largely gone unexamined in Oedipal family lineages. For an ethical ecosophical activism, Oedipal families are considered microcosmic equivalences of state and nationalist identifications, because the values attached to blood and lineage are arbitrary and most often superstitious (e.g. DNA and paternity tests would not be needed if people inherently knew they were related, so perceived genetic relation is a projection). Donna Haraway calls to create a sense of kinship with all entities as persons (a syntactic shift also seen in abolitionist animals rights). Haraway states:

> I think that the stretch and recomposition of kin are allowed by the fact that all earthlings are kin in the deepest sense, and it is past time to practice better care of kinds-as-assemblages (not species one at a time). Kin is an assembling sort of word. All critters share a common 'flesh', laterally, semiotically, and genealogically. Ancestors turn out to be very interesting strangers; kin are unfamiliar (outside what we thought was family or genus), uncanny, haunting, active. Too much for a tiny slogan, I know! Still, try. Over a couple hundred years from now, maybe the human people of this planet can again be numbered 2 or 3 billion or so, while all along the way being part of increasing well-being for diverse human beings and other critters as means and not just ends. So, make kin, not babies! It matters how kin generate kin. (2016: 103)

Haraway's reductionist argument trails those problems of who breeds, but even more problematic is the equivalent question of 'who kins?' Her calls to activist and thought actions are needed in a world of kin walls based on violence and colonialist histories. Yet there remains a sense it is Anthropos who imposes the making of kin, the decisive turn and what that relation would look like. Is making kin an act of grace or a non-consenting forced relation? Is there such a possibility to extricate kin from kind, which Haraway cites as coming from Shakespeare's punning of the single etymological root. Kind returns us to the world of division, of species, the imposition of definition which Serres calls a human violence against nature. Serres and Haraway both foster creativity and generative relations as that which is necessary to create a plane of Venus, a territory of love. Yet there is a residual aspect of human decisiveness imposed upon the unlike other which would not resonate with the ahuman focus on our actions and our continuation or extinction, even while of course my insistence on 'we' and 'our' is a species homogenization and obviously non-consensual. Under current conditions in the world, it remains humans who impose, upon other humans, upon nonhuman animals. The least empowered human remains in higher consideration, legally if not actually, than the nonhuman. Human cessation of species can divert all of our attention to all lives which remain, human and nonhuman, and the overwhelming need for specific and attentive care each needs. Ahumanism fosters symbioses with all entities (or what Haraway and abolitionist activism would call 'persons', human and nonhuman) without imposing a relation of kinship with them. This critique is not of Haraway's ideas, but more of the tendency in Anthropos to relegate new entities into old diachronic structures which Haraway herself criticizes in *Simians, Cyborgs and Women* (1991), especially in her coining of the 'amodern'. Haraway's joy in reinvigorating and proliferating stories which challenge the singular narratives of history and thus futurity differ from ahumanism's seeking escape routes from any stories being told which may risk assimilating or incorporating non-consenting persons/entities. Both techniques embrace strangeness, hybridity, unlike and unnatural participations. Ahumanism dies drowning in the unknowable other, a delicious and uncomfortable refusal to seek to know. The unknown and unknowable but also the unseen, the never perceived and adamantly never seeking to perceive the other, who, after Irigaray, like us must be allowed to be born to themselves without our imposed ontology or epistemology to vindicate their liberty. Making kin retains a dialectic of enforced relation that then validates ethical consideration. Can we go beyond this very human idea of relationality between two or more entities or kinds, unravel ourselves without the need for the other to ever exist through our perception, our language, our identification, our storytelling, our Martian impositions?

The psychological institutional relationship between analyst and patient is a reflection of many other resonant versions of anthropocentric relations – the master/slave, the parent/child, and particularly the human/nonhuman or more generally, man/nature. All primary dominant entities both structure and impose the system of knowledge upon the other, while the other is seen as somehow failing, 'sick' or in need of that system imposed. It can be argued all primary dominant terms simply perform their duties of rectification for their own benefit even under a rubric of benevolent ordering of disorder. The second term, a differend, must be incorporated or is destined to failure and death, but blamed themselves for their own resistance to be incorporated. There is no option of an escape route offered. The relation could even be pushed to the philosopher or theorist and the world or object of study, say, for example, the kin-maker and the made-kin, or the ahumanist antinatalist and the human species. What would my own defence against this claim be? Perhaps, that traditionally the antinatalist, especially the woman, is considered the 'sick' party in need of re-incorporation into normal human socio-physiological functioning. Perhaps that I am a traitor to my species and am myself under the interrogators spotlight to recant my call for human extinction. These simply reverse the dialectic while retaining the isomorphic power imbalance. What I request is for the 'what else is there' or the 'what then' of how we can create, foster symbioses and relate to seen and unseen others, human, nonhuman and the environment. It sometimes feels to me as if humans (again especially women) are only offered one route, some see as an escape route, others a prison, which is reproduction. Removing reproduction from the singular diachronic narrative, as Haraway would call it, of heteronormative anthropocentric subject history (birth, marriage, breeding, death) makes all of life escape routes. We queers know this, already liberated from the narrative if we have escaped the interrogator's lamp.

Guattari's reconfiguration of the relationship between interlocuter and other (patient, child, citizen, whatever) is transversality. Guattari discusses Freud's identification of anxiety as born, not of danger, but the impossible conversation between the ego-ideal and the super-ego (2015: 105). Many of philosophy's unanswerable questions are borne of what Bataille calls our accursed share which resonates with the conversion of danger to anxiety, from necessary energy expenditure to excess energy which transforms itself via anthropocentric rituals into, often, damage to the Earth and excess greed for the self. The claim we need to reproduce can be reduced to an immortality anxiety, equivalent to the excessive accumulation of wealth we see hoarded by ageing patriarchal figureheads and oligarchs, or the quieter leaving behind of art, of writing, all the horrible and beautiful excesses we form to deny the banality of death or extend our life afterwards. Anxiety prevents life unfurling as lived, exchanging the duration for accumulation of signifiers, yet in late capitalism, this is the way normal life is lived: through children and things bringing meaning to what is assumed to be a meaningless life, suggesting life without breeding or objects is inherently without meaning, conversely suggesting life has meaning. Neither is correct, as nature is amoral, so life is neither meaningful or meaningless, it is life. The obsession we have with legacies of all kinds is more about making our deaths meaningful than our lives, investing anxiety into death alone, which is why Guattari calls the impossible conversation between the super-ego and the ego-ideal a death drive repetition: 'The persistence is really a repetition, the expression of a death instinct. By seeing it merely as a continuity, we miss the question implied in it. It seems natural to prolong the resolution of the Oedipus complex into a "successful" integration into society' (2015: 105). Big 'L' signifier 'Life', that which society super-ego demands we live with excess of meaning, includes breeding both as fulfilling the mono-narrative of life and as control over death, which the ideal-ego repudiates:

> But surely it would be more to the point to see that the way anxiety persists must be linked with the dependence of the individual on the collectivity described by Freud. The fact is that, barring some total change in the social order, the castration complex can never be satisfactorily resolved, since contemporary society persists in giving it an unconscious function of social regulation. There becomes a more and more pronounced incompatibility between the function of the father, as the basis of a possible solution for the individual of the problems of identification inherent in the structure of the conjugal family, and the demands of industrial societies, in which an integrating model of the father/king/ god pattern tends to lose any effectiveness outside the sphere of mystification. This is especially evident in phases of social regression, as for instance when fascist, dictatorial regimes or regimes of personal, presidential power give rise to imaginary phenomena of collective pseudo-phallicization that end in a ridiculous totemization by popular vote of a leader. (2015: 105)

In this account, by extension, compulsion to reproduce is a phallocentric impulse seeking to resolve the lack of logic, which the lack of (phallic) power fosters, but which the ideal-ego craves and the super-ego seeks with which to belong. The romantic, blurry and cinematic mystical images of fascism by which the right strives to seduce through a perceived national Oedipalization of the state, giving control to the powerless by making themselves their own minor kings over oppressed and marginalized groups while in awe of the king/God/father, is a familiar and frightening warning. It would seem sacrilegious to think this of reproduction, except the demand to reproduce within traditional families is the foundation of many religions, Western and other patriarchal cultures and the 'mystical' nature of childbirth has turned much of social media into a postmodern gallery of Madonna with child posts, blogs and huge industrialized investment in reproductive technology which prioritizes genetic reproduction over care of children already in existence and the millions of animals tortured in medical experiments for reproductive technological 'advancement'. About what are we anxious? For a mystical idea that 'something' uniquely genetically 'I' will be passed down and create an eternity. The rhetoric seems frighteningly similar to that of neo-fascist nationalism. Add to this anxiety-driven death displacement – love for one's 'own' seeks the death of the other while concealing the anxiety which is one's own death drive – the obligation to love as one which is supposedly unconditional. Love becomes impossible both with or without genetic filiation – love due to genetic relation is conditional, lack of love due to lack of genetic filiation is unethical. Love needs no legitimacy, of nation or relation. We all have anxiety, as a bioevolutionary aspect of life it can be argued all organisms have it (though the word *anxiety* holds anthropocentric qualities). Human anxieties over death and legacy, over the meaning (meaningful and/or meaningless) of life, the same questions of why are we here, what happens after death, these are all questions belonging to Anthropos. What can we do with anxiety when we ask different questions to Anthropos? Could removing or reorienting the anxiety which becomes a death drive that leads to both reproduction and nationalism create new trajectories of care, a making strange of kinship as consensual or distant or gracious?

Without death-drive anxiety, without the late capitalist *want*, without the questions and drives of Anthropos, how can we live? When we enter into a becoming which repudiates being the patient to the analyst, or the child to the parent, or the citizen to the state, thereby also removing the desire to be in the position of power of analyst, parent, state, we enter into a becoming-with, the symbioses. Guattari calls this shift from transference transversality:

> As a temporary support set up to preserve, at least for a time, the object of our practice, I propose to replace the ambiguous idea of the institutional transference with a new concept: transversality in the group. The idea of transversality is opposed to: (a) verticality, as described in the organogramme of a pyramidal structure (leaders, assistants, etc.); (b) horizontality, as it exists in the disturbed wards of a hospital, or, even more, in the senile wards; in other words a state of affairs in which things and people fit in as best they can with the situation in which they find themselves. (2015: 112)

In transversality, 'all movement is from the summit to the base' (2015: 113). Were humans to shift life lived as if the Earth were for us, instead listening as if we are for Earth, we could minutely and massively change our dancing with and around the base which is all nonhuman life and environments. We could begin to extract ourselves instead of the devastating extraction mining by which we annihilate the Earth. Being interpellated or indoctrinated into anthropocentric narratives involves an obedience to the many patriarchs who reflect the practitioner – church and its priests, state and its leaders, the family and its father, the nation/race and its icon. Just as the analyst reincorporates the patient into normalcy, so too the price of being kin and incorporated into groups of belonging is a continuation of the narratives of kin through conversion, production and reproduction. Guattari states: 'Henceforth, the authority of this social reality will base its survival on the establishment of an irrational morality in which punishment will be justified simply by a law of blind repetition, since it cannot be explained by any ethical legality' (2015: 104). Were I brave enough I could go so far as to say reproduction, following Guattari's critique of the hierarchical pyramid of transference, is an ideological and capitalist Ponzi/multi-level marketing scheme. However, I will suspend that possibly outrageous claim, suffice to say it follows the death instinct as an expression of anxiety, perception of fulfilment and belonging, within an economic model of desire more than an ecosophical model of undifferentiated love. From the collective perspective, the drive to reproduce is often based on a need to reincorporate into one's own family/tribe/group while simultaneously having something for oneself, thus fitting in as best one can within the perceived routes Anthropos allows for its own perpetuation. It is tragic to think that escape routes from the genetic demands of Anthropos produce phenomenal unlike and unlikely kinship with myriad entities, human and nonhuman, from the millions of children and adults in need of fostering and care to the many rescue and domestic nonhuman animals desperate for care, to the wild animals and environments who benefit from the gracious care of technological and scientific investment in allowing habitats to thrive and rectifying decimation of species and terrains, polluted oceans and mined lakes. Transversal kinship spans the intimacy of the immediate rescue to the grand scale collective attempt to care for distant, nameless, faceless humans, animals and environments assisted with liberty and thriving. When all is kin, the Earth is delivered from being a series of territories of war, Orders of Mars, becoming terrains of love, Orders of Venus, a series of conceptual complexities (as Deleuze and Guattari in *What Is Philosophy* remind us, all concepts are problems), no longer friend or foe or even a demand to love the other in spite of not being kin. Antinatalism is the very antithesis of violence and exclusion of humans (after all, how many years and how much conceptual initiative will it take to care for the Earth right now?) It is, akin to Guattari's transversality of the anxiety of the death drive in the super-ego, a movement of positive initiative: 'its object is to try to change the data accepted by the super-ego into a new kind of acceptance of "initiative," rendering pointless the blind social demand for a particular kind of castrating procedure to the exclusion of anything else' (2015: 106).

For Guattari, transversality delivers the group of patients from dependence on the institute and language to escaping through independence via decipherment (of language and action) and collectivity without participant recognition and hence a form of tribal totem and taboo. He states:

> The key questions have been asked before likes and dislikes have hardened, before sub-groups have formed, at the level from which the group's potential creativity springs – though generally all creativity is strangled at birth by its complete rejection of nonsense, the group preferring to spend its time mouthing clichés about its 'terms of reference', and thus closing off

the possibility of ever saying anything real, that is, anything that could have any connection with other strands of human discourse, historical, scientific, aesthetic or whatever. (2015: 108)

Resonant with Serres's critique of the violence of recognition, and perception slaughtering creation, Guattari emphasizes relation before the crystallization of signification. Were we as living organisms to be and act in reality – real activism, real connectivity – before identifying for whom and thus why we act, the ecosophical networks of the Earth could flourish devoid of warring conflicts between signifiers of nation, state, family, all those other institutes Guattari critiques as equivalent to the hospital for their psychological indoctrinating enslavement to arbitrary anthropocentric, nationalistic, ideological signifiers. For Guattari, critically epistemic discretion too becomes transversal, where art and science are able to create together. History exists without demanding a mirrored futurity:

> Take the case of a political group 'condemned by history': what sort of desire could it live by other than one forever turning in upon itself? It will have incessantly to be producing mechanisms of defence, of denial, of repression, group phantasies, myths, dogmas and so on. Analysis of these can only lead to discovering that they express the nature of the group's death wish in its relation to the buried and emasculated historic instincts of enslaved masses, classes or nationalities. (2015: 108)

The human patients of Guattari's institute in antinatalist radical compassionate ecosophy include all organisms beyond species, as transversality 'tends to be achieved when there is maximum communication among different levels and, above all, in different meanings' (2015: 111). Can humans accept that reproduction as giving meaning to life reflects that life has no meaning and the question itself is unanswerable; hence, the answer of reproducing simply repeats the vacuity of the question, a death drive perpetuating the actual death of the planet? Can our desire for meaning transcend family, nation and species barriers, as well as discursive barriers, to transform into a work of non-hierarchical care? As a species, can we face Guattari's call to transversality: 'It is my hypothesis that there is nothing inevitable about the bureaucratic self-mutilation of a subject group, or its unconscious resort to mechanisms that militate against its potential transversality. They depend, from the first moment, on an acceptance of the risk – which accompanies the emergence of any phenomenon of real meaning – of having to confront irrationality, death, and the otherness of the other' (2015: 118). Nothing dies in the death of the human species, but the potentialities of life when care is rerouted are infinite.

7

Goth culture, occulture, aesthetic death culture

We are nearing the end of some of the ways death activism might look. Real-world activisms that we face with terror and love can be exhausting even in hope. Just as Chapter 1 was a playful dance with aesthetics to ease in, as a fulcrum balance chapter to the Danse Macabre, this chapter will discuss the enigmatic and largely similarly aesthetic role of death in contemporary areas of the goth and occult communities, encompassing primarily the last forty years. For most of us even in times of deep grief, apprehending death feels more like the impossibility of our inability to understand absence when another has been so fully present in our material lives and experiences. Death in these instances can seem like an exhaustingly incomprehensible concept, while our beloved are corporeally concealed or reconstructed as effigies of both life and themselves. The inaccessibility of death is not finally exposed when we encounter its affects. That indeed could make grief easier. Arguably, with exceptions such as deeply traumatic experiences, for example genocide, undercover animal investigations or personal encounters with violence and murder, death is largely conceptual. A thing to think about, a looming ultimately unsolvable problem, a Real which converts to aesthetic even in times of trauma, as evinced by the power of representational footage to move us without impacting the reality of death as something which could possibly be surmountable. Much aesthetic navigation of death involves surmounting, catharsis or bearing witness to the unrepresentable. Death activism works from the perspective of activism being essential to the work, so art is part of activism, a feature of catalysts to enhancing immanent focal needs for death democracy, care, compassion and distribution. Such art belongs with activism undifferentiated and is less divided into a death aesthetic from its source in the Real. This chapter, like Chapter 1, is less attentive to trauma and catharsis, real-world activism and confronting death, and more interested in two elements of what I would call death cultures, primarily in Western culture but which have been exported globally – goth subculture and occulture. I focus on these for three purposes. First, the divide between the anthropologist and the subject-turned-object of analysis in death studies carries a large risk of totemic Western fetishization of othered cultures as somehow more deeply insightful in their 'primitivism' and 'animism' or simply presented as oddities. Goth and occulture are cultures in which I am deeply enmeshed, so I place my own self within the environment, preventing any colonizing dialectic. The second is that both goth and occulture embrace and emerge via a 'death rhythm' of cyclical rebirth, which sees their perceived transgressive aspects incorporated, diluted and spat out by neo-capitalism when their marketability is exhausted, yet we who I could call perpetual neophytes find ourselves objects of analysis varyingly every five or ten years based on whatever has ignited a re-trending of the cultures, be it fashion, film and television, or music. Finally and pragmatically, this book, as all activisms, needs a touch of fun. While goths and Western occultists can take themselves altogether very seriously, both demand a highly imaginative aspect of play, experiment and dismantling and recreating oneself in various ways. There is nothing too dreadfully serious about goth or occultism, though each can include elements taken seriously, such as passion for and exhaustive knowledge of music and film in the former, and a lifelong deep commitment to learning and practice in the latter. My discussion of death within these cultures is decidedly queer, so even their labelling should not be adhered to with too much gravity, although the perpetual battle between the authentic and inauthentic neophyte is definitely one which is apparent in both arenas, to the amusement of many. Goth and occultism take both seriously and lightly the necessity of looking and being alive as a sovereign subject imbued with a healthy recognizable signification and subjectification, asking what value is found in 'passing' as mainstream, aesthetically pleasing, adherent to state, religious or Oedipal institutes and these elements they share with queer culture. The chapter is designed to be a brief play with the death aspects of these two cultures, and for more exhaustive studies, histories or descriptions, they will not be forthcoming beyond the peculiar status of death within their remit. Because death can be taken lightly, playfully and as fun, which is the goal of the focus of death activism's take on goth and occulture.

Before schematically defining what I mean by goth and occulture, their crucial shared aspect is important to mention. While death in art shares an aesthetic focus with death in goth and occulture, what the latter devote themselves to is the lived experience of experiments in death and where the self is taken as the object. The art of goth and of occulture is living as, with and through the focal concepts. Exteriorizing the concepts into a 'work' occurs in the creation of art objects – music, paintings, totemic objects, rituals – but these objects are expressive affects of the intensities which flow through individuals and collectives, such as during a group ritual or a concert or gig. Critical to thinking about the subcultural aspects of goth and occulture in relation with death is that they are corporeally and materially self-involved. The division of exterior and interior, of art and self and world, of subject and object, is involuted, folded and blurred. Ironically, perhaps, the relation of self and world within the goth subculture is less gothic and more baroque, a multi-pleated series of enfolded aspects and intensities. The Kantian notion of aesthetics being ascendent through the imperceptibility of artifice, through a work's independent higher state of being, its perfection in itself, 'independent of charm and emotion' (Kant 2005: 43), independent of any concept or judgement, is corporeal and ritual within goth and occulture. Paul Gruyer emphasises the freedom of the artwork (1994: 275–276), which for the purposes of this book could be understood as freedom from Anthropos. Kant's critique is for art and against judgement, which frees art's affects beyond intent or comprehension. This could have a parallel drawn with the goth or occultist within their scene, external to what we call 'normie' culture (a largely apocryphal sense that there is a normal culture judging us, even though there is but it is not monolithic). But it would be naïve to claim the self as an aesthetic work is independent of its rhizomatic relationality with its immediate, extended and increasingly digital environmental affects and expressions. So the subcultures fail at being integrated into a Kantian framework because we do not exist independent of our own artifice and find in it a performative and indulgent element of pleasure. Not that I was attempting to succeed but to describe a different kind of use of the term *aesthetic*. Another obvious failure is the way in which art functions to work through affects. There is often a sense that art should take death seriously or the purpose of art is to expiate serious affects. For example:

> Art does not mourn death nor does it, as an aesthetic act, commemorate death. It does not attempt to control death nor does it try to understand it as we understand the laws of aerodynamics or the aetiology of a disease. In contrast with all these, in the arts we find ourselves confronting the event of death. This is not to say that art is a rehearsal for death, for a rehearsal is never the genuine event. It is rather that through the arts we have an actual encounter with the fact of death, engaging ourselves with its human reality and realizing some of the many conditions, forms, and nuances of that experience. (Berleant 2004: 130)

Like the danse macabre art of Chapter 1, the purpose of aesthetics for goth and occulture is to have fun with a serious subject, to (both metaphorically and literally) dance where we feel atrophied by death. As a final proviso, I am also not delving into the sociology of subcultures because, while these are in some ways subcultures and in others not, the sociologist/group-for-study dialectic has power dissymmetry and an old-fashioned lack of immersion which is discursively violating and is indebted to colonizing practices that have been performed far more violently with other non-Western cultures, and which have no place in a transversal baroque relation.

Baroque goth death aesthetic

Popular culture studies have demarcated subcultures based primarily on the two intersections of music and 'youth' (simultaneous with the advent of 'the teenager') since the 1950s. In this sense, goths belong to the 1980s (beginning c. 1977, continuing until today) just as Mods and Teds belong to the 1950s, Hippies belong to the 1960s and Glam kids, Ska Kids, Punks and Disco

Queens to the 1970s. Each bleed into other decades and other sub-subcultures ad infinitum. The transience and blurriness of subcultures in resistance to attempts to define them lend their affects well to being clinamen collectives, certain stabilized vibratory bodies shimmering together in more or less volatile and incandescent ways. The 1980s included the quickening of goth as one of its subcultures, and like all subcultures, its name is both a misnomer and a somewhat reflective label applied to many who have little in common but who, in general, were collected from a music and youth scene. For the purposes of this chapter that is sufficient discussion of subculture (the Order of Venus is anti-sociology), except to add that in 2023, three popular culture books were published on goth as a subcultural music scene by three authors involved in that scene (Unsworth 2023, Robb 2023 and Tolhurst 2023), evincing persistence among generations, from original 'trad' goths to so-called 'baby-bats'. For the purposes of death activism, goth is a fascinating punctuation in culture for four reasons. First, both popular and various self-identifying goths interpret the aesthetic as looking dead; second, this dead look is highly gender ambiguous if not gender irrelevant, goth being a particularly queer identity both aesthetically and within spaces such as gigs and clubs; third, unlike many other subcultures, goth has not been broken and dissipated by shattered ideals or musical irrelevance; rather, it has become a global aesthetic with new music and new artists each year, in spite of looking dead; fourth, goth appears in its aesthetic to embrace death with joy, with imaginative flair, being a decidedly optimistic performance of 'deathiness'. These are not entirely separate tenets, so I will address them simultaneously. Goths, for the uninitiated, currently and globally, register to other goths and to the world as stereotypically pale of face. Critically, goths of colour are included in this; pale does not mean white and while the goth scene has as much racism as other scenes, it is not exclusionary and pale means sickly or dead-looking. The word 'pale' exists in relation only to what should be 'healthy', which may also explain why the goth scene is highly inclusive of disability. Goths can have ratty hair or no hair; what seems to matter is the look being somewhat 'dishevelled' even in a polished version, such as teased hair or giant hair more akin to the 1960s teen beehives or a John Waters movie coupled with 1980s crimped hair. *Dishevelled* is a forensic term to describe the autopsy procedure, so my use of the term cements the relation between aesthetics and death deliberately. Here is where the connection becomes strange, or perhaps more correctly 'queer' though – goths typically wear dark make-up and clothing can be anything from 'fresh from the grave' torn fishnets to high Victorian frills, reflecting the influences of punk coupled with an imagined connection with the Victorian obsession with death meeting cinematic representations of zombies and vampires. Goths definitely look dead while not looking like dead people. They are real-life 'undead', kin to vampires, werewolves, zombies.

Goth takes what it means to look dead as an imagined phantasy of the romanticism of death at its extreme. All genders partake in a selection of stylistic elements, and the finished look utterly defies the faciality biunivocalizations of gender, race, sexuality, often age. The only selection seems to be dead/alive, or as minoritarians, (q)we(e)irdo/normal. Choosing to embrace the goth aesthetic may seem obnoxious in comparison to those minoritarian tells which may not 'pass' such as being BIPoC, non-cis, visibly disabled or a woman, but expressing one's persona aesthetically as a goth is not, contrary to much analysis, an act of rebellion or transgression alone, but an act of creative connectivity with one's own sense of self and others. The risks posed to goths is materially violent, as seen in such a rise in incidences of aggression towards goths that reached its most tragic moment with the murder of Sophie Lancaster in 2007, leading Manchester Police in 2013 to become the first force to make crimes perpetrated against people for looking alternative a hate crime. Goths are also blamed for everything from Columbine to Satanic panic, suggesting that the biunivocalization of looking goth weighs heavily on subjectification and signification in criminology. Covertly, some writers on goth have celebrated uncritically the 'beauty' of the 'dark aesthetic' in predictably heteronormative ways (Hodkinson 2002 and Baddeley 2017) or from a musical and less-mansplaining way (Scharf 2011). What remains is a persistent fascination with explaining goth or having to explain ourselves or any other such adherence to the 'why' of embracing a dark, dead aesthetic. Explicating the significations of goth from the outside holds no purpose for death activism. I am interested in exploring goth as a form of death activism from the inside, simply adventuring around the desire for a queer death aesthetic that is evident in goth.

Like corpses, goths are docile. Unlike corpses, goths are docile in the Foucauldian sense. Between being murdered and causing Columbine in criminology, being more (Young 2006) and simultaneously less (Phillipov 2006 Taubert and Kandasamy 2006) likely to self harm in psychiatry, and being less and more seeking to belong (Gaia 2006) in sociology, goths are enforced by and forced into epistemological institutes to discursively explain the inexplicable. Technically not a queer subculture, goths are nonetheless queer in encompassing everything and nothing; all evil yet benevolently macabre, mentally ill yet stable in spite of looking odd. Why goths pique analysis so much is a question for a different book. The capacity to be exemplar of oppositional traits in various epistemes leads me to include goths in an unsurprising collective belonging with the most abject object – the corpse. Abjection, as Kristeva (1982) describes it, shares with both goth and corpse the primary quality of being a non-quality. Taking the opening lines from Kristeva's seminal work, we are immediately given qualities of, not the abject, but how it is experienced by the subject:

NEITHER SUBJECT NOR OBJECT

There looms, within abjection, one of those violent, dark revolts of being, directed against a threat that seems to emanate from an exorbitant outside or inside, ejected beyond the scope of the possible, the tolerable, the thinkable. It lies there, quite close, but it cannot be assimilated. It beseeches, worries, and fascinates desire, which, nevertheless, does not let itself be seduced. Apprehensive, desire turns aside; sickened, it rejects. A certainty protects it from the shameful – a certainty of which it is proud holds on to it. But simultaneously, just the same, that impetus, that spasm, that leap is drawn toward an elsewhere as tempting as it is condemned. Unflaggingly, like an inescapable boomerang, a vortex of summons and repulsion places the one haunted by it literally beside himself. (1982: 1)

Aligning those elements and intensities in which goths are interested is easy regarding abjection's relation with horror. But reading Kristeva's opening lines, it is striking that the subject is not with whom we identify. That would presume the psychiatrist, the sociologist, the criminologist. Guattari's first term of transversality. What happens when we claim the abjection as the experience of self, expressed and felt, externally, internally, within infinite baroque folds of their indeterminability within us and us within the world? Deleuze states the baroque is that which is 'not adjusted to structure' (2001: 29) – 'folds seem to be rid of their supports' (2001: 34). Goths are nostalgic for a gothic sensibility which was never quickened into a consistent definition. Goth is contemporary (1977ish onwards) music youth culture and also fantasies of eighteenth- and nineteenth-century literature, and all ages of horror cinema, and . . . and . . . and . . . (an indeterminable number of additions) Goths are the abnormal/pathological (to the idea of being a normal/healthy subject) and dark (aesthetically, thematically, physically) revolt(ings)s (against Matthew Arnold's idea of sweetness and light, truth and beauty) which seduce ourselves to ourselves. We are the undefinable object, just as queer reclaims its own indefinability converted from insult to an insult against classification. Can goths reclaim abject for our own tactically? Of the baroque Deleuze states it is 'form–matter . . . but temporal modulation that implies as much the beginnings of a continuous variation of matter as a continuous development of form . . . The object here is manneristic, not essentializing: It becomes an event' (2001: 19). Queer and abject are not synonymous, and associating a term like *gay* taken in its literal sense with the perceived deathbound misery of goth seems a stretch. Except that misery is imposed from without as an arbitrary perception. Goths are miserable optimists, jolly pessimists, asexual seducers, blood-drenched suppurating vampires, too much and meagre corporeally. Events of tenebrous affect. Goth really can be reduced to a crepuscular aesthetic with a deviation and reclassification for every individual example. Of baroque desire, Deleuze states it is 'occasions for meanders and detours' (Deleuze 2001: 37), reminiscent of Deleuze and Guattari's escape routes for minoritarian becoming-animal. We find ourselves through film and music in homes in which we belong but which never existed – unheimlich but more florid. From German Expressionist horror through Universal, Hammer and via European films of vampires, ghosts, werewolves, somnambulists and mad scientists, the beauty of disgust and pleasure of horror permeates goth. So too the transformation from antagonistic punk to entrancing goth in the music and image of bands such as The Damned, Bauhaus, Siouxsie and the Banshees as very few examples (and only from England, designated as the birthplace of goth but certainly not the only place from whence it rose from the crypt) created soundscapes and poetry that merged historical fantasies of monsters with experimental fashion and subcultural belonging. We find pleasure in fear – the film or song is not catharsis but succubus. The crepuscular aesthetic includes an ambiguous trembling jouissance at disgust and unpalatability. It may be hinted at by Freud's Uncanny. Freud writes:

> It is only rarely that a psychoanalyst feels impelled to investigate the subject of aesthetics even when aesthetics is understood to mean not merely the theory of beauty, but the theory of the qualities of feeling. . . . The subject of the 'uncanny' is a province of this kind. It undoubtedly belongs to all that is terrible – to all that arouses dread and creeping horror; it is equally certain, too, that the word is not always used in a clearly definable sense, so that it tends to coincide with whatever excites dread. Yet we may expect that it implies some intrinsic quality which justifies the use of a special name. One is curious to know what this peculiar quality is which allows us to distinguish as 'uncanny' certain things within the boundaries of what is 'fearful'. (1955: 217)

Freud continues with a slew of adjectives: 'Unheimlich, uneasy, eerie, bloodcurdling; "Seeming almost unheimlich and 'ghostly' to him." "I had already long since felt an unheimlich, even gruesome feeling." "Feels an unheimlich horror." "Unheimlich and motionless like a stone-image." "The unheimlich mist called hill-fog." "These pale youths are unheimlich and are brewing heaven knows what mischief"' (1955: 219). The pale youths alone could be describing Bram Stoker's bloofer ladies of *Dracula* or goths of any decade. More prevalent is the insinuation that these adjectives, qualities and intensities are malignant, mentally unhealthy or at least not to be embraced. The contribution to becoming-abject/uncanny is the ambiguity of Freud's definition of intensity, and the interiorization of the external threat which, in its homely unhomeliness, is still a place where the body dwells, more than the body in which the self dwells simultaneously within and without.

Kristeva claims abjection besets us but without an 'it' with which it besets as. From a death activism perspective, could we, the becoming-dead aesthetically, be acknowledging the myth of sovereign subjectivity which besets Anthropos, we as selves not invested in the imago or refined neo capitalist self, haunted by our own never-arrived ego-ideals and so living as ghosts or harpies or spectres and indulging in the playful experimentation with the abjection at the heart of the demand for being a human subject, rather than an ahuman organism? Freud states of the uncanny it is nothing more than an intensity. Whether goth is thought of as a style of music or dress or taste in film and literature, whether it is trad goth, neo-goth, a subculture or fractal sub-subculture, only intensities resonate beyond and without classifications, whispers of intersections which speak of decay and delight simultaneously that ensures we who doubt the impenetrability of desire for power can stave off death.

> The corpse (or cadaver: *cadere*, to fall), that which has irremediably come a cropper, is cesspool, and death; it upsets even more violently the one who confronts it as fragile and fallacious chance. A wound with blood and pus, or the sickly, acrid smell of sweat, of decay, does not signify death. In the presence of signified death – a flat encephalograph, for instance – I would understand, react or accept. No, as in true theater, without makeup or masks, refuse and corpses show me what I permanently thrust aside in order to live. These body fluids, this defilement, this shit are what life withstands, hardly and with difficulty, on the part of death. There, I am at the border of my condition as a living being. My body extricates itself, as being alive, from that border. Such wastes drop so that I might live, until, from loss to loss, nothing remains in me and my entire body falls beyond the limit – cadere, cadaver. If dung signifies the other side of the border, the place where I am not and which permits me to be, the corpse, the most sickening of wastes, is a border that has encroached upon everything. It is no longer I who expel, 'I' is expelled. (Kristeva 1982: 3–4)

Performance art, representational documentary, frontline activism and trauma show us the real corpse. It is eviscerating, bearing witness to the unthinkably present which goes so far beyond representationality and symbol that even when witnessing death, death cannot be seen. Often this leads to secondary trauma, to catatonia, to atrophy, at least to grief. In between this and aesthetics is the taboo of corpse concealment in banal death, so as to conceal the absence of subjectivity of a loved one or turn it into an idol or effigy. These are not uncanny, playful, aesthetic deaths. To play with death, to enjoy inhabiting a vacant corpse, is part of the spectrum of death that lives and jokes and reminds us that death is as individual as life and is not part of a historical or familial event. The baroque occupation of playing with/at becoming-abject in goth may be as purposeless as the aesthetic aspect of death but, unlike the male poets and painters who only fetishize dead women to affirm their living gaze, goths fetishize their own deathbound presence as spectacle involuted upon itself to collapse every diachronous binary term. I look at me. I look at me dead. But the dead do not look like me. I breach life and death, succubus and siren, dream and materiality, and the moebian band of play continues so that death belongs with experiment, with encounters with the unthinkable in excess of trauma. Goths do not wear masks or make-up, because we are not metaphors for corpses; we are living beings, in our becoming-corpse mediating, occupying and being the borderlands of how we aesthetically, materially encounter thinking death as a vitalistic creative force.

Occulture and death practice/practising for death

Apparently, occulture is currently enjoying heightened popularity, a claim also made of the much younger phenomenon of goth. Also like goth, occulture since its (far more ancient) inception has never gone away, but its visibility rises and falls depending on its capacity for conversion to marketability and neo-capital assimilation for consumption. Occulture is an enormous field, much as one would use the term *philosophy*, although has only recently entered serious academic study due to being perceived as aberrant – anti-scientific, superstitious, delusional or simply weird. Academic occultists in the last fifteen years have increasingly come out of the esoteric closet, and unsurprisingly some are very queer in every sense of the word. This section is a brief and tactical exploration, as was the section above on goth, of one aspect of occulture and its relationship with death as a form of activist practice, collective and individual. This is the area of chaos magick but can be applied to a number of other occult practices just as many other occult areas, especially paganism and goddess worship, have applications for ecological activism. An important proviso arises in differentiating chaos magick, the stream of magick inspired by the work of early twentieth-century artist and visionary Austin Osman Spare, from that of twenty-first-century meme culture and the rise of the racist neo-folk right, both of which claim attachments to chaos magick in different forms. Like all neither-good-nor-evil practices, chaos magick is defined by its expressions and affects, not through a claim to essence, so the chaos magick in this section follows a particular, and queer, trajectory. I will begin with a long but valuable quote from Saidiya Hartman, who brings together the occult, the baroque, queering, revolt and the escape routes of creative paths for the minoritarian, here speaking of the lives of young Black women:

> Wayward, related to the family of words: errant, fugitive, recalcitrant, anarchic, willful, reckless, troublesome, riotous, tumultuous, rebellious and wild. To inhabit the world in ways inimical to those deemed proper and respectable, to be deeply aware of the gulf between where you stayed and how you might live. Waywardness: the avid longing for a world not ruled by master, man or the police. The errant path taken by the leaderless swarm in search of a place better than here. The social poesis that sustains the dispossessed. Wayward: the unregulated movement of drifting and wandering; sojourns without a fixed destination, ambulatory possibility, interminable migrations, rush and flight, black locomotion; the everyday struggle to live free. The attempt to elude capture by never settling. Not the master's tools, but the ex-slave's fugitive gestures, her traveling shoes. Waywardness articulates the paradox of cramped creation, the entanglement of escape and confinement, flight and captivity. Wayward: to wander, to be unmoored, adrift, rambling, roving, cruising, strolling, and seeking. To claim the right to opacity. To strike, to riot, to refuse. To love what is not loved. To be lost to the world. It is the practice of the social otherwise, the insurgent ground that enables new possibilities and new vocabularies; it is the lived experience of enclosure and segregation, assembling and huddling together. It is the directionless search for a free territory; it is a practice of making and relation that enfolds within the policed boundaries of the dark ghetto; it is the mutual aid offered in the open-air prison. It is a queer resource of black survival. It is a beautiful experiment in how-to-live. Waywardness is a practice of possibility at a time when all roads, except

the ones created by smashing out, are foreclosed. It obeys no rules and abides no authorities. It is unrepentant. It traffics in occult visions of other worlds and dreams of a different kind of life. Waywardness is an ongoing exploration of what might be; it is an improvisation with the terms of social existence, when the terms have already been dictated, when there is little room to breathe, when you have been sentenced to a life of servitude, when the house of bondage looms in whatever direction you move. It is the untiring practice of trying to live when you were never meant to survive. (2019: 227–8)

Herself an occult visionary, Hartman's influence on contemporary occulture derives from her extraordinary refusal of traditional concepts of transcendence in politics, philosophy and artistic practice, which in Western esotericism aspires to the typical Vitruvian godhead, transcending the flesh while remaining, paradoxically, adamantly within white male representation. Her concept of enfolding speaks of a baroque self and collective indivisible, while her waywardness is an activity of determined intent liberated from preformed narratives of how-to-be liberated, embracing chaos as the emergent potentiality of as-yet-unformed and perpetually unforming leaderless swarms who have repudiated the myth of equality through verisimilitude. Hartman's is an empathic chaos, a logical chaos, a chaos of refusal and positive material imagination, antagonistic to the use of the term *chaos* in psychology which insinuates malevolent conditions, of family and state. Order is the enemy for minoritarian politics, because it subjugates through signification and subjectification. If chaos is the enemy of order, then chaos minoritarianism is the enemy of ordered majoritarianism, at its worst, fascism. The very use of 'chaos' in chaos magick is therefore misrepresented in current examples by the right, because they ultimately seek to annihilate potential wayward behaviour and wayward swarms. Chaos for the alt-right is a distraction technique towards an atrophied end goal of hyperreal and compulsory order. Chaos magick for the queer wayward is a proliferation of escape routes, lines of flight, intensities by which one is occupied, modes of subjectivity as fluid and multiple simultaneously, making chaos of linear time and nationality space through durational immanences and hybrid becomings.

On a practical level this is enacted through various forms of ritual, utilizing dramaturgy, which can be anything from public demonstrations to private solitary meditations. What is shared across all rituals, and what differentiates chaos magick from intent based esoteric practice, is that chaos magick is increasingly against results. In twentieth-century magick tradition, such as Spare's chaos and Crowley's Thelema, will is understood as a Nietzschean force (Spinoza's *potentia*, Foucault's puissance) that first requires the undoing of self. Other forms of magic require a self who utilizes power (Spinoza's *potestas*, Foucault's *pouvoir*) to achieve predicted outcomes. This is a tremendous oversimplification necessary in such a small section. Suffice to say that popular perception insinuates there is a black/left hand path magic and a white/right hand path magic usually based on the intent (will/power) of the sorcerer and the outcome (malevolent/benevolent) of the intent via the ritual (black/white) and servitors (demons or mischievous gods/angels or good gods) utilized. While this whole system was long ago debunked by most fields of occult practice and is popular only in the realm of Wheatley-esque fiction, Hollywood and tele-evangelists, breaking down this perception shows clearly that chaos, like most occulture, first takes the collapse, involution and dissipation of bifurcations and then the dismissal of pseudo-capitalist narratives of ritual=outcome as given.

Chaos magick, like most occulture, is aligned in these presumptions with non-Western traditions of, for example, Tao, Buddhist, Tantra and other non-dualistic philosophies. Hakim Bey calls the work of Chuang Tzu 'chaos linguistics' through its freedom, while the work of Saussure he names 'nihilistic linguistics' due to its vertiginous spiralling into no meaning. According to Bey, in the chaos linguistics evinced by Chuang Tzu 'There IS a name but also there is NO name' (1999: 6). In Spare's *The Book of Pleasure*, 'beyond will and belief is self love' (2011: 59). Spare creates postures for releasing the lifeforce – kia – from what he sees as the tyranny of will (as *pouvoir*) and knowledge and faith. Only through death, primarily the death posture and subsequently the transformation of ego to ecstasy, can creativity be accessed. The death posture is described in detail in 'The Death Posture' chapter of *The Book of Pleasure* (2011: 65–69). It is a chaos magick (before the label was applied) ritual which involves practices that lead to death-like states and which require adept training in self-hypnosis as preparation (as there are risks of actual death). Due to their risk I will not describe them here. The death of self, an experience of a death of being one's own subjectivity and the preliminary trance state are all dissolutions of ego requiring death as the first step in creative self-love. The ecstasies which follow the death of ego are illustrated by Spare with glorious visions of animal human hybrids with multiple gendered organs coalescing into innovated versions of Eliphas Levi's Baphomet, who themself lives by the law of solve/coagula (dissolve and reform). The adoption of Spare as a muse for chaos magick embraces the radically strange, frightening, fascinating and weird (seen in chaos magick's other muse being Lovecraft). These experiences can only be accessed through first destroying the self, dying to one's self, learning to love one's self without signification – but where Lovecraft finds horror, Spare finds ecstasy. Like Serres, Spare sees knowledge as antagonistic to love. To know, to define, even to will in slavery to power, are tenets of the Order of Mars. Self-love loves the self without knowing, far from the transcendental aspirations of knowing oneself of philosophy or new age wellness. It loves the infinity of the self, the germinal Nietzschean child, the *potentia* of nature's organism independent of Anthropos, formed of animal, human, god, insect, molecule, cosmos indistinguishable. While the description could easily seem a slogan for the new age, or Green neo-capitalism ('greenwashing'), or reformed fundamentalist religion of any kind, it aligns at the level of physics with chaos theory, particularly complex chaos theory, seen, for example, in the works of Gaffney (2010), Bell (2006), Ansell-Pearson (1999), Scholtz , feminist ecology and new materialism's embrace of Barad and entanglement at a molecular emergent level.

In *Queerying Occulture* Phil Hine discusses a pseudo-personal history of the heteronormativity of the condensation of various magickal practices of the twentieth century, including paganism, Thelema, Wicca, Tantra, even macrobiotics. Magick of course refers to Aleister Crowley's demarcation of occulture from the trickery of magic, so even though I will be addressing more than just Crowley's Thelema, I will maintain the 'k'. Many established magical orders are adamantly hierarchical, subjectification-driven in ways which reflect both religious and secular state. Part of the subjectification involves the nuances of a perceived necessity of balance, a micro-to-macro cosmic vision which sometimes suggests but often demands a division of that which is feminine from that which is masculine. At worst this can lead to abuse of power through sexual means, at the very least there is a maintenance of gender as one of a binary selection, even though the polarities are attempted to be redeemed in equality and delivered from isomorphism. The in-between-ness integral to pre-Judeo-Christian religious understandings of, for example, paganism and Wicca, or even the chaos which would be presumed to be part of chaos magick, are often either seen as illicit in the name of balance or denied as desires purely on a magickal plane, further separating occultism from 'life'. The latter repudiation is particularly maligned throughout Hine's book due to his defining of queer as an ethical stance. Hine emphasises the binarism of Western esotericism threatens to create opposition where it seeks balance (2023: 6). Against both results-based magick and the enforced heteronormativity in seeking results, Hine details the deep vulnerability of all practitioner's required in opening to potentiality during invocation, using the invocation of Baphomet as an example, both tender and terrifying, while deconstructing a default hyper-masculinity in historic and artistic representations of Baphomet because 'sissy Baphomet' (2023: 74) insinuates simultaneously homosexuality (presumed male because gods are men, even those with breasts) and excess of libidinal feeling over desire for power. Far from the high camp, Hine criticizes Levi's quickening of Baphomet as an amorphous bringer of intensity into form (2023: 76). Invoking Baphomet through Serres's Lucretian physics, the point of least turbulence, the clinamen, of this god(dess) figure, in their perpetual coagula/solve, is their apprehensible form, the most boring moment between dying and becoming. Spare's many images of goat and ram-headed Baphomet creatures end with whisps of smoke which could not be turned into stone icons but remain conceptual personae, different among themselves and to Levi's Baphomet. Cyclical rebirth and redeath (the former a popular term, the latter less so) hinge on each being a difference of a repetition, where no death or birth is the same. What matters is the duration of the dying and the becoming, rotting and reforming. In this sense Inanna would make a better icon than Baphomet. These durations exist within the indivisibility of the dissolving self as indivisible from their environments and other entities. All is balance because each molecule is singular and brings shimmering turbulent forms into temporary imperceptible forces. Narrative is alien to the 'form' and 'force' of entities in queer chaos, making it incommensurable with most religions. When death is frequent, the afterlife and Nirvana are too transcendental and punctuative.

Chaos magick experiments in dying to oneself and being born anew require deep vulnerability and a desire for absolute loss of control which makes them antagonistic to the desire for power typical of many rituals both within and beyond traditional chaos magick as espoused by, for example, Peter Carroll (1987). Carroll's tradition of utilizing Lovecraftian entities relies on a sense, adherent to Lovecraft himself, that Anthropos should be the true form of the sorcerer. The mind-annihilating Elder Gods and Ancient Ones, which for Lovecraft are horrific because they diminish the power and relevance of Anthropos, for Carroll are entered into ritual with in order to absorb their power towards typical results such as wealth and success with the opposite sex. In Hine's *Pseudonomicon* (2004) the terror of Lovecraft's 'gods' (they have neither gender nor technically perceptible Euclidean form) is embraced so that the relevance of the self can be put in service of becoming-otherwise, a kind of death by fear, a queer relationship with the unseeable and unknowable. From the imperceptibly infinite to the domestically ordinary, Hine devotes a chapter of *Queerying Chaos* to the queerness of a kiss, storytelling the biography of this most ordinary act in opening the world to being a queer person in a heteronormative scene and society. No virgins on sacrificial alters, no rampant sodomites engaged in Sadean transgressions, cliches and the ordinariness of prejudice are far less chaotic than what is nearly available to catalyse our dissolving states and our self-love.

Feminist occultists also share a history of storytelling of libidinal becomings with entities. The domestic yet explicit marriages Ida Craddock (2017) advocated for with angelic entities saw her banned for obscenity, institutionalized and ultimately resulting in her suicide in 1902. More recently, ecofeminism has queered Wicca and paganism while fighting against the desire for power and fascism over compassion and care. The history of witches and animals as 'familiars' is also a shared history of persecution, escape routes, denial of experiments in thinking-otherwise and the collecting of women, racial others, sexual others, the disabled, the non-reproductive crone, animals, nature itself as of use in the outcomes of power, or expendable. All are monsters, demons, invoked by someone other than god of religion, state, church or family. 'Occult' means hidden or secret knowledge. The Sorcerer or mage, the Anthropos of magic, seeks that knowledge as something awaiting revelation in service to power, often by using we expendable monsters. The witch understands knowledge is experiments in thought and action, in expressivity in affecting, which begins with a willingness to refuse power as belonging to flows of desire. The clinamen of witchcraft in magic seeks a turbulent ease for every aspect of relationality by comprehending no forms or functions beyond the critical singularity of the whole rhizomatic field of relations. In this sense when we experiment with chaos, with dying and becoming, being is only a vibrating moment of potentialized activism as a collective, the collective we are as individual witch or as a coven of activists, a swarm of wanderers, who see no value in individuality being a form of catatonic clinamen but seek opening liberty for all entities by experiments in dying to the value of sovereign subjectivity and its unbreakable bond with power. We are becoming-death, creator of worlds.

Conclusion

The difficult joy of death activism

There is nothing for the self after the event. The event itself insinuates an imperceptible moment of becoming-absent, of something annihilated, of the still undetermined and undefined status of consciousness, sentience and the precarious definition of what constitutes 'life' that the idea of contemplating death emphasizes. Desire for death knows there is no after. Yet we remain compelled to phantasize the after of death, whether it be through institutes of religious, familial or artistic legacy or acknowledging our flesh feeding the Earth in whichever ways this may occur. The medical definitions of death which vary globally, coupled with forensic narratives and excavations of death that continue a life's story long after it is extinguished, confound the temporality of death as both and neither the infinitesimal instant and the slow organ-by-organ elongated process of cessation. *Death* is currently a technical or legal term, with a cause, manner and mechanism. So we turn again to attempting to apprehend life in as much as these interdependent terms teach very little and too much about death's voluminous capacity for nothingness and life's humble capacity for being everything. Both terms, while opposing thus contradicting each other, illuminate their own internal paradox. Bare life is, in being life nonetheless, too much life to disavow. Basic death is the devastating finitude of all, regardless of whether it is a spectacular or unremarkable death. Cause, manner and mechanism make sense of what makes no sense of the base reality of being living, which is that its only absolute is its guaranteed end.

The posthuman turn has utilised nonhumans as theoretical models to think humans otherwise, with greater and lesser degrees of fetishism, co-option or empathy, but the eternal life of becoming-hydra and transhuman turns is yet to succeed in eradicating death. Animal rights and various life-affirming activisms for humans, be they fascist and genocidal in affirming certain life only, or demanding equality and liberty, seek the line between the life that counts and that line where life matters less or not at all. Category, genus, species, subject – each recognizes life before the fact. The organism does not need a category in which to live. Life defies definition as to its nature. While this means all life is as valuable to an organism and the Earth as any other, it also insinuates that a life is because it persists not because of what it is that persists being convertible to ontological apprehension. So there is a means by which there can be a presence, a spectre of death, in how we think the world, which includes death within our too anthropocentric knowledge of life. Beginning with those lives deigned to count the most, life as defined is qualified as 'mattering'. The greater, more refined and detailed categorical language that props any given life seems correlative with anxiety over death. Our own lives cultivate reasons for their living, through capital (work, including breeding), state (citizenship/nationality), church (morality) and Oedipal regimes of belonging. The lives of those who suffer and are denied life also have their murder vindicated through reasons, usually designated as 'produce' for agricultural animals, 'inconvenience' for animals in the way of development or 'undesirables' for humans and animals seen as a degenerative form of life, vindicating the interchangeability of metaphors used for their thriving (such as vermin or invasive). We can go entirely the other way, in a posthuman turn that devolves the hyper-refined linguistic and scientific classification of life. What if we declassify life into thinking lives beyond genus, species, gender, race? Life, as instances, involves the death of defining what someone, human or nonhuman, is and the reasons and limitations of their life that precede their instance of life, thereby authorizing licit and illicit forms of death. Much posthuman adaptations of philosophy, from continental philosophy and posthumanism to the rise of Buddhist and occult theory in art and ritual experiments with subjectivity, share one maxim, directly antagonistic to that of the cultivated semiocapitalist subject. The message: 'lose yourself, die to yourself'. There are diverse pieces of evidence for how this could be considered adaptations of what psychoanalysis, existentialism and nihilism had already produced. The Lacanian concept of *spaltung* is one example where one never existed, but at the first moment of being separated from the mother, the self, through the mirror phase, was realized as a simulacrum, an unattainable idea. Or Lacan's exploration of symptoms which lead to becoming-*rien*, the becoming-nothing of anorexia and other habits of disappearing. Existentialism's emphasis on becoming into existence as an arbitrary series of ultimately meaningless practices culminates more interestingly in the work of, for example, Clarice Lispector than Jean-Paul Sartre. Both find life viscerally nauseating, but in Lispector there is love and transformation. Transformation is what divides these modern un-becomings in art and philosophy from nihilism. Dadaism, surrealism, feminism, queer, post-colonialism, post-structuralism all embraced the death of the sovereign subject, its reasons, its desirability, its bad ethics. The creeping presence of juxtapositions of Buddhism with fantasy literature and shamanistic practices with cinema in Deleuze and Guattari's work, especially *A Thousand Plateaus*, is a series of ways of exemplifying the death of subjectivity. Foucault's archaeology from pre-modernity to modernity could be described as a history of the subject as never having been real. Irigaray and Kristeva both utilize experiments in language and in flesh as encounters with difference that can only be germinal and not-yet-made. Lyotard's ambivalent relationship with postmodernity evinces the paradox of 'anything goes' subjectivity based only on empty signifiers with the Holocaust as the outcome of life reduced to a signifier alone. While postmodernism's simulacrum subjectivity is devoid of corporeal, material existence as enfleshed experience, it makes life lesser not because categorized lives are not recognized, but because the phenomenology of living, of organism-ing, for every individual instance of life, is reduced to species or subject. The eternal deferral of life to signs makes empathy and any understanding of suffering impossible. Capitalism's conversion of that signifier to use/credit value alone – semiocapitalism – exacerbates this technique of 'un-lifing'. Deferral also over-values signs, not what they signify, or more, precisely, that they signify life, hence the right to be-unto-oneself as an organism. In this way, death is not the end of life. Language is death. Epistemology is death. All lives are already dead when they can be acknowledged only through anthropocentric, and increasingly semiocapitalist, signifying regimes. Poststructuralist, posthuman theatres of experiments with language and thought make the subject die, or perhaps show it had never really arrived, but both are not sites of lament; they are sites which can be celebrated as joyful, because they liberate life from its motives and reasons and reorient death as one instant out of millions within a life. There is great liberty in living without being defined for the living being one is, whether that is to oneself or to society. This goes for both benevolent and malevolent definitions, so through the death of life as life defined, the person and the pig are given a reprieve from the anthropocentric war machine of signification. To be dead is a great way to live.

The responsibility of death

In an ambiguous and oscillating discussion of what it means to have the right to be responsible, Nietzsche demarcates morality from ethics in a way equivalent to habit from will:

> The enormous labour of what I have called the 'morality of custom' – the special work of man on himself throughout the longest era of the human race, his whole endeavour *prior to the onset of history*, all this finds its meaning, its great justification – regardless of the degree to which harshness, tyranny, apathy, and idiocy are intrinsic to it – in the following fact: it was by means of the morality of custom and the social straightjacket that man was really *made* calculable. (1996: 40, original emphasis)

When we invoke the power of anthropocentrism as the dominating *potestas* of Earth, Nietzsche reminds us there is value neither intrinsically good nor evil, but driven by banal phantasies of excessive greed and an overflow of mindless stupidity which propels an imposition of evaluations of what is right and wrong, showing morality as utterly arbitrary and, as in his time of writing, driven still by the pyramid of subjectification that is based on wealth and exploitation over the more expected evil and good, or powerful and powerless (or rather how each fosters the other empty signifiers interchangeably). Strangely and continuously it is the woman, the queer, the 'brute', the animal, who is evil, and the exploiter who is designated as good because they designate at all. Humans love power not because we are evil, but because we are mindless and fleshless. This insinuates an address to the question of what is of value in human consciousness that is perceived as far exceeding nonhuman consciousness, when the absolutely unknowable consciousness of another species is at the very least, true to the nature of its own being, in the Spinozist sense. When Nietzsche states the only free human worthy of being entitled to responsibility is 'the individual who resembles no one but himself' (1996: 41), we are reminded of Spinoza's definition of an organism: 'Everything, insofar as it is in itself, endeavours to persist in its own being. The endeavour, wherewith everything endeavours to persist in its own being, is nothing else but the actual essence of the thing in question' (1957: 35). This reading of Nietzsche insinuates that humans, when driven by a morality that has as its frame, the *potestas* of anthropocentric love of power (however that manifests, from accruement of wealth, to reproduction, to oppression) denies the *potentia* of the self as an autopoietic organism unto itself and capable of inevitable (benevolent and malevolent) ethical interaction with the world and other organisms. Nietzsche emphasizes that an individual without the capacity to manifest their own being, not within signification and subjectification, but, Spinoza-style, unto themselves, is also incapable of making promises, of being responsible (1996: 41–42) and thus of claiming to have a conscience.

This claim challenges human exceptionalism in two ways. First, it shows that humans cannot compare themselves to other organisms as superior or inferior, while they remain within the bondage of anthropocentrism, and outside that bondage comparison would be redundant because the individual is a singularity. Second, it interrogates the paradox of humans, at whatever level of power, being enthralled by signifying regimes which precede them to such an extent that to speak of individuality at all is a fallacy. Put simply, just as many theorists have claimed we have always already been posthuman, after Nietzsche we can claim we have *always already been dead*, because our selves are not our unknowable essences, they are navigations of human regimes, at certain points upon which we alight. From a posthuman perspective this can ignite two positive outcomes for ethical death activism. First, if we were never alive, who cares if we now embrace death? Second, this demands we become-born, in the sense Irigaray advocates in *To Be Born*:

> Becoming oneself means winning this unique being that we are, but of which our culture and the milieu in which we live constantly deprive us. It means discovering the sole and irreducible nature of our own being and caring about cultivating it as such towards its blossoming, however difficult the task may be. Indeed becoming oneself requires one to give up the quietness that the fact of assimilating to the world in which we stay brings to ourselves and to take on the anguish of solitude and decisions on the way to follow in order to favour a development which is both suitable for us and concerned with what and who partake in our existence. And this asks of us to distinguish ourselves from them so that we become capable of respect for their own being. Becoming oneself requires as much heroism as being born, and also needs resorting to our breath in order to emerge from the family and sociocultural background which, too often, substitute themselves for the maternal placenta in which we started living. (2017: 41–42)

To be born, to cultivate a Nietzschean liberty or will, to relate ethically as best we can is far from the cultivation of the subject to which semiocapitalism incites us. In many ways, the so-called culture wars have been criticized for indoctrinating a new set of reified subject positions, as ossified as the old white Empire men they denounce as defining human history. The culture wars have never been about exchange of one dominant for another, or even one included for another, although identity politics and 'me first' equality risks this as a strategy. The strangely apt slurs of 'woke' and 'snowflake' mask what these contemporary terms include as their quality of emergence (in addition to the former co-opting African American vernacular). To be awakened to compassion and radical empathy would suggest the denouncer is himself asleep, which sounds surprisingly like the somnambulist of Nietzsche, who obeys without even knowing that he obeys and is incapable of will or responsibility. Similarly, snowflakes as unique singularities, and as ephemeral, correspond with what tactical subjectivity is within activist movements – metamorphic, hard to catch, unlike yet collective and ultimately seeking not exchange, but perpetual change. The velocity of what it means to be a human subject in these 'culture wars' is one part of the speed capital of the twenty-first century that is evidence that we are being born constantly and anew. Those who are not snowflakes or woke are usually those who desperately adhere to the scaffolds of their subjectification, and thus were never born, while being already dead. The question is, for death activism, how can we embrace the dead that we are if we seek recognition within established human subjectification while also opening the Earth for those to be born who these dead human dominating subjects continue to oppress, harm and actually make materially dead?

Queering death activism

Currently, in a large percentage of the world, to be queer is to be technically illegal, definitely immoral, at risk of censorship and death. While most of the human world still defines queer as LGBTQIA+, currently law reform in eight states of the United States is seeking to ban drag of any kind (which translates as men acting feminine in practical terms, see Helmore: 2023), and in the UK the government has sought to ban the teaching of LGBTQIA+ relationships in primary schools, various anti-trans bills are being proposed and outrage against everything from queer performance to non-binary inclusive school sports days is spouted in the press. Additionally, major global sporting events and luxury tourism experiences are being sponsored in countries where homosexuality is punishable by death, and the definition is very loose, amounting to any disobedience, by men or women, to the phallocratic governing regimes. To exist within the Nietzschean moral structure is to be a legal citizen. For many who do not conform in gender, sexuality, human performativity (whatever that may mean) or even activist alliance (e.g. the current UK government has listed Greenpeace and animal rights activists as terrorists under the Prevent act 2015, updated 2020), not counting as alive means our very existence is an act of defiant activism. To be, whatever that being may be, is too much for the human world. Being queer is being dead to the human world, but if humans are dead to the Earth, to which realm do we Earth activists and queer activists belong? As interstitial beings we straddle both worlds, and the tenacity of our existence with the tenuous of our 'subjectivity' as more relegated than defined is a jubilant space for exploitation. Neither human nor animal – potentially ahuman. Alive but never born into a recognizable life, we are not living humans. And the paradox is that the more of a human subject one is, the less of a living entity unto oneself one is. Humans are then all dead, aren't they? While death is absolute and not conceptual, the playful use of conceptual death of subjectivity is a tool by which we can de-hierarchize the value and definitions of various lives. It can become the playfulness by which we challenge hypocritical Anthropos on life and death, while attesting to the trauma to which we are awakened where life and death are without any signification except their absolute truth.

Dead if we do, dead if we don't

Although we have liberated the world to an extent from the Aristotelean and Christian hierarchy of God(s)/man/woman/animal (openly, in practice and reality not so much), have we aligned our logic to an overlapping species hierarchy where classification always attaches to use and value, not simply being-in-itself? Can we queer species? This involves a Spinozan ecosophy or what Jean-Luc Nancy suggests as *co-ipseity*:

> What comes to light, then, is not a 'social' or 'communitarian dimension' added onto a primitive individual given, even if it were to occur as an essential and determining addition. (Just think of the numerous circumstances of ordinary discourse in which this order is imposed on us: first the individual, then the group; first the one, then the others; first the rights-bearing subject; then real relationships; first 'individual psychology', then 'collective psychology'; and above all, first a 'subject', then 'intersubjectivity' – as they astonishingly persist in saying.) It is not even a question of a sociality or alterity that would come to cut across, complicate, put into play, or *alter* the principle of the subject understood as *solus ipse*. It is something else and still more. It does not so much determine the principle of the *ipse*, whatever this may be ('individual' or 'collective', insofar as one can speak in these ways), as it codetermines it with the plurality of *ipses*, each one of which is co-originary and coessential to the world, to a world which from this point on defines a coexistence that must be understood in a still unheard-of sense, exactly because it does not take place 'in' the world, but instead forms the essence and the structure of the world. It is not a nearness [*voisinage*]

or community of *ipses*, but a co*ipseity*: this is what comes to light, but as an enigma with which our thinking is confronted. (2000: 44)

The impulse to want to be heard is strong among minoritarian individuals and communities. The conundrum occurs when these subjectifying belongings recreate the moral and legislative categories of the majoritarian but at lesser value, with all the same performative and moral arbitrary implications. Subjectification also always prizes the separation from, even when being with. Someone inevitably loses in this Order of Mars. There is a lack of porosity or what Irigaray would call mucosity. The mucosal nature of queer, as an open question with a thousand tiny unheard-of responses, none of which are answers, confronts us with what is really important in activism. We are faced with a decision: do we want to be recognized, to be born into a catatonizing subjectivity among the humans, or can we thrive with no defined existence, in the spaces between the spaces between? Queer is enigma, to embrace the birth with which we have never been endowed, into the heteronormal and adamantly white male human world involves many deaths, a being born into death. It also risks closing off our coipseities with those unlike-others who are the Earth's nonhuman (and capital H non-counting-as-Human) occupants. The value of being a subject who counts, and especially one who ascends the hierarchy, must itself be slaughtered. We must massacre the sovereign subject manifest as the icon of Anthropos, with his pouches of gold and his reproductive capacity as that of power and status, just as anthropocentrism has massacred so many bodies, actually and politically. Queer death activism is always simultaneously queer anti-death activism. I can write with Nietzsche on the human who, if not liberated from subjectivity, is dead, or with Irigaray on how we can learn to be born, but it is the site of the flesh where Guattari emphasises the revolution happens, just as it is the site of the flesh where billions of nonhuman animals a day experience death at the hands of human oppression. The drive of this flesh is desire, for Guattari all revolution is desire, and desire is the definitive intensity of queer living: 'These are the people, of both sexes, who have finally broken that perennial barrier between "politics" and reality as it is actually lived – a barrier that has served the interests of both the bourgeois society and those who have claimed to represent and speak for the masses' (1996: 31). Being seduced into a faith that the recognition of a minority identity will allow for queer becomings to continue is a technique of capital, where subjectivity is converted to currency and will advocate any mouthpiece who persists in speaking with anthropocentric language. As Nancy states, it is the unheard, and for Lyotard's differend, those who speak in ways we cannot understand but to whom we must still attend, abide, ally, that show human language is always a limited and limiting closing off of ecosophical communication. Guattari states: 'There are people of both sexes, who have opened the way for the great uprising of life against the forces of death – even as the latter continues to infiltrate our organisms in order to subjugate, with greater and greater subtlety, our energies, our desires and our reality to the demands of the established orders' (1996: 31). Dead if we do, dead if we don't, so let us cease the forensic autopsy of being-a-subject for ourselves and all anti-anthropocentric organisms to cease the equivalence of our signification dictating our value and capacities. Finally,

> we can no longer sit idly by as others steal our mouths, our anuses, our genitals, our nerves, our guts, our arteries, in order to fashion parts and works in an ignoble mechanism of production which links capital, exploitation and the family. We can no longer allow others to turn our mucous membranes, our skin, all our sensitive areas into occupied territory – territory controlled and regimented by others, to which we are forbidden access. We can no longer permit our nervous system to serve as a communications network for the system of capitalist exploitation, for the patriarchal state; nor can we permit our brains to be used as instruments of torture, programmed by the powers that surround us. We can no longer allow others to repress our fucking, to control our shit, our saliva, our energies, all in conformity with the prescriptions of the law and its carefully defined little transgressions. We want to see frigid, imprisoned, mortified bodies explode to bits, even if capitalism continues to demand that they be kept in check at the expense of our living body. (1996: 31)

It is both harrowing and enlightening the extent to which Guattari's visceral and corporeal collapse of metaphor politics and lived reality ecologically joins the queer body with the incarcerated body, the raped body, the factory farmed nonhuman body, the vivisected nonhuman body. The Oedipal violence of the family structure that resonates everywhere from farm rape-racks to insular households to heterotopic institutions, dependent on gendered, heterosexual, racist, ableist, speciesist but utterly human acts of control, conscious and unconscious, leads us to queer death activism. Death to the Oedipal patriarchal family structure, which maps itself from macrocosms to microcosms of oppression, and death to Anthropos, the eternal unchanging figurehead who denies the perpetual metamorphosis of the Earth as the persistence to life.

Death of self, opening of life

Numerous cultures reflect upon the death of what we would name, with and beyond Freud, the ego (or capital Ego proper). While most neo capitalist societies advocate in favour of the ego, others such as those who engage with Buddhism and tantric practices see the ego as that which causes suffering. The Tantraloka states:

> He should not become attached through prejudice to anything that is not real. [So] he should immediately exorcize as though they are evil spirits (grahāh) the eight 'possessors'... namely [pride of] caste, learning, lineage, orthopraxy, physical appearance, country, virtue, and wealth. 'I am a brahmin. How can I perform any rites other than those ordained by the Veda?' Such is the pride of caste, which [must be removed because it] blocks one's access to the higher [teachings]. The other [seven] too may readily be exemplified along the [same] lines. These have been called 'possessors' grahāh – in this [passage of scripture] because they are indeed analogous to possessing spirits. Though individuals are autonomous [agents] these factors make them appear to take on a nature that is alien to their own, concealing their true identity. Such conceptual constructs as caste cannot apply to one's real identity as consciousness. [But] once established they [like invasive spirits] completely occlude that nature with their own. Each and every conceptual construct that causes the undivided reality of consciousness to contract [in this way] is such a 'possessor' and should be discarded. (Abhinavagupta 2013: 17)

What the Tantraloka and Western philosophy and psychoanalysis share is that most trace a trajectory of the development of ego as a navigation of gender, race, status and corporeal signifiers buttressing against the capacity to live as intensities and corporeal affects. I cite the Tantraloka here not to fetishize Tantric alterity from a Western perspective (though I may indeed be guilty of this), but rather to show that the sophisticated seduction of signification leads via various manifestations to a self that is rarely conscious or corporeally present as immanent intensity. Instead it is enslaved by regimes of subjectivity-defining strata that make other forms of presence a struggle. Whether these navigations are desired, should be defied or are distractions is arbitrarily dependent on attitudes towards what it means to live or die. The traditional configuration of the ego is the self's desires struggling against reality, yet here we see the self struggles with being a self against the demands of or default to signification. Being a sovereign subject is death to self as consciousness or corporeal immanence, but it is also a perpetual induction into a trauma of simulation existence. If signification is a war machine (as Serres would suggest), Freud's words resonate: 'We remember the old proverb: *Si vic pactem, para bellum*, if you wish to preserve peace, arm for war. This might be the time to alter it to read as follows: *Si vis vitam, para mortem*. If you wish to endure life, prepare yourself for death' (2005: 194). Freud suggests the disjunct between the desire for the death of the other and the utter repudiation of conceiving the death of the self. Inverted within a radical compassion framework of care, death activism's commitment to liberation of the other, no matter the what, who or why of the other, makes the self absorption of both neocapitalist subjectivity and identity politics irrelevant.

Because equality based on ascension to majoritarianism is, like many psychoanalytic projects of desire, one punctuated with repetitive frustrations and eternal lack as its foundation; it is neither a project of consciousness nor a project of ethical relationality. Unless the only relation that counts is the one between one's idea of the primacy of one's own liberty (which, compared to many other humans and nonhumans, is usually greater) and one's actual existence. This is adamantly not to say that the self is unworthy of liberty. Radical compassion through death activism is neither sacrifice nor martyrdom, those tedious lamentations of a self that never was. *It ceases to covet and idolize the self as majoritarian*. Death of the ego is death of the ego as *potestas*, as part of an overarching system of atrophied power. The self, in conscious material immanence, can use the unconscious to develop escape routes and deviations, lines of flight from power towards *potentia*. Death of ego, death of self as signified, subjectified and stratified, these deaths are deaths of desire for power, necessary to death activism in order to fully comprehend the impossible but critical project of liberation of other lives and organisms beyond wishing to comprehend their alterity and even one's own relation with them as two (or more) entities defined by relations of seriality (this is to this) and proportionality (this is to this as that is to that), two ruses of subjectification which, according to Deleuze and Guattari, block becomings, escape routes and relations with alterity.

And so we return to responsibility, that which Nietzsche demands can only happen outside of moral subject in servitude to social structures/strictures. On responsibility Derrida states:

> The simple concepts of alterity and of singularity constitute the concept of duty as much as that of responsibility. As a result, the concept of responsibility, of decision, or of duty, are condemned a priori, to paradox, scandal and aporia. Paradox, scandal and aporia are themselves nothing other than sacrifice, the revelation of conceptual thinking at its limit, at its death and finitude.... But I am sacrificing and betraying at every moment all my other obligations: my obligations to the other others whom I know or don't know, the billions of my fellow (without mentioning the animals that are even more other others than my fellows), my fellows who are dying of starvation or sickness. (1995: 68–69)

Derrida uses the often invoked example of Abraham, as treacherous to his own in his faith to God. If we think about the limits of this scene another way, it is, in ecosophical terms, time that we become treacherous to our species in order to show our faith in the Earth. But where God is the demander and the bearer of power (and coercion, let's be clear), the victim is now not Isaac but the Earth itself and the billions of occupants who are sick and dying at the hands of our species, through direct consumption and collateral greed. And the demand comes from us; we have split into both the demander of sacrifice and those making the demand. We are, as a species and as individuals, the paradox of how to allow life to thrive. We are the aporia of how to be alive and not operate as war machines against ourselves and others. And as activists we must become the scandal of allying ourselves with the nonhuman. For those of us who never counted fully perhaps this is easier or perhaps more difficult because the arbitrariness of who flourishes and who is oppressed can ignite a desire for self-liberty. Following Guattari's call to action, society demands self-liberty at the expense of the body and immanent consciousness. We are massacred, meaning that thinking activisms will also require a reactivation of our own flesh, and this requires death of the strive for equality on the terms of the state, family and other anthropocentric institutes. We are both already dead and can die joyfully in order to transform our selves and their capacities. Derrida's tone of being overwhelmed by responsibility and obligation is all too poignantly real at this time, but if we die to ourselves first it may be easier to see the denial of lives in reality for those whose cries we cannot translate into human reasons or vindications. Ethical empathy and radical compassion require a death of self·in so many ways. The death of ourselves as subjects can be the way we create radical collectives and individual direct action, unleashing thought and expression, obligation becoming, not lament, but liberty for the other(s).

References

Adams, Carol J. (1995), *Neither Man nor Beast: Feminism and the Defense of Animals*, New York: Continuum.
Adams, Carol J. (1995), *Neither Man nor Beast: Feminism and the Defense of Animals*, New York: Continuum.
Adams, Carol J. (2014), 'The War Against Compassion', in Patricia MacCormack (ed), *The Animal Catalyst: Toward Ahuman Theory*, 15-26, London: Bloomsbury.
Aldana-Reyes, Xavier (2016), 'Discipline…But Punish! Foucault, Agamben and Torture Porn's Thanatopolitical Scaffold', in Mark De Walk (ed.), *Screening the Tortured Body*, 51–70, London: Palgrave.
Alexander, Jeffrey C., Eyerman, R., Giesen, B., Smelser, N. J., and Sztompka, P. (2004), *Cultural Trauma and Collective Identity*, Berkeley: University of California Press.
Andersson, N. W., Gustafsson, L. N., Okkels, N., Taha, F., Cole, S. W., Munk-Jørgensen, P. and Goodwin, R. D. (2015), 'Depression and the Risk of Autoimmune Disease: A Nationally Representative, Prospective Longitudinal Study', *Psychological Medicine*, 45 (16): 3559–69.
AnimalsInMind. (2018), *PTSD and Trauma in Animal Activists*. https://animalandmind.com/2018/02/25/trauma-and-animal-activists/#:~:text=Following%20exposure%20to%20animal%20suffering,of%20what%20they%20saw%20in (accessed 25 December 2023)
Ansell-Pearson, Keith (1999), *Germinal Life: The Difference and Repetition of Deleuze*, London: Taylor & Francis Group.
Baddeley, Gavin (2017), *Goth Chic: A Connoisseur's Guide to Dark Culture*, London: Plexus.
Barad, Karen (2007), *Meeting the Universe Halfway : Quantum Physics and the Entanglement of Matter and Meaning*, Durham: Duke University Press.
Bar-On, Yinon M., Phillips, Rob and Milo, Ron (2018), 'The Biomass Distribution on Earth', *PNAS*, 115 (25): 6506–11. https://doi.org/10.1073/pnas.1711842115
Bataille, Georges (1992), *Theory of Religion*, trans. Robert Hurley, New York: Zone Books.
Baudrillard, Jean (1981), *For a Critique of the Political Economy of the Sign*, trans. Charles Levin, Candor NY: Telos Press.
Baumeister, R. F. (1990), 'Suicide as Escape from Self', *Psychological Review*, 97: 90–113.
Bell, Jeffrey (2006), *Philosophy at the Edge of Chaos: Gilles Deleuze and the Philosophy of Difference*, Toronto: Toronto University Press.
Berardi, Franco 'Bifo' (2015), *Heroes*, London: Verso.

Berardi, Franco (2019), *Futurability: The Age of Impotence and the Horizon of Possibility*, New York: Verso

Bergson, Henri (1937), 'Le possibile et la réel' *Nordisk Tidskrift*, cited in Berardi, Franco (2019), *Futurability: The Age of Impotence and the Horizon of Possibility*, New York: Verso, 2–3.

Bergson, Henri (1992), *The Creative Mind: An Introduction to Metaphysics*, New York: Citadel Press.

Berlant, Lauren Gail (2011), *Cruel Optimism*, Durham: Duke University Press.

Berleant, Arnold (2004), *Re-Thinking Aesthetics: Rogue Essays on Aesthetics and the Arts*, Florence: Taylor & Francis Group.

Bersani, Leo (2009), *Is the Rectum a Grave? And Other Essays*, Chicago: Chicago University Press.

Bey, Hakim (1999), *Aimless Wanderings: Chuang Tzu's Chaos Linguistics*, Portland: Dagon Publishing and Carbondale: Tumultus Publications.

Bichat, Xavier (1801), *Anatomie générale appliquée à la physiologie et à la medicine*, Paris: Brosson and Chaudé.

Biggs, Sarah J. (2014), 'The Three Living and the Three Dead', *British Library Medieval Manuscript Blogs,* https://blogs.bl.uk/digitisedmanuscripts/2014/01/the-three-living-and-the-three-dead.html (accesses 24 December 2023).

Blanchot, Maurice (1997), *Friendship*, trans. Elizabeth Rottenberg, Stanford: Stanford University Press.

Blanchot, Maurice (2000), 'The Instant of My Death', in Maurice Blanchot and Jacques Derrida (eds), *The Instant of My Death/Demeure: Fiction and Testimony*, trans. Elizabeth Rottenberg, Stanford: Stanford University Press.

Blau, Herbert (1987), *The Eye of Prey: Subversions of the Postmodern*, Bloomington: Indiana University Press.

Boisseau, Will (2019), 'What We Can Learn about Vegan Education from Anarchist Philosophy and the Animal Liberation Activists', in Agnes Trzak (ed.), *Teaching Liberation: Essays on Social Justice, Animals, Veganism and Education*, 137–56, Brooklyn: Lantern.

Boje, D., Gephardt, R. P. J. and Thatchenkery, T. J., eds. (1995), *Postmodern Management and Organization Theory*, SAGE Publications, Incorporated, Thousand Oaks.

Breuer, Josef and Freud, Sigmund (1895) *Studies on Hysteria,* trans. James Strachey, Hogarth Press, London 1955.

Brevard, A., Lester, D. and Yang, B. (1990), 'A Comparison of Suicide Notes Written by Suicide Completers and Suicide Attempters', *Crisis*, 11: 7–11

Butler, Judith (2020), *The Force of Non-Violence*, London: Verso.

Canguilhem, Georges (1989), *The Normal and The Pathological*, trans. Carol R. Fawcett with Robert S. Cohen, New York: Zone Books.

Canguilhem, Georges (1994), 'The Death of Man, or Exhaustion of Cogito?', trans. Catherine Porter. In Gary Gutting (ed.), *The Cambridge Companion to Foucault*, 71–91, Cambridge: Cambridge University Press.

Carroll, Peter (1987), *Liber Null and Psychonaut*, York Beach, ME: Weiser.

Clark, James M. (1950), *The Dance of Death in the Middle Ages and the Renaissance*, London: Phaidon.

Colebrook, Claire (2014), *Death of the Posthuman: Essays on Extinction Volume 1*, London: Open University Press.
Colebrook, Claire (2023), *Who Would You Kill to Save the World?* Lincoln: University of Nebraska Press.
Craddock, Ida (2017), *Heavenly Bridegrooms, Psychic Wedlock, The Heaven of the Bible, The Wedding Night, Right Marital Living and Other Papers on Marriage and Sex*, City Not Known: McAllister Editions.
Daigle, Christine and McDonald, Terrance H. (2022), 'Introduction', in Christine Daigle and Terrance H. McDonald (eds), *From Deleuze and Guattari to Posthumanism: Philosophies of Immanence*, 1–22, London: Bloomsbury.
Deleuze, Gilles (1988), *Spinoza: Practical Philosophy*, trans. Robert Hurley, San Francisco: City Lights.
Deleuze, Gilles (1990), *The Logic of Sense,* trans Constantin V. Boundas, New York: Columbia UP.
Deleuze, Gilles (2001), *The Fold: Leibniz and the Baroque,* trans. Tom Conley, London: Athlone.
Deleuze, Gilles and Guattari, Fèlix (1986), *Kafka: Toward a Minor Literature*, trans. Dana Polan, Minneapolis, MN: University of Minnesota Press.
Deleuze, Gilles and Guattari, Fèlix (1987), *A Thousand Plateaus: Capitalism and Schizophrenia II*, trans. Brian Massumi, London: Athlone.
Deleuze, Gilles and Guattari, Fèlix (1994), *What is Philosophy?* trans. Hugh Tomlinson and Graham Burchell, New York: Columbia University Press.
Derrida, Jacques (1995), *The Gift of Death*, trans. David Wills, Chicago: University of Chicago Press.
Derrida, Jacques (2000), 'Demeure: Fiction and Testimony', in Maurice Blanchot and Jacques Derrida (eds), *The Instant of My Death/Demeure: Fiction and Testimony*, trans. Elizabeth Rottenberg, Stanford: Stanford University Press, 13-103.
Dickson, A., Toft, A., and O'Carroll, R E. (2009), 'Neuropsychological Functioning, Illness Perception, Mood and Quality of Life in Chronic Fatigue Syndrome, Autoimmune Thyroid Disease and Healthy Participants', *Psychological Medicine,* 39 (9): 1567–76.
Dube, Shanta R., Fairweather, DeLisa, Pearson, William S., Felitti, Vincent J., Anda, Robert F. and Croft, Janet B. (2009), 'Cumulative Childhood Stress and Autoimmune Diseases in Aadults', *Psychosomatic Medicine*, 71 (2): 243–50.
Dué, Casey (2006), *The Captive Woman's Lament in Greek Tragedy*, Berlin: University of Texas Press.
Durkheim, Emile (2006), *On Suicide*, trans. Robin Buss, London: Penguin.
Edelman, Lee (2004), *No Future: Queer Theory and the Death Drive*, Durham: Duke University Press.
Edwards, Paul (2007), 'Kant on Suicide', *Philosophy Now* 61, https://philosophynow.org/issues/61/Kant_On_Suicide (accessed 5 September 22).
Eustace, Frances with King, Pamela (2011), 'Dances of the Living and the Dead: A Study of Danse Macabre Imagery within the Context of Late-Medieval Dance Culture', in Sophie Oosterwijk and Stefanie Knöll (eds), *Mixed Metaphors: The Danse Macabre*

in Medieval and Early Modern Europe, 43–72, Cambridge: Cambridge Scholars Publisher.

Farberow, N. L. and Shneidman, E. S., eds. (1961), *The Cry for Help*, New York: McGraw-Hill.

Freud, Sigmund (1955), 'The "Uncanny"' [1919], in *The Complete Psychological Works*, Vol. XVII, 217–56, London: Hogarth Press.

Freud, Sigmund (2005), *On Murder, Mourning and Melancholia*, trans. Shaun Whiteside, London: Penguin.

Friedman, H. (1972), 'Aspects psychosomatiques de la polyarthrite chronique évolutive (PCE) ou polyarthrite rhumatoïde: revue de la littérature', *Acta psychiatrica Belgica*, 72 (1): 117–41.

Fuchs, Barbara (2021), *Theater of Lockdown: Digital and Distanced Performance in a Time of Pandemic*, London: Bloomsbury, 2021.

Gaffney, Peter, ed. (2010), *Force of the Virtual : Deleuze, Science, and Philosophy*, Minneapolis: University of Minnesota Press.

Gaia, Vince (2006), 'Goth Subculture May Protect Vulnerable Children', *New Scientist*, 14 April 2006.

Gairola, Rahul K. (2017), 'Bastardly Duppies and Dastardly Dykes: Queer Sexuality and the Supernatural in Michelle Cliff's Abeng and Shani Mootoo's Cereus Blooms at Night', *Wagadu: A Journal of Transnational Women's and Gender Studies*, Winter, 18: 15–54.

Goldstein, Caroline (2017), 'How Many Animals Have Died for Damien Hirst's Art to Live? We Counted: Nearly One Million, by Our Conservative Estimate', *Artnet News*, 13 April. https://news.artnet.com/art-world/damien-whats-your-beef-916097

Granovetter, S. (2021), 'Activist as Symptom: Healing Trauma within a Ruptured Collective', *Society & Animals*, 29 (7): 659–78. https://doi.org/10.1163/15685306-bja10051

Guattari, Fèlix (1996), *Soft Subversions*, trans. David L. Sweet and Chet Wiener, New York: Semiotext(e).

Guattari, Fèlix (2000), *The Three Ecologies*, trans. Ian Pindar and Paul Sutton, London: Athlone.

Guattari, Felix (2015), *Psychoanalysis and Transversality: Texts and Interviews 1955-1971*, trans. Ames Hodges, New York: Semiotext(e).

Haraway, Donna (1991), *Simians, Cyborgs and Women*, New York: Routledge.

Haraway, Donna (2016), *Staying with the Trouble: Making Kin in the Chthulucene*, Durham: Duke University Press.

Hartman, Saidiya (2019), *Wayward Lives: Beautiful Experiments*, New York: W.W. Norton.

Häyry, Matti and Sukenick, Amanda (2023), 'Imposing a Lifestyle: A New Argument for Antinatalism', *Cambridge Quarterly of Healthcare Ethics*, 33 (2): 1–22. https://doi.org/10.1017/S0963180123000385

Helmore, Edward (2023), 'Republican Legislators Introduce New Laws to Crack Down on Drag Shows', *The Guardian*, 21 January 2023. https://www.theguardian.com/world/2023/jan/21/anti-drag-show-laws-bans-republican-states

Hiddema, Krista (2023), 'The Power of Love to Transform Animal Lives: The Deception of Animal Quantification', in C. J. Adams, A. Crary and L. Gruen (eds), *The Good it Promises, the Harm it Does: Critical Essays on Effective Altruism*, 176–88, Oxford: Oxford University Press.

Higgins, Kathleen (1998), 'Death and the Skeleton', in Jeff Malpas and Robert C. Solomon (eds), *Death and Philosophy*, 39–49, London: Routledge.

Hine, Phil (2004), *The Pseudonomicon*, Tempe, AZ: Falcon Press.

Hine, Phil (2023), *Queerying Occulture*, Tempe, Arizona: The Falcon Press.

Hodkinson, Paul (2002), *Goth: Identity, Style and Subculture*, London: Bloomsbury.

hooks, bell (2001), *All about Love*, New York: HarperCollins.

Hume, David (2005), *On Suicide*, London: Penguin.

Hyrd, Myra J. and Yusoff, Kathryn (2021), 'Lines of Shite: Microbial-Mineral Chatter in the Anthropocene', in Andres Jacque, Marina Otero Verzier and Lucia Pietroiusti (eds), *More-Than-Human*, 49–60, Rotterdam: Het Nieuewe Instutuut.

Irigaray, Luce (2002), *The Way of Love*, trans. Heidi Bostic and Stephen Pluháček, London: Continuum.

Irigaray, Luce (2017), *To Be Born*, London: Palgrave: MacMillan.

Ivic, Sanja, (2007) 'Spinoza and Kant on Suicide', *Res Cogitans,* 1 (4): 132–44.

Jackson, Zakiyaah Iman (2020), *Becoming Human: Matter and Meaning in an Antiblack World*, New York: New York University Press.

Jameson, Frederic (2003), 'Future City', *New Left Review* 21, May–June: 65–79.

Joiner, T. (2005), *Why People Die by Suicide*, Cambridge, MA: Harvard University Press.

Jones, P. (2007), *Aftershock: Confronting Trauma in a Violent World*, New York, NY: Lantern Books.

Joy, M. (2018), *Beyond beliefs*, Brooklyn, NY: Lantern Books.

Kant, Immanuel (1949), *Fundamental Principles of the Metaphysics of Ethics*, trans. Thomas Kingsmill Abbott, London: Longman Green and Co.

Kant, Immanuel (1987), *Critique of Judgement*, trans. Werner S. Pluhar, Indianapolis and Cambridge: Hackett.

Kant, Immanuel (2005), *Critique of Judgement,* trans. J. H. Bernard, Mineola NY: Dover.

Kinch, A. (2013), *Imago Mortis: Mediating Images of Death in Late Medieval Culture*, Leiden: BRILL.

Koutny-Jones, Aleksandra (2015), *Visual Cultures of Death in Central Europe: Contemplation and Commemoration in Early Modern Poland-Lithuania*, Leiden: BRILL.

Kràlovà, Jana (2017), 'What is Social Death?', in Jana Kràlovà and Tony Walter (eds), *Social Death: Questioning the Life Death Boundary*, 1–14, London: Routledge.

Kristeva, Julia (1982), *Powers of Horror: An Essay on Abjection,* trans. Leon S. Roudiez, New York: Columbia University Press.

Kristeva, Julia (2002), *Revolt, She Said*, trans. Brian O'Keeffe, New York: Semiotext(e).

Lemmens, Willem (2005), 'The Melancholy of the Philosopher: Hume and Spinoza on Emotions and Wisdom', *The Journal of Scottish Philosophy*, 3 (1): 47–65.

Lester, David and Mahboubeh Dadfar (2022), 'Sociotropy, autonomy, depression and suicidality, *Suicide Studies*, 2022, 3(4), 2-10.

Levinas, Emmanuel (1989), *The Levinas Reader*, trans. Alphonso Lingis, London: Blackwell.

Lotringer, Sylvere, ed. (1981), *Polysexuality*, New York: Semiotext(e).
Lykke, Nina (2022), *Vibrant Death: A Posthuman Phenomenology of Mourning*, London: Bloomsbury.
Lykke, Nina and Marambio, Camila (2020), 'A Triptych Of Viral Tales', *Kerb Journal of Landscape Architecture: Decentre: Designing for Coexistence in a Time of Crisis*, 28: 102–7.
Lyotard, Jean François (1988), *The Differend: Phrases in Dispute*, trans. Georges Van Den Abbeele, Minneapolis: University of Minnesota Press.
MacCormack, Patricia (2020), *The Ahuman Manifesto*, London: Bloomsbury.
Malabou, Catherine (2012), *The New Wounded: From Neurosis to Brain Damage*, Fordham University Press, 2012.
Mann, C. (2018), *Vystopia: The Anguish of being Vegan in a Non-vegan World*, Sydney: Communicate31 Pty Ltd.
Maturana, Humberto R. and Varela, Francoise J. (1987), *The Tree of Knowledge: The Biological Roots of Human Understanding*, Boston: New Science Library.
Mbembe, Achille (2003), 'Necropolitics', trans. Libby Meintjes, *Public Culture*, 15 (1): 11–40.
McCrystal, Rachel (2023), 'The Wisdom Gained from Animals Who Self-Liberate', in C. J. Adams, A. Crary and L. Gruen (eds), *The Good it Promises, the Harm It Does: Critical Essays on Effective Altruism*, 198–203, Oxford: Oxford University Press.
McRuer, Robert (2006), *Crip Theory: Cultural Signs of Queerness and Disability*, New York University Press.
Moretti, S., Arunachalam, M., Colucci, R., Pallanti, S., Kline, J. A., Berti, S. Lotti, F. and Lotti, T. (2012), 'Autoimmune Markers in Vitiligo Patients Appear Correlated with Obsession and Phobia', *Journal of the European Academy of Dermatology and Venereology*, 26 (7): 861–7.
Nancy, Jean-Luc (2000), *Being Singular Plural*, trans. Robert D. Richardson and Anne O'Byrne, Stanford: Stanford University Press.
Nietzsche, Friedrich (1996), *On the Genealogy of Morals*, trans. Douglas Smith, Oxford: Oxford University Press.
O'Brien, Martin (2019), 'You are My Death: The Shattered Temporalities of Zombie Time', *Wellcome Open Research*. https://wellcomeopenresearch.org/articles/5-135#ref-10 (accessed 06 July 2023).
O'Brien, Martin and Bouchard, Gianna (2019), 'Zombie Sickness: Contagious idea in Performance', In Alan Bleakley, (ed.), *Routledge Handbook to the Medical Humanities*, 257–63, London: Routledge.
O'Conner, Mary Frances (2022), *The Grieving Brain: The Surprising Science of How We Learn from Love and Loss*, San Francisco: HarperOne.
Oosterwijk, Sophie (2011), 'Dance, Dialogue and Duality: Fatal Encounters in the Medieval Danse Macabre', in Sophie Oosterwijk and Stefanie Knöll (eds), *Mixed Metaphors: The Danse Macabre in Medieval and Early Modern Europe*, 9–42, Cambridge: Cambridge Scholars Publisher.
Osborne-Crowley, Lucia (2021), *My Body Keeps your Secrets*, London: The Indigo Press.
Paltrinieri, Luca (2015), 'Between (bio)-Politics and (Bio)-Ethics: What Life', in Miguel de Beistegui, Guiseppe Bianco and Marjorie Gracieuse (eds), *The Care of Life*:

Transdisciplinary Perspectives in Bioethics and Biopolitics, 33–46, London: Rowman and Littlefield.

Parkes, C. M. and Prigerson, H. G. (2009), *Bereavement: Studies of Grief in Adult Life*, fourth edn, London: Taylor & Francis Group.

Parsons, Talcott (1951), *The Social System*, London: Routledge.

Patterson, Charles (2002), *Eternal Treblinka: Our Treatment of Animals and the Holocaust*, New York: Lantern Books.

Peta Facts and Statistics About Animal Testing. https://www.peta.org/issues/animals-used-for-experimentation/animals-used-experimentation-factsheets/animal-experiments-overview/ (accessed 12 April 23).

Phillipov, Michelle (2006), 'Self Harm in Goth Youth Subculture: Study Merely Reinforces Popular Stereotypes', *BMJ* (letter to the editor), 332 (7551): 1215–16.

Plato. (2010), *The Last Days of Socrates: Euthyphro, Apology, Crito, Phaedo*, trans. Christopher Rowe, London: Penguin.

Prevent Act, UK Government. (2018), https://www.oscb.org.uk/wp-content/uploads/2020/04/Safeguarding-from-Radicalisation-Reference-Guide.pdf. (accessed 13 April 23).

Radomska, Marietta, Mehrabi, Tara and Lykke, Nina (2020), 'Queer Death Studies: Death, Dying and Mourning from a Queerfeminist Perspective', *Australian Feminist Studies*, 35: 104, 81–100. https://doi.org/10.1080/08164649.2020.1811952

Reed, D. E., Cobos, B., Nagpal, A. S., Eckmann, M., and McGeary, D. D. (2022), 'The Role of Identity in Chronic Pain Cognitions and Pain-related Disability within a Clinical Chronic Pain Population', *The International Journal of Psychiatry in Medicine*, 57 (1): 35–52. https://doi.org/10.1177/0091217421989141

Robb, John (2023), *The Art of Darkness: The History of Goth*, Manchester: Manchester University Press.

Rodier, Kristin (2018), 'Fat Temporality, Crisis Phenomenology, and the Politics of Refusal', in Sara Cohen Shabot, and Christinia Landry (eds), *Rethinking Feminist Phenomenology: Theoretical and Applied Perspectives*, 137–52, London: Rowman & Littlefield.

Rodowick, D. N. (2014), *An Elegy for Theory*, Harvard: Harvard University Press.

Samuelson, Charles (2016), 'Queering Temporality and the Gender Binary in *Flamenca*', *Postmedieval: A Medieval Journal of Cultural Studies*, 7 (3): 431–55.

Scarry, Elaine (1985), *The Body in Pain: The Making and Unmaking of the World*, New York: Oxford University Press.

Scharf, Natasha (2011), *Worldwide Gothic: A Chronicle of a Tribe*, Church Stretton, England: Independent Music Press.

Schönegger, Philipp (2022), 'What's up with Anti-Natalists? An Observational Study on the Relationship between Dark Triad Personality Traits and Anti-Natalist Views', *Philosophical Psychology*, 35 (1): 66–94. https://doi.org/10.1080/09515089.2021.1946026

Schopenhauer Arthur (2007), *Studies in Pessimism: On the Sufferings of the World*, New York, NY: Cosimo.

Segal, Charles (1993), *Euripides and the Poetics of Sorrow*, Durham, N.C.: Duke University Press.

Sekowski, Martin and Lester, David (2022), 'The Complex Relationships between Dependency and Self-Criticism and Suicidal Behavior and Ideation in Early Adulthood', *Personality and Individual Differences*, 198: 111806. https://doi.org/10.1016/j.paid.2022.111806

Serres, Michel (1997), *Genesis*, trans. Genevieve James and James Nielson, Ann Arbor: The University of Michigan Press.

Serres, Michel (2000), *The Birth of Physics*, trans. Jack Hawkes, Manchester: Clinamen.

Serres, Michel (2002), *The Natural Contract*, trans. Elizabeth MacArthur and William Paulson, Ann Arbor: The University of Michigan Press.

Serres, Michel (2011), *Betrayal: The Thanatocracy*, trans. Randolph Burks. https://issuu.com/randisi/docs/serres__betrayal?fbclid=IwAR3HIonPXcA9x8L8nwhwtQ6ZPx7kBVHXoFtKdwyqVTguAC65E2oz2rKd8O4 (accessed 6 September 22).

Serres, Michel (2014), *Times of Crisis*, trans. by Anne-Marie Feenberg-Dibon, London: Bloomsbury.

Sherif Xenoph Ibn El (Zafer Aracagok). (2013), *I Want to be a Suicide Bomber*, Constantinople: Somnambulist Situationists.

Shildrick, Margrit (2022), *Visceral Prosthesis: Somatechnics and Posthuman Embodiment*, London: Bloomsbury.

Sholtz, Janae, Desire (2022) 'Delirium, and Revolutionary Love: Deleuzian Feminist Possibilities', *Philosophies*, 7 (3): 61.

Schopenhauer, Arthur (2007), *Studies in Pessimism*, New York: Cosimo Classics.

Spare, Austin Osman (2011), *The Book of Pleasure*, London: Jerusalem Press.

Spinoza, Baruch (1957), *The Road to Inner Freedom*, trans. Dagobert D. Runes, New York: Philosophical Library.

Spinoza, Baruch (1996), 'Tractatus de intellectus emendatione', in Herman De Dijn (ed.), *The Way to Wisdom, Commentaries and introduction to Tractatus de intellectus emendatione*, with the Latin text and English translation by Edwin Curley, West Lafayette/Indiana: Purdue University Press.

Stevenson, R. and Morales, C. (2022), 'Trauma in Animal Protection and Welfare Work: The Potential of Trauma-Informed Practice', *Animals* (Basel), 12 (7): 852. https://doi.org/10.3390/ani12070852

Stiegler, Bernard (2018), *The Neganthropocene*, trans. Daniel Ross, London: Open Humanities Press.

Taubert, Mark and Kandasamy, Jothy (2006), 'Self Harm in Goth Youth Subculture: Conclusion Relates Only to Small Sample', *BMJ* (letter to the editor). 332 (7551): 1216.

The Save Movement. https://thesavemovement.org/trauma/ (accessed 25 December 2023).

Thomas, Carol (2007), *Sociologies of Disability and Illness: Contested Ideas in Disability Studies and Medical Sociology*, Basingstoke: Palgrave Macmillan.

Tolhurst, Lawrence (2023), *Goth: A History*, London: Quercus.

Understanding Animal Research Organisation. https://www.understandinganimalresearch.org.uk/what-is-animal-research/numbers-animals

Unsworth, Cathi (2023), *Season of the Witch*, London: Nine Eight Books.

Van der Kolk, Bessel (2014), *The Body Keeps the Score: Brain, Mind, and Body in the Healing of Trauma*, New York: Viking Press.

Virilio, Paul (2003), *Art and Fear*, trans. Julie Rose, London: Continuum.
Waldschmidt, A., Berressem, H. and Ingwersen, M., eds. (2017) *Culture—theory—disability: Encounters between Disability Studies and Cultural Studies: Disability Studies*, Vol 10, Bielefeld: Transcript Verlag.
Warda, Susanne (2011), 'Dance, Music, and Inversion: The Reversal of the Natural Order in the Medieval Danse Macabre', in Sophie Oosterwijk and Stefanie Knöll (eds), *Mixed Metaphors: The Danse Macabre in Medieval and Early Modern Europe*, 73–100, Cambridge: Cambridge Scholars Publisher.
Wilson, Elizabeth (2004), *Psychosomatic: Feminism and the Neurological Body*, Durham: Duke University Press.
Woods, Simon (2006), *Death's Dominion:Ethics at the End of Life,* Buckingham: McGraw-Hill Education.
Wrye, Jen (2015), '"Deep Inside Dogs Know What They Want"', in Patricia J. Lopez and Kathryn A. Gillespie (eds), *Economies of Death: Economic Logic of Killable Life and Grievable Death*, London and New York: Routledge.
Young, Robert (2006), 'Goths "More Likely to Self-harm"', *BBC,* 13 April 2006. http://news.bbc.co.uk/1/hi/health/4905898.stm (retrieved 29 November 2023).

Index

#BLM   61, 67
#metoo   61

abjection   7, 52, 54, 147, 177–81
abolition   33, 73–7, 94, 103, 107–19, 122–4, 155, 161–2
activism   15, 33–4, 61, 73–9, 97, 107, 109, 113–17, 122–4, 127, 142, 149, 171–2, 188, 190, 195, 202
Adams, Carol J.   9, 17
affect   xiii, xiv, 6–7, 9–10, 22, 24, 37, 41, 53, 58, 62, 82, 86–9, 96–8, 111, 122–4, 136, 140, 178
ahuman   19, 153, 161–3, 180, 195
AIDS   18, 64, 67, 146
Aldana-Reyes, Xavier   57
Alexander, Jeffrey C.   63
Andersson, N. W.   132
animal rights   73–5, 94, 109, 122, 160, 190, 195
AnimalsInMind   73
Ansell-Pearson, Keith   185
apocalypse   33, 104–5, 123, 149–52, 156–8
Apocalypse Now (film)   157
Arnold, Matthew   178
Artaud, Antonin   55, 139
Arunachalam, M.   132

Baddeley, Gavin   176
Baldung, Hans   50
Barad, Karen   185
Bar-On, Yinon M.   105
Bataille, Georges   118, 163
Baudrillard, Jean   7

Bauhaus (band)   178
Baumeister, R. F.   94
becoming   ix, xi–xiii, xiv, 3, 15, 18, 20–4, 27, 39, 41, 47, 56, 66–7, 77–9, 82, 86, 89–90, 94–8, 100–1, 113, 116, 124, 132, 137–41, 157, 159–60, 165–7, 178–83, 186–94, 198, 201–2
Beham, Hans Sebald   50
Bell, Jeffrey   185
Berardi, Franco 'Bifo'   10, 88, 126, 130, 141, 147
Bergson, Henri   136, 137, 147
Berlant, Lauren Gail   132
Berleant, Arnold   174
Bersani, Leo   16
Berti, S.   132
Bey, Hakim   184
Bichat, Xavier   143
Biggs, Sarah J.   49
biogea   74, 110–11
biunivocalization   90, 176
Blanchot, Maurice   68–71, 149, 151–2
Blau, Herbert   55
Boisseau, Will   75
Boje, D.   93
breeding (reproduction)   19, 34, 109, 115, 142, 154, 158–64, 190
Brevard, A.   97
Buddhism   191, 199
Buonamico (artist)   49
Butler, Judith   56, 64

Canguilhem, Georges   143–6
Carroll, Peter   187
Cave, Nick   103

chaos magick 35, 181–7
Clark, James M. 45
clinamen 11–15, 17, 27–8, 45–50, 86, 111, 119, 175, 186, 188
co-ipseity 196
Colebrook, Claire 6, 9, 17, 137, 157–8
Cole, S. W. 132
Colucci, R. 132
conatus 82
corpse 37, 40, 46–59, 67, 90, 114, 125, 177, 180–1
Covid 19 18, 21, 33, 61, 64–8, 70–4, 150
Craddock, Ida 187
Crowley, Aleister 184–5

Daigle, Christine 13
Damned, The (band) 178
danse macabre 32, 35, 38–9, 44–53, 55–9, 171, 174
death and the maiden 32, 38, 49–51, 55, 59
death camps 54, 111
Deleuze, Gilles 13, 20, 23–4, 42–3, 59, 74, 75, 86, 90–1, 94–7, 138–9, 159–60, 167, 178, 191, 201
demourance 70–2, 77
deprivileging 16, 89, 93–4
Derrida, Jacques 56, 65–71, 127, 201–2
desire xi–xiii, 9, 10, 18–22, 27–31, 33, 35, 39–40, 49–53, 56–9, 66, 73, 81–5, 89, 93, 96–101, 144–6, 150, 165–8, 176–8, 180, 186–91, 197–8, 200–2
Deutsch, Niklaus Manuel 50
dialectics x, 51, 111, 113
Dickson, A. 132
differend 7–9, 74–5, 111, 116, 163, 198
Dracula (novel) 179
Dube, Shanta R. 132
Dué, Casey 120
duppy 126
Durkheim, Emile 91

Earthlings (film) 75
Edelman, Lee 16
Edwards, Paul 84

efilism 20, 77, 152
Epicurus 117–19
equality xi, xiv, 3, 33, 82, 93, 156, 183, 186, 190, 194, 200, 202
equivalence 74, 106–7
Eustace, Frances 51
existentialism 81, 191
Extinction Rebellion 149
Eyerman, R. 63

Farberow, N. L. 97
fascism 21, 22, 54–5, 57, 108, 165, 183, 187
feminism 16, 17, 22, 61, 73, 106, 133, 187, 191
Fisher, Mark 84
Flamenca (troubadour poem) 56
Flanagan, Bob 141
Freud, Sigmund 62–3, 66, 70–2, 76, 89, 134, 163–4, 179–80, 199–200
Friedman, H. 132
Fuchs, Barbara 65

Gaffney, Peter 185
Gaia, Vince 177
Gairola, Rahul K. 126
genocide 5, 8, 10, 34, 38, 40, 55, 57, 60–3, 68, 75, 114, 153, 155, 171
Gephardt, R. P. J. 93
German Expressionism 54, 178
Giesen, B. 63
Goldstein, Caroline 40
goth 171–81
grace 2, 35, 69, 94, 99, 101, 124, 133–4, 157, 161
Granovetter, S. 73, 114–15
Grien, Hans Baldung 50
Guattari, Fèlix 13, 20, 21, 23–4, 46, 59, 75, 86, 90–1, 94–5, 97, 121, 138–9, 159–60, 164, 166–8, 177, 191, 197–8, 201, 202
Gustafsson, L. N. 132

Hagen, Gunther von 54
Hamilton, Ann 54

Hammer films 178
Haraway, Donna 161–3
Hartman, Saidiya 182
Häyry, Matti 154
Heart of Darkness (book) 157
Heidegger, Martin 48
Helmore, Edward 195
Hiddema, Krista 109–10
Higgins, Kathleen 48
Hine, Phil 185–7
Hirst, Damien 40
Hodkinson, Paul 176
Holbein, Hans 47, 59
holocaust 54, 106, 111, 191
hooks, bell 112
hope 10, 33, 35, 74, 95, 116, 150, 171
Hume, David 85–7
Hyrd, Myra J. 24

Irigaray, Luce 98–9, 123, 162, 191, 193, 197
Ivic, Sanja 82

Jackson, Zakiyaah Iman 18
Jameson, Frederic 103–4
Joiner, T. 95
Jones, P. 114
jouissance xiv, 39, 56, 179
joy xi, 2, 4, 9, 22, 35, 41, 55, 60, 76–8, 85–8, 96, 103, 108, 113, 117, 123, 137–8, 148, 162, 175, 192, 202
Joy, Melanie 115

Kandasamy, Jothy 177
Kant, Immanuel 44, 45, 48, 66, 82–4, 87, 158, 173–4
Karenina, Anna (Tolstoy character) 84
Kinch, A. 58
King, Pamela 51
Kline, J. A. 132
Knoblochtzer, Heinrich 47
Koutny-Jones, Aleksandra 58
Kràlovà, Jana 5
Kristeva, Julia 52, 54, 56, 59, 177, 179–80, 191

Lacan, Jacques 10, 17, 43, 91, 191
Lancaster, Sophie 176
Lemmens, Willem 85
Lester, David 9, 94
Levi, Eliphas 185
Levinas, Emmanuel 39–41
Lispector, Clare 191
Lotringer, Sylvere 58
Lotti, F. 132
Lotti, T. 132
love 66, 67, 74, 84, 86, 88, 94, 98, 100, 103–4, 107–13, 115–24, 159, 161, 165–7, 171, 182, 184–5, 187, 191
Lovecraft, H. P. 185, 187
Lykke, Nina 23–5, 31, 72–3, 77–8, 84, 100
Lyotard, Jean François 7, 75, 111–12, 191, 198

McCrystal, Rachel 108–9
McDonald, Terrance, H. 13
McRuer, Robert 142
Malabou, Catherine 72, 76, 79
Mann, C. 114
Marambio, Camila 23, 25
Marchant, Guyot 46
Maturana, Humberto R. 6
Mbembe, Achille 155
melancholy 59, 62, 71, 85
Milo, Ron 105
monsters/teratology xii, xiii, 39, 46, 49, 126, 130–2, 179, 188
Moretti, S. 132

Nancy, Jean-Luc 196, 198
Nietzsche, Friedrich 81, 158, 184–5, 192–5, 197, 201
nihilism xiv, 84, 184, 191

O'Brien, Martin 125–9, 137, 139, 141, 143, 145
O'Conner, Mary Frances 72
obligation xiii, 33, 111–13, 117, 124, 143, 165, 201–2
Oedipus Rex (Sophocles play) 64

Okkels, N.   132
Oosterwijk, Sophie   47–9
Order of Mars   12–15, 29–32, 74, 94, 107, 109, 118, 157, 159, 167
Order of Venus   12–15, 29–32, 74, 86, 94, 98, 107, 109, 111, 118–19, 124, 157, 159, 161, 167, 175
Orpheus   84
Osborne-Crowley, Lucia   135

Pallanti, S.   132
Paltrinieri, Luca   131
Parkes, Colin Murray (and Prigerson, H. G.)   103–4, 113, 117
Parsons, Talcott   143
Patterson, Charles   106
Peta Facts and Statistics About Animal Testing   105
Phillipov, Michelle   177
Phillips, Rob   105
plague   xii, 4, 29, 46, 52, 64–5, 72, 91
Plath, Sylvia   89, 96
Plato   41–2, 90, 158
Prevent Act, UK Government (2018)   107
psychosomatics   132–5
PTSD   31, 33, 62, 67, 73, 114–16, 140
punk   174, 176, 178

Queen Elizabeth II   103

Radomska, Marietta   31
Reed, D. E.   139–41
revolution   60, 197
Robb, John   175
Rodier, Kristin   142
Rodowick, D. N.   66

Samuelson, Charles   56
Satre, Jean-Paul   191
The Save Movement   73
Scarry, Elaine   8–9, 129
Scharf, Natasha   176
Schönegger, Philipp   154
Schopenhauer, Arthur   154

Segal, Charles   120
Sekowski, Martin   94
semiocapitalism   1, 3, 6, 9–10, 82, 88–9, 91, 98, 104–5, 108–10, 121, 126, 129–35, 139, 141–2, 151, 190–4
Serres, Michel   10–15, 28–9, 46, 56, 74–5, 86, 88–90, 98, 110–12, 117–21, 124, 161, 168, 185–6, 200
Sherif Xenoph Ibn El (Zafer Aracagok)   89
Shildrick, Margrit   25–6
Shneidman, E. S.   97
signification/subjectivication   ix, xii, 1, 6–10, 16, 26–7, 31, 37–43, 47–9, 52–3, 57–60, 74, 88, 90–4, 108, 127, 130–1, 137–41, 153, 164, 168, 172, 176, 180, 183, 185, 191–3, 198, 200
Singer, Peter   160
Siouxsie and the Banshees   178
Smelser, N. J.   63
spaltung   91, 191
Spare, Austin Osman   182, 184–5
Spinoza, Baruch   44, 74, 81–3, 85–7, 160, 184, 193, 196
Stevenson R, Morales C.   73
Stiegler, Bernard   22
Stokes, Marianne   50
Stuart, Meg   54
suicide   33, 34, 73, 75, 81–101, 126, 128, 130, 138, 141, 187
Sukenick, Amanda   154
Sztompka, P.   63

Taha, F.   132
Tantra   184, 199–200
Taubert, Mark   177
terrorism   74, 94, 107, 116, 149, 195
Thatchenkery, T. J.   93
Thomas, Carol   143
three living and three dead   38, 47–51
Tolhurst, Lawrence   175
torture porn   57, 59
transgression   62, 92, 172, 176, 187, 198
transhumanism   190

transversality 21, 163, 166–9, 174, 178
trauma 3, 33, 62–79, 111, 113–17, 132–5, 140, 171–2, 180–1, 196, 200
troubadour 56–8

uncanny 41, 60, 161, 179–81
universal horror films 178
Unsworth, Cathi 175

vampires xii, 176, 178
Van Der Kolk, Bessel 133–5
Varela, Francoise J. 6
Versalius 59
Virilio, Paul 54–7

war 1, 11, 15, 27, 30, 34, 41, 55, 57, 60, 63, 67–9, 76, 83, 86, 88, 90, 94, 107–13, 117, 119, 124–5, 127, 150, 167, 192, 194, 200
Warda, Susanne 47
Waters, John 175
werewolves 176, 178
Werther (Goethe character) 84–5
Wilson, Elizabeth 134–5
witches/witchcraft xii, 187–8
Woods, Simon 82
Woolf, Virginia 96, 100
Wrye, Jen 14

Yang, B. 97
Young, Robert 177

Zizek, Slavoj 103
zombies 125, 135, 148, 176